REACTING TO SOCIAL PROBLEMS

CANADIAN SOCIAL PROBLEMS SERIES

LONGMAN CANADA LIMITED

Reacting to Social Problems

Richard L. Henshel

To Robert Merton

GENERAL EDITOR
Anne-Marie Henshel
YORK UNIVERSITY

PREVIOUSLY PUBLISHED TITLES IN THE CANADIAN SOCIAL PROBLEMS SERIES:

Perspectives on Social Problems, by Richard L. Henshel and
    Anne-Marie Henshel
Sex Structure, by Anne-Marie Henshel
Forgotten Canadians: The Blacks of Nova Scotia, by Frances Henry
Natives Without A Home: The Canadian Indian, by Mark Nagler
Fertility Control: Canada's Lively Social Problem, by Gary D. Bouma and
    Wilma J. Bouma
The Tyranny of Work, by James W. Rinehart

The publishers wish to thank the following persons and organizations for permission to reproduce copyright material. If any errors or omissions have been made, we will gladly correct them in the next printing.

p.42, from *The Captive Mind*, by Czeslaw Milosz, translated by Jane Zielonko, copyright © 1955 by Alfred A. Knopf, Inc. Pp. 83-86, reprinted by permission from *Being Mentally Ill: A Sociological Theory* (Chicago: Aldine Publishing Company), copyright © 1966 by Thomas J. Scheff. P. 150, from *Love and Will*, by Rollo May, copyright © 1969 by W. W. Norton & Company, Inc., reprinted by permission of the publisher.

Printed in Canada by Web Offset Publications Limited

ISBN 0-7747-3025-0

1 2 3 4 5 6 7 82 81 80 79 78 77 76

Contents

congeniality of human plasticity idea to interventionism—*Social "Laws" and Social Reality*—inexorable "laws" as objections to intervention—Ricardo's iron law of wages—its historical significance—other examples: prelogical savages, unilinear evolution—laissez faire economics—*Faith in Progress*—belief in progress versus a golden past—strong belief during the Age of Reason—reasons for declining faith—revolutionary optimism and the death of progress—complex effects of faith in progress for intervention—sociological optimism—*Summary and New Issues*—choice laws: unemployment or inflation.

Examples of unintended consequences of intervention—technologism—immigration chains—the prohibition era—four types of unintended consequences—problem of ethical relativity—*Manifest and Latent Functions*—types of functionalism—definitions—inherent conservativism of early functionalists—functionalist illustrations: latent dysfunctions of a meritocracy—functions of stratification—counterarguments and functional alternatives—functionalist conservativism reconsidered; counterexamples—functionalism as a style of thought—functionalism used as an objection to intervention—*Internal Contradictions; Marxian and Weberian Conceptions*—the dialectic—unanticipated consequences from the unfolding development of a system—dialectical materialism—examples: Marx's analysis of capitalism—imperialism and monopoly—importance of the dialectical mode of analysis—the dialectic applied to ideas in history—Weber: the "tragedy of the idea"—examples—utility of functionalism and the dialectic for anticipating consequences—*Labeling: A "Case Study" of Unanticipated Consequences*—manifest function of official labeling—marginality of many deviants—possible unintended consequence: perpetuating the problem—primary versus secondary deviation—*The Labeling Process in Greater Detail*—Matza on effects of potential labeling—the hearing: aura of impartiality, majesty of officialdom, sharp cleavage between citizens and the adjudged—reference group changes—institutional dynamics; new life experiences—Scheff's stages in accepting a mental label—labeling as a self-fulfilling prophecy—the perpetration of stereotypes through labeling—effects of police and judicial discretion—*Present Status and Implications of the Labeling Viewpoint*—principal advocates of labeling theory—theoretical criticisms—empirical criticisms—the labeling school as a social movement—labeling as a radical use of the latent function; as an unintended consequence of intervention.

—background versus training—technicism in public opinion control—relevance to social problems—"the engineering of consent"—technicism on the left—*The Ethical Blindness of Technicism*—pragmatism in bureaucracies—organizational self-perpetuation—ritualism—secrecy—ignorance of the experts—"trained incapacity" of experts—shifts in modal personality; "other directedness"—Roszak: "objective consciousness"—cyclical nature of reform: juvenile courts; mental hospitals—ethical myopia in social science—examples—blindness of leftist technicism—the mystique of revolution—revolutionism without programme—*In the End: The Advantages of Competence*—one-sidedness of the critiques—tendencies are not insurmountable—the obvious advantages of competence—new forms of consciousness—the inevitability of impersonal agencies—toward the compassionate expert.

Preface

As one can see immediately by examining the extended table of contents, this is not a typical textbook on social problems or even on the resolution of social problems. Most books of the latter sort provide illustrations of specific remedies for specific problems. I would doubt that a reader could find many such detailed discussions in this book. What will be found is a treatment of the broader issues which nag at both students and practitioners when dealing with social problems. What are the basic strategies of intervention? What are the possible alternatives? How did we get where we are today in terms of society's means of coping with social problems? Are we becoming more or less effective in dealing with problem conditions, and why? What are some of the effects of increased expertise? of the increased use of social science? Why did people of earlier eras not intervene in certain problems? How did today's intervention institutions come into existence in the form we now see? What are some of the hidden pitfalls, the unanticipated consequences of intervention? How can we be sure we are producing any results, and how can we choose between competing remedies?

These are basic, essential questions, yet the average social problems text ignores them. As Lowry notes in one of the very few social problems texts to depart from a problem-by-problem format:

> The traditional approach concentrates on particular issues
> (war, race, pollution, crime, narcotics use, sexual deviance,
> and the like) as though they were generally unrelated to one

another and, more importantly, as though they were unrelated to the way in which scientists and laymen define, identify, investigate, and attempt to resolve them.[1]

Obviously it is impossible, especially in a book the size of this one, to examine every facet of the issues cited in the opening paragraph, but at least the student can encounter them and begin to think about policy questions.[2] Obviously, too, some of the answers which have been proposed are subject to controversy, and whenever it seemed important this fact has been mentioned in the text. The book breaks with what has become a *de facto* tradition by providing at the *introductory* level the type of subject-matter usually found only in advanced seminars on social problems: evaluation research, latent functions, labeling, fatalistic and deterministic philosophies, the problem of technologism, historical development of institutions, and conflicting intervention strategies. Clearly the advanced seminar can treat each of these issues in greater depth than the introductory social problems course, but the writer has found through his own teaching that such subjects do come up again and again at an early stage, that they can be dealt with at more than a cursory level, and, finally, that students are *interested* in such issues — as indeed they should be.

This book examines a set of topics involving social action to cope with recognized social problems. As such it intentionally omits a number of topics which have been or will be covered in other works in the Longman social problems series. The reader is directed particularly to Henshel and Henshel for discussions of the nature of social problems; a history of the concept itself and of the conceptualization of selected problems in earlier periods; approaches to the causes of social problems; and the role of moral entrepreneurs, victims, intellectuals, and the mass media in the selecting and defining of social problems.[3] Other books in

1. Ritchie P. Lowry, *Social Problems*, Lexington, Mass.: Heath, 1974, p. ix.
2. One requirement of the Longman social problems series is that monographs be short. All that one can attempt, then, is to outline the high points of each topic. An effort has been made throughout to supply extensive references for those students (and other readers) wishing to pursue matters further.
3. Richard L. Henshel and Anne-Marie Henshel, *Perspectives on Social Problems*, Don Mills: Longman, 1973.

the series, completed or planned, discuss specific social problems — crime, delinquency, alcoholism, addiction, mental illness, poverty, racism, sexism, and others. The present work is the logical sequel to Henshel and Henshel: whereas the earlier book focused on the definition and recognition of social problems, we now consider issues surrounding their treatment and resolution. "Intervention" in this context refers to all of the ways that human beings have reacted to recognized social ills.

The book frequently adopts an historical perspective, focusing on how institutions, ideas, and modes of intervention emerged and developed instead of treating them at a single point in time. (This treatment can be seen most clearly in Chapters 1, 2, and 5.) The historical emphasis was not initially a conscious strategy, but it was adopted as a seemingly natural outgrowth of the topics presented. The student can thus begin to acquire both the historical and theoretical understanding which are so essential to insight into social problems, especially into the prevailing treatment of social problems by a society. What the book does not provide is equally clear: discussions of specific problems, their apparent causes, and methods of treatment. The book is, therefore, intended to be used in conjunction with one or more traditionally oriented texts.

The sociology of knowledge as a perspective has also seemed congenial for the subjects of the book. I disagree with those who feel that this orientation is too difficult for students who lack extensive experience in sociology — again using my own classes as guides. It is true, however, that I have not found standard works in the sociology of knowledge very helpful in preparing this book, and the sociology of knowledge is not treated as a separate topic; rather, it seeps through in numerous discussions of other subjects.

The usual aids for students and researchers are included in the form of a bibliography and an index. In addition to this traditional back-matter the table of contents has been extended beyond the usual chapter and subchapter headings to include the principal topics of each section of material. This is a teaching aid which I have found helps the student to grasp the connection of material and to have some idea of what he is going to read next. Indeed, because it provides a précis, an overview, the extended table of contents can be a useful tool for anyone read-

extended table of contents can be a useful tool for anyone reading the book for the first time.

I should like to extend my thanks to those who helped in the preparation of this book. The draft benefited from the substantive and editorial suggestions of Anne-Marie Henshel and the advice provided by S.D. Clark, Arthur K. Davis, Laura Hollingsworth, Craig McKie, Alice Propper, James Rinehart, and Jay Turner. I have felt free to maintain a scholarly disagreement on certain points. Gwineth Andrews helped locate historical material, Anne Bowen and Vince Sacco provided me with numerous Canadian references, and Alex Berljawsky put the index together. Helen Fowler and Judi Smith contributed their ever efficient services in preparation of the manuscript. And a grant from the University Research Council at Western Ontario provided funds for library research and services. For all of these aids I am very grateful.

R.L.H.

1 In The Beginning:
   The Strategies of Intervention

AN INTRODUCTION

Throughout history mankind has attempted to surmount two very basic sorts of ills: the physical problems represented by such disasters as famine and plague, and social problems brought about by difficulties in relations among people. Over the years, the conception of what constitutes resolvable social problems has changed, as have the strategies for handling them. But some form of intervention — as we will call *all* of the conscious, organized efforts to alleviate social problems — is ubiquitous in human society.[1] The process of intervention, however, is replete with pitfalls. This book examines some of the problems and special features surrounding intervention itself, the issues and the strategies in the treatment or management of social problems.

In particular we want to look at the basic alternative strategies of intervention, at the problem of unanticipated consequences from society's reactions (including the labeling controversy), and at the approaches and difficulties of evaluating the effectiveness of intervention programmes. Along the way we will consider how some of the present means of coping with social problems arose, whether society is growing more effective in dealing with problem conditions, and the effects of social sci-

---

1. Let us note briefly that some writers restrict the term *intervention* so that it applies only to certain forms of reaction to social problems, typically those which we will call amelioration of problem conditions. That convention is not followed here.

ence expertise. An examination of why earlier periods did not envision some social problems as resolvable, or chose not to interfere in them, furnishes valuable insight into contemporary issues and the genesis of contemporary problems.

Our objectives will be pursued under the following line of development. Chapter 1 takes up the alternative strategies of intervention, from deterrence to moral regeneration, which, at one time or another, have been proposed as solutions to social problems. A great number of objections have been raised to various forms of intervention; Chapter 2 examines these conceptual obstacles and the content and significance of each. Intervention does not necessarily accomplish its proclaimed objectives; more significantly there may be unintended consequences of intervention, and Chapter 3 considers these possibilities via theory and illustration. In the latter part of the chapter, a specific form of unintended consequence known as labeling is examined in greater detail. Chapter 4 deals with the promise and the difficulties, practical and political, of evaluating the effectiveness of intervention. Finally, Chapter 5 looks at the emergence and triumph of expertise in social intervention and the ethical difficulties and pragmatic advantages which accompany this development.

As we begin our study it is worth emphasizing that we shall be examining *conscious*, planned intervention. Obviously, social problems can at times be alleviated or even eliminated by unconscious or semiconscious means of social control, such as informal expressions of disapproval or choice of partners or acquaintances. There may also be new sociocultural developments occurring for reasons entirely extraneous to a given problem which help to alleviate it. More questionably, some people have argued that there is a "natural" or "spontaneous" recovery rate for some social problems paralleling that sometimes found for physical illnesses.[2] These possibilities are interesting, no

2. For instance, extreme fads or "crazes" have been viewed as having a limited life-span. See Rolf Meyersohn and Elihu Katz, "Notes on a Natural History of Fads," *American Journal of Sociology*, 62, 1957, pp. 594-601. On the other hand it may be argued that these seemingly consistent reversions to the norm only *appear* spontaneous because we do not yet have sufficient knowledge of the causes that govern the return to the status quo.

doubt, but we shall ignore them in order to concentrate on the issues, strategies, and consequences of concerted social action. To repeat the point of the opening paragraph, we are interested in all of the conscious, organized efforts to alleviate social problems — those sponsored by governments, those that are private but cooperative with government, and those in active opposition to the established government. That is, we are interested in the progress and pitfalls of intervention.[3]

STRATEGIES OF INTERVENTION: EARLIER PATTERNS

In the sweep of human efforts to control social problems — classical and modern, self-conscious and unreflective — only a limited number of basic "strategies" have appeared. Although it may not be recognized, each strategy is based on a theory of the problem's cause and on a theory of human nature — on a distinctive "model of man." The causes and solutions which have been proposed for *specific* problems will not be discussed here; instead, the chief concern of this chapter will be to lay out the total span of possible strategies in a rough historical development.[4] Toward the end we will try to organize these approaches into a meaningful pattern. Although the order of presentation here is roughly chronological, it should be clear that most of the early strategies are still with us today.

Although all of the measures described have been consciously articulated at one time or another, some of them are not ordinarily presented in the same form as they are here. To differentiate these, when the proposed reaction has often been articulated as described here, it will be called a *doctrine* (for instance, the doctrine of deterrence). Where, on the other hand, we are collecting scattered proposals into a single category of our own

3. For a complete discussion of the meaning of the social problem concept itself, readers are referred to Chapter 1 of Richard L. Henshel and Anne-Marie Henshel, *Perspectives on Social Problems*, Don Mills: Longman Canada, 1973. For present purposes, a social problem will be understood to be (1) a condition that affects a significant number of people (2) in ways they consider undesirable (3) about which it is felt something can be done through collective social action. For the development of the concept through the years, see Henshel and Henshel, *op. cit.*, Chapter 2.
4. The historical plan follows what is generally known as Western civilization; it makes no attempt to follow the development of other major cultures.

making, the result will be called a *strategy* (as, for instance, the strategy of social reorganization). All doctrines are also strategies, but the reverse is not true: strategy is the more general term.

The earliest known historical doctrines responded to social problems quite explicitly in terms of a general strategy of *reward and punishment*, most often the latter.[5] Recorded history begins during an era of "hydraulic civilizations," which display to the archeologist a number of elements in common. Organized around large-scale irrigation agriculture, these were empire states, possessing tributary dominions and a hierarchical system of power and authority. All possessed a rigid class structure with a small élite and a very large number of slaves. Unity tended to rest more heavily on compulsion than consent.[6] Individuals, groups, social classes, or whole captive societies were expected to behave in certain ways and to refrain from behaving in other ways. Those persons or groups who did not received negative sanctions.[7] The containment of social problems in this era was virtually synonymous with the achievement of social control.

The system had the virtue of simplicity. Like the social structure, the theories of social problems and their remedies were straightforward. Underlying factors were not understood, so that problems were seen as produced by the actions of specific individuals. And, in a system of heavy-handed domination which had little room for subtlety, the obvious response to undesirable behaviour was the negative sanction. Through long periods of history, concepts of limited responsibility, which today would be applied to mental incompetents, the insane, and small children, were often minimal, in many cases nonexistent.

---

5. It is impossible to ascertain the extent of various doctrines among prehistoric cultures, although punishment can occasionally be discerned in fossil remains. Comparisons with contemporary non-literate cultures are stimulating, but anthropologists consider them inconclusive for purposes of historical reconstruction. See E. Adamson Hoebel, *The Law of Primitive Man*, Cambridge, Mass.: Harvard University Press, 1954.
6. Karl Wittfogel, *Oriental Despotism: A Comparative Study of Total Power*, New Haven: Yale University Press, 1957, especially Chapters 4 and 5.
7. For ideas on why punishment has been so extensively used throughout history, see B.F. Skinner, *Beyond Freedom and Dignity*, New York: Knopf, 1971.

Punishments were meted out to such persons, and, indeed, records exist of trials of children and even animals who had been the cause of injury. As will be seen momentarily, several other explicit doctrines fit under the broad umbrella of punishment.[8]

A policy of *retribution* (or revenge) for wrongs or injuries was at one time in wide use as an explicit doctrine. The desire for retaliation, for *lex talionis*, "an eye for an eye," undoubtedly remains as a concealed motive for some more recent doctrines, but the explicit doctrinal basis has been shifted to other grounds. When developed overtly, retribution involves some conception of a loss of "balance" which can only be restored or "righted" by subjecting the perpetrator to an equivalent unpleasantness. (Punishment, of course, need not be conceptualized in such terms.) As the state has come to monopolize the legitimate use of force, the rationale behind such retributive institutions as the duel or the blood feud has declined, and the institutions themselves have gradually disappeared.[9] The legitimacy of vengeance has diminished to a point where it appears, if at all, only as a *sub-rosa* feature of other doctrines.[10]

Two doctrines which have an obvious connection with punishment are *deterrence* and *incapacitation*. Paradoxically, they are based on opposing conceptions of human nature. Deterrence assumes that knowledge of unpleasant consequences for proscribed acts will either prevent the commission of such acts altogether or minimize their frequency. The doctrine is usually divided into general and special deterrence. General deterrence refers to effects on the general population — the population as a whole — from the knowledge that someone else has been punished.[11] Special deterrence refers to the effects of

8. For a good historical study see George Rusche and Otto Kirchheimer, *Punishment and Social Structure*, New York: Russell and Russell, 1968 (original, 1939).

9. Arthur S. Diamond, *The Evolution of Law and Order*, London: Watts, 1951. The thrust of this work is an attempt to relate legal codes to the type of society in which they were formulated.

10. For instances of the policy in modern times one can turn to some Indian cultures. See T.C. McLuhan, ed., *Touch the Earth*, Toronto: New Press, 1971.

11. See E.A. Fattah, *A Study of the Deterrent Effect of Capital Punishment with Special Reference to the Canadian Situation*, Ottawa: Office of the Solicitor General, 1972. An excellent general treatment of deterrence is found in Franklin Zimring and Gordon Hawkins, *Deterrence*, Chicago: University of Chicago Press, 1973.

sanctions on the specific persons who receive them. Deterrence assumes that if sufficient pressure is brought to bear, people can and will change their behaviour. Incapacitation, on the other hand, assumes either that certain persons have an incorrigible tendency to behave in certain ways, or that society's responses are ineffectual in altering their behaviour. This doctrine therefore sees a reduction in the *capacity* of such persons to do damage as the only viable solution. Early versions of incapacitation consisted of such intentionally frightful actions as branding the forehead with a letter signifying the act committed, thereby warning others to beware of the branded individual. Other responses were equally cruel: a thief's hand might be severed, a liar's tongue cut out.[12] Death and exile were other forms of incapacitation. Today, incapacitation survives in the form of incarceration and, in some societies, the death penalty. Ordinarily, a felon while in prison cannot menace the outside populace. Periodically, demands surface for other types of incapacitation — castration of convicted child rapists would be one example. Imprisonment, contrary to popular belief, is a relatively recent approach to incapacitation. Prior to the eighteen hundreds, confinement was principally a temporary means to insure the whereabouts of the offender until the real punishment could be imposed.[13] Confinement as punishment was initially regarded as a progressive and humanitarian reform.

Although the doctrines of deterrence and incapacitation were based on diametrically opposed conceptions of the alterability of human nature, in practice they were not often in conflict because what was incapacitating was nearly always also extremely punishing and, hence, thought to be capable of exerting a deterrent effect. Indeed, paradoxical as it may appear today, imprisonment was at first opposed on the grounds that, while incapacitating, it could not really be expected to *deter* proscribed activities because inmates would find themselves pro-

---

12. This treatment for thieves was recently revived in Libya under a puritanical religious government. So-called poetic justice seems to exert a strong appeal to certain individuals.
13. See Chapter 3 of Rusche and Kirchheimer, *op. cit.*, "Mercantilism and the Rise of Imprisonment."

vided with free food, clothing, and shelter. Imprisonment, iron-ically, marked the first shift toward a rehabilitative philosophy.[14]

Before we leave the concept of incapacitation, it should be noted that sanctions which left a permanent visible mark on the individual were obviously self-confirming in terms of incorrigi-bility. Such persons could never again take part in normal soci-ety because other people would not deal with them; hence they were destined to engage in marginal, proscribed activities in order to live. In certain historical periods whole sectors of cities developed which housed these wretched individuals who banded together in order to survive.[15] The connection between this doctrine and the labeling controversy (taken up in Chapter 3) is most intriguing.

Two other early doctrines were expiation (for the sins in-volved in breaking moral rules) and restitution by the wrong-doer to those who had suffered from his actions. Like retribu-tion, *expiation* involved some conception of "balance" which had to be restored, but it implied reconciliation of man with God (through atonement), not reconciliation of man with other men. (In some pre-Christian cultures the expiatory act "cleansed" and purged the deviant from his ritual pollution and appeased the gods.) It was a doctrine highly dependent on popular conformity to theological dogmas and the practice of the confessional. Clergy set the penalties involved in expiation. Because of the lapse in the use of the confession, this doctrine is no longer a viable strategy, although it is still occasionally advocated.[16] *Restitution*, on the other hand, is still the rule in civil suits (e.g., as monetary compensation for damages) and has lingered on in

14. We shall examine the nineteenth-century movement towards asylums in Chapter 5.
15. See Gideon Sjoberg, *The Preindustrial City*, Glencoe, Ill.: Free Press, 1957.
16. Rioux and Martin make the point that the parish priest is still the dominant moral voice in rural French Canada. The confessional (and hence expiation) thus remains a potential strategy in some areas. M. Rioux and Y. Martin, *French Canadian Society*, Volume I, Toronto: McClelland & Stewart, 1965. But see Horace Miner, "A New Epoch in Rural Quebec," *American Journal of Sociology*, 62, July, 1956, pp. 1-10.

criminal cases in a number of jurisdictions. Currently it is enjoying a limited return to favour in thinking about criminal law.[17]

We can now see why an essentially punitive reaction to social problems persisted for so long. The several doctrines and strategies hung together; explicit punishment, retribution, deterrence, incapacitation, expiation, restitution—all demanded the calculated infliction of some sort of misery on the offending party. Only the specific form of misery might vary in terms of the doctrine most favoured.[18]

In terms of non-punitive strategies, *denial of opportunity* for wrong-doing has a venerable heritage. City walls and other fortifications to keep out raiders and bandits are found among the most ancient ruins uncovered. Personal seals to prevent forgeries of correspondence have also been unearthed in the ancient Near East. And simple keys and locks have a very long history. Recently there has been a revival of such protective measures because of the growth in crime, with the attention now devoted to urban housing and office architecture.[19] Denial of opportunity has been an especially commonplace approach in dealing with minors. Laws forbidding the sale of alcohol or cigarettes to minors or the provision of contraceptive information are measures (increasingly futile) to deny minors the opportunity to acquire "sinful habits" when they "do not know better." At least that was the strategy intended.

A campaign of *moral regeneration* is another ancient non-punitive strategy which reappears periodically to combat social ills. Biblical accounts of the Old Testament prophets testify to the antiquity of this response, and of course, references

17. Stephen Shafer, "Restitution to Victims of Crime — An Old Correctional Aim Modernized," in *Criminological Controversies*, edited by Richard Knudten, New York: Appleton Century-Crofts, 1968.
18. Harry Elmer Barnes, *The Story of Punishment: A Record of Man's Inhumanity to Man*, Montclair, N. J. : Patterson Smith, 1972. Original is dated 1930, but still excellent. Also see W.T. McGrath, *Crime and Its Treatment in Canada*, Toronto: Macmillan of Canada, 1965; and Stanley Grupe, ed., *Theories of Punishment*, Bloomington: Indiana University Press, 1971.
19. See C. Ray Jeffery, *Crime Prevention through Environmental Design*, Beverly Hills: Sage Publications, 1971; Oscar Newman, *Defensible Space: Crime Prevention through Urban Design*, New York: Macmillan, 1973.

appear in the sacred works of other ancient religions as well.[20] The solution to rampant problems is seen either in a return to an earlier, presumably more moral style of life (perhaps extensively exaggerated and idealized), or, alternatively, adoption of a new and radically different moral code.[21] Advocates of the radical shift as the preferred solution tend to emerge during periods of deep social malaise. Cases in point are Jewish messianism in the time of Christ, the growth of Christianity in the late Roman Empire, the Ghost Dance religion among the plains Indians in the late 1800's, the Cargo cults of Melanesia.[22] The Union Nationale is an example from French Canada of a moral regeneration movement.[23] Such movements are of great interest to sociologists and anthropologists of religion, and extensive study has been made of what are known as nativistic, chiliastic, revitalist, and messianic movements. In the non-religious case, such drives have been termed "ideological renewal."[24]

Another non-punitive doctrine has always been available for those relatively few individuals whose inability to support themselves was recognized as a legitimate social problem. Throughout most of human history, the greater part of the dependent population has been ignored or, worse, scourged as lazy, shiftless, or weak-willed. What today we call "unemployment" and regard as a systemic problem of the economy was for long regarded as the problem of "idleness."[25] In the case of

20. An excellent treatment is contained in James G. Frazer, *Folklore in the Old Testament*, New York: Tudor, 1923.
21. Wilson D. Wallis, *Messiahs: Their Role in Civilization*, Washington: American Council on Public Affairs, 1943.
22. See Weston LaBarre, *The Ghost Dance: The Origins of Religion*, New York: Delta Books, 1972; Wallis, *ibid.*; Peter Worsley, *The Trumpet Shall Sound*, London: Macgibbon and Kee, 1957.
23. See H.F. Quinn, *The Union Nationale: A Study in Quebec Nationalism*, Toronto: University of Toronto Press, 1963.
24. As an example, see J. Irving, *The Social Credit Movement in Alberta*, Toronto: University of Toronto Press, 1959.
25. As an example, Henry Mayhew entitled one volume of a study of the poor *Those That Will Not Work*, London: 1861. In times of exceptional distress, this attitude was often mitigated. But Richard Splane observes that in the history of Upper Canada the "idleness" interpretation carried a special appeal because of supposedly unlimited opportunities for employment. For examples of this frame of mind in the Ontario context, see his *Social Welfare in Ontario*, Toronto: University of Toronto Press, 1965, pp. 15-16.

"madness" the person's problem was even seen as the result of divine retribution.[26] But there was always a residual group to whom such forms of derogation could not be applied — the crippled war hero, the blind, the orphaned. Most of these individuals were cared for privately by family and kinfolk, like children or the aged, but a *programme of relief* was applied to the small remaining sector acknowledged to be a genuine social problem. The "worthy poor" were seen as legitimate problems, but these were to be resolved by the individual charities of Christian men, or perhaps of the parish in which the poor lived. In the Western world the church was the usual agency through which such assistance was provided; until relatively recent times the state assumed few responsibilities, although it might regulate the clergy's humane work.[27] Mutual aid between neighbours, practised especially on the frontier and in Old World peasant communities, was another closely related means of providing assistance.[28] The doctrine of relief has extended unbroken to contemporary times, with a vast expansion in the number of cases of misfortune considered to be genuine social problems and, concomitantly, the elaboration of new relief programmes into areas previously untouched.

ALTERNATIVE STRATEGIES: THE BREAK WITH PURE PUNISHMENT

In the modern era of Western culture the first major break with punitive doctrines came in the late 1700's. In England and British North America a new spirit centred around the work of

26. Throughout long periods of history the concern of the state for the "madman" was virtually nil. See George Rosen, *Madness in Society: Chapters in the Historical Sociology of Mental Illness*, New York: Harper & Row, 1968. For historical studies of attitudes toward poverty and wealth, see Robert Bremner, "Shifting Attitudes," in *Social Welfare Institutions: A Sociological Reader*, edited by Mayer Zald, New York: Wiley, 1965.
27. For the development of public welfare in Canada see Margaret K. Strong, *Public Welfare Administration in Canada*, Chicago: University of Chicago Press, 1930. Implicit within the book are the various philosophies of treatment which characterized each stage of public welfare history. Although useful, readers will find its own outlook badly out of date.
28. P. Kropotkin, *Mutual Aid*, London: 1902.

the Quakers and other reform elements.[29] A call was issued for efforts to achieve the moral reformation of offenders. The movement illustrates that terrible disparity of doctrine and practice which is possible in reaction to social problems. "Meditation in solitude is reformative," the movement said, and drove some prisoners insane through lack of social stimulation. "Hard work is uplifting," the movement said, and virtually broke the backs of its victims with unprecedented drudgery. The emphasis was not on physical pain, however, but rather on an attempt to remold the deviant person. He was required to work, read the Bible, and meditate in solitary confinement or silence. Extreme regimentation, discipline, and daily routinization of activities were expected to reshape the character of the person confined. The Auburn and Pennsylvania systems of confinement, both of which drew world-wide attention, laid the foundations for modern penal approaches in their contention that rehabilitation was possible, a contention that became a focus of debate for many generations.[30]

The new doctrine of *rehabilitation* called for the "salvage" of wrongdoers. Helped by the development of asylums and institutional centres, programmes of rehabilitation were developed around religious and work-centred themes. Parole and probation were added to the repertory of legal responses. Prisons became penitentiaries, then reformatories, finally "rehabilitation centres." In many cases the changes were more linguistic than actual, and it can be questioned whether reform actually took place within the walls. But there was no doubt that the rehabilitation orientation continually gained in strength.

Several reasons for this shift toward rehabilitation can be

29. See Sidney V. James, *A People among Peoples: Quaker Benevolence in Eighteenth Century America*, Cambridge, Mass.: Harvard University Press, 1963.
30. See Chapter 18 of Elmer H. Johnson, *Crime, Correction, and Society*, rev. ed., Homewood, Ill.: Dorsey Press, 1968; Chapter 25 of Donald R. Taft, *Criminology*, 3rd ed., New York: Macmillan, 1956. The doubts about rehabilitation continue. As a striking illustration note the lack of theoretical consideration for rehabilitation in two recent Canadian government reports: Department of Justice, *Juvenile Delinquency in Canada*, Ottawa: Queen's Printer, 1965; and Canadian Committee on Corrections, *Toward Unity: Criminal Justice and Corrections*, Ottawa: Queen's Printer, 1969.

isolated. First, there was increasing belief in human malleability —in the plasticity of human nature. The reformability of individual deviants was emphasized through the recounting of successful examples. Bold pioneers created treatment-based institutions, not always successfully and sometimes at great personal cost. The long-term trend was toward a decline in the belief in incorrigibility.[31] Later the rehabilitation trend was strengthened by the emergence of deterministic theories of human nature which maintained that individuals were not wholly responsible for their actions. Offensive behaviour was now seen as the result of social conditions or childhood experiences beyond the individual's control. He was seen as a "product" rather than as a free agent. A third force in the direction of rehabilitation has been a growing adherence among intellectuals to the relativity of legal standards. Holders of the position of ethical relativity maintain that no moral absolutes exist.[32] The growth of historical and anthropological studies which revealed the diversity of human cultures and standards of ethical conduct, and contact with advanced non-Western cultures with distinctive ethical traditions, stimulated the development of this relativistic point of view.

These same forces led not only to the growth of rehabilitation doctrines with respect to wrongdoers but also, for the first time, to forms of intervention that concentrated on changes *not related to individual miscreants.*

There now emerged movements to alter the conditions which were thought to foster the social problems—to attack the "roots" of the problem, as it was put. These were based on a new set of causal theories which gradually displaced traditional conceptions of free will. With increasing frequency, behaviour which led to social problems was seen as traceable to pre-existing conditions, and more and more efforts were directed at these "underlying" conditions themselves. This strategy of *amelioration of conditions* is increasingly in evidence today, although it is by no means universally accepted.

31. See Chapter 2 for greater detail.
32. See Chapter 3 for a more extensive treatment of ethical relativity.

The new perspective made its appearance in several ways.[33] It might be cheaper and more effective to safeguard the health of the poor than to treat epidemics, so there arose a new emphasis on such measures as public sanitation, mosquito control, and mass inoculation. The supposedly debilitating features of city life brought about a demand for recreation spaces, parks, and rural-like areas for "spiritual renewal."[34] The teaching of hygiene, dietetics, and proper family budgeting was a prominent welfare activity in the early twentieth century. All activities of this sort represented a rudimentary increase in sophistication in the sense that they reacted to underlying factors instead of to specific events. This is not to say that the approaches were always, or even typically, successful.

We have concentrated thus far on the individual as offender or deviant because through most of human history he has been the major social problem recognized as such. General conditions such as war or poverty were regarded either as the inevitable fate of man, as desirable for religious reasons, or perhaps as good in themselves. Cases of insanity seemed the result of individual sins or faults, not of social factors.[35] The same was true for most cases of poverty. Those social problems not regarded as inevitable were viewed as the product of the behaviour of a limited number of persons (as indeed, strictly speaking, they were), and social reaction took the form of outlawing such activity under one or more of the doctrines previously described.

Of course this is no longer true today. Although there are still sophisticated theorists who regard such conditions as war, aggression, or racial animosity as invariable components of human society,[36] a large and growing segment of the community now

33. Some would call these measures "preventative" rather than "ameliorative." We shall discuss this distinction later in the section.
34. Stephan Thernstrom and Richard Sennett, eds., *Nineteenth Century Cities: Essays in the New Urban History*, New Haven: Yale University Press, 1969.
35. M. Foucault, *Madness and Civilization*, New York: Pantheon Books, 1965. In contrast, see M. Harvey Brenner, *Mental Illness and the Economy*, Cambridge, Mass.: Harvard University Press, 1973.
36. See as one recent example Pierre Van den Berghe, "Bringing Beasts Back In: Toward a Biosocial Theory of Aggression," *American Sociological Review*, 39, December, 1974, pp. 777-788. See older theorists with this viewpoint reviewed in Pitirim Sorokin, *Contemporary Sociological Theories*, New York: Harper

regards them as social problems with possible resolutions.[37] Some of the proposed solutions continue to rely on the outlawing of selected forms of behaviour, but a considerable number revolve around amelioration of conditions, and a growing number involve the basic restructuring of society.

This perspective, what we might call the strategy of *social reorganization*, is a relatively new and radically different approach to the solution of social problems. Far from regarding the acts of specific individuals as the source of the problem, its advocates tend to see these acts as symptoms only of a deeper flaw. Individuals are seen as victims of the system they live under, acting out what they are constrained to do by the impositions of a radically defective set of social arrangements.[38]

In terms of social reorganization, three great historical foci of discontent can be discerned, each demanding the reordering of a particular aspect of the society. The first to appear was a revolt against *legal inequality*, beginning with attacks on the distinction between commoners and nobility which culminated in the French and American revolutions. Then in succession came revolts against the superiority in law of landholders, the institution of slavery, peonage or economic slavery (as in company towns), and, finally, dominance by whites and males.[39] The last struggle continues in the present, while on the horizon looms a new conflict over the inequality between adults and children.[40]

A second focus for social restructuring has been *economic inequality*. Its philosophical roots lie in the socialist, and espe-

Torchbooks, 1928. The old Durkheimian viewpoint that crime is inevitable may actually be gaining in strength. See, for example, Kai Erikson, *Wayward Puritans*, New York: Wiley, 1966.

37. Lester Pearson, *Peace in the Family of Man*, London: Oxford University Press, 1969.

38. See as examples Lewis Yablonsky, *Robopaths*, Indianapolis: Bobbs-Merrill, 1972; William Ryan, *Blaming the Victim*, New York: Vintage Books, 1971.

39. This historical sequence fits most closely the progression in North America and Western Europe. These events, however, were the springboards for similar events elsewhere in the world. See S.M. Lipset, *The First New Nation*, New York: Basic Books, 1963.

40. See Richard Farson, *Birthrights: A Bill of Rights for Children*, New York: Macmillan, 1974; David Gottlieb, ed., *Children's Liberation*, Englewood Cliffs, N.J.: Prentice-Hall, 1973.

cially Marxian, reactions to the doctrines of classical economics. Ignoring early writers of little influence, its period of origin was in the early 1800's, considerably later than the philosophical doctrines which spawned the first revolutions against legal inequality. Many of the early economic struggles have since been resolved: although often abrogated in specific cases, the essential rightness of collective organization by workers, old age security, and a progressive income tax have become so much a part of the contemporary international scene that the bitter, often violent struggles which greeted their emergence have been virtually forgotten. And some of the old demands for social restructuring, such as public ownership of industry, have come to seem of less consequence to many contemporary reformers.[41] But as income disparities and differential access to services remain acute, new points of contention arise, and the past decade has witnessed a dramatic resurgence of demands for the radical reorganization of the economic sphere.[42] The demand for national control of industry is a case in point.[43] Originally, economic inequality referred to inequality of opportunity; hence the demand for greater mass education.[44] Most recently there has been a shift in emphasis toward inequality of results or outcomes.

A final, considerably newer source of discontent is more amorphous; it lacks a straightforward label such as "legal inequality," yet it is sufficiently pressing so that again demands

41. See C.G. Benello and D. Roussopoulos, ed., *The Case for Participatory Democracy*, New York: Viking Press, 1971, "Introduction." Also see chapter 23 of Fred Polak, *The Image of the Future*, Amsterdam: Elsevier, 1973 (original: 1952).
42. See, for example, Paul A. Baran and Paul H. Sweezy, *Monopoly Capital*, New York: Monthly Review Press, 1966; Irving Zeitlin, ed., *American Society, Incorporated*, Chicago: Markham, 1971; Mark Starowicz and Rae Murphy, eds., *Corporate Canada*, Toronto: James Lewis and Samuel, 1973; R.M. Laxer, ed., *Canada Ltd.*, Toronto: McClelland & Stewart, 1973. An immensely influential book of the early 1960's, in terms of reinvigorating economic protest, was Michael Harrington's *The Other America: Poverty in the United States*, New York: Macmillan, 1962. For specific recommendations see Ian Adams, *et al.*, *The Real Poverty Report*, Edmonton: Hurtig, 1971.
43. A.E. Safarian, *Foreign Ownership of Canadian Industry*, Toronto: University of Toronto Press, 1973.
44. See Chapter 6 of John Porter, *The Vertical Mosaic*, Toronto: University of Toronto Press, 1965.

for social restructuring are being brought forward. It is perhaps its very vagueness which is the hallmark of a deep sense of unease, of aimlessness, lack of purpose, futility. There is a growing demand for personal fulfillment, for "self actualization," for meaning in life. On one level this can be translated as *alienation* in a fairly rigorous sense. The discontent of assembly line workers, as an example, can best be understood not in a legalistic or economic sense but in terms of lack of control over some of the most important conditions of their lives. Alienation of man from his work — the reduction of workmanship to labour — can be approached in terms of reasonably straightforward industrial reforms.[45] Other forms of dis-ease, of existential despair, are more difficult to diagnose, yet they evoke equally pressing cries for fundamental change.[46]

Some of the demands call for a change in the traditionally dominant *values* of Western culture rather than for alteration of institutions or social structures *per se*. It might be appropriate to term this a strategy of *value substitution*, or reorganization.[47] People of this persuasion tend to agree with Freud's position, presented in his old *Civilization and its Discontents*, insofar as Freud maintained that modern civilization is constraining or crushing man.[48] Thus we hear calls for the checking of the Protestant work ethic, for the substitution of a social ethic in place of an all-consuming struggle for success. We must, it is said, learn to live again in harmony with nature instead of seeking its mastery, realize that bigger and faster do not mean better, that in the realm of technology "can" does not imply

45. For current developments in worker control see C. George Benello and Dimitrios Roussopolous, *op.cit.*; Jerry Hunnius, ed., *Participatory Democracy for Canada*, Montreal: Black Rose Books, 1971.
46. Hollander points out the novelty of this attitude: "While individual misery and deprivation has often and justly been blamed on social institutions, the derivation of *highly personal [psychiatric] problems* ... from the defects of society was [a claim] usually absent from the utterances of revolutionaries of other periods." See Paul Hollander, "Sociology, Selective Determinism, and the Rise of Expectations," *The American Sociologist*, 8, November, 1973, pp. 147-153. Quote is from p. 147. Italics added.
47. Such a change, or even reversal, of traditional values is also seen as essential in resolving such problems as pollution which are not strictly social in nature.
48. See also in this regard Erich Fromm, *Escape from Freedom*, New York: Holt, 1941; and Herbert Marcuse, *Eros and Civilization*, Boston: Beacon Press, 1955.

"ought."[49] Economic growth, it is increasingly realized, does not automatically lead to a more satisfactory existence, even in materialistic terms. In 1971, for example, a high level commission of Japanese economists suggested adopting Gross National Satisfaction instead of Gross National Product as a measure of progress.

These views, and others like them, are at considerable variance with the explicit or implicit orientations which have dominated Western thinking for centuries.[50] Value substitution prescribes a shift in personal orientations as fundamental and demanding as that required by social reorganization. The similarity between value substitution and what we earlier called moral regeneration should be clear; the former could in fact be considered the modern, secularized equivalent of this very old tradition. The newer version, however, tends to be more individualistic and less of a formal, integrated ideology.[51]

Philosophers as divergent as Sartre and Dewey have observed how radical, in an historical sense, is the advocacy of a strategy of social reorganization by the intellectual members of the privileged classes. Prior to comparatively recent philosophical innovations the intellectual élite formed a bulwark of conservatism, a pillar of the status quo unrecognizable in today's liberal or radical intelligentsia.[52] Some of the principal reasons

49. Hasan Ozbekhan, "The Triumph of Technology: 'Can' Implies 'Ought'," in *An Introduction to Technological Forecasting*, edited by Joseph P. Martino, London: Gordon and Beach, 1972.

50. Not only Western thinking may be affected. Examine George A. De Vos, *Socialization for Achievement: Essays on the Cultural Psychology of the Japanese*, Berkeley: University of California Press, 1973.

51. See Kenneth Westhues, *Society's Shadow*, Toronto: McGraw-Hill Ryerson, 1972.

52. See S.M. Lipset and R.B. Dobson, "The Intellectual as Critic and Rebel: With Special Reference to the United States and the Soviet Union," *Daedalus*, 101, 1972, pp. 137-198. Only if religious schism or heresy might be considered a social problem (for some cultural contexts) could we perhaps find in earlier periods in Western civilization advocacy by the literati of basic restructuring of social arrangements as a counter to a social problem. A true "adversary culture" among the intelligentsia develops only under relatively unique historical conditions. (See Lionel Trilling, *Beyond Culture*, New York: Viking Press, 1965, pp. xii-xiii.) Eric Hoffer and Edward Shils have offered some ideas on what these conditions might be. See E. Hoffer, *The True Believer*, New York: Mentor, 1951, pp. 121-123; E.A. Shils, "Introduction," to Georges Sorel, *Reflections on Violence*, New York: Collier Books, 1961.

for this state of affairs can be found in the next chapter.

To counter the threat of radical ideas, which some have seen as a social problem in itself, a doctrine/strategy of *idea suppression* has often been used. It can be considered either as a doctrine or a strategy since sometimes it has been expressly viewed as a way to stop the spread of heretical thought (as in the Soviet Union, with a theory of the place of the press as an instrument of struggle) while sometimes this aspect is played down (as in the West, where although only the rich can own newspapers, this is not overtly regarded as censorship). The doctrine of suppression is an old one, as the Catholic Church's Index of prohibited books demonstrates, but in the twentieth century the approach has been elaborated. To control ideas we now see control of the press, censorship, rewriting of history, jamming of foreign broadcasts, teacher surveillance, visitor control, and similar totalitarian measures. Such "solutions" are problems in themselves.

Some modern viewpoints have arisen which can be called doctrines of *reduced intervention*, that is, arguments for the *removal* of the apparatus of intervention from certain areas in which it has hitherto been active. This strategy has more than one theoretical basis. Following the growth of cultural and ethical relativism there may be a moral concern with the apparent persecution by the law of deviants who do no one any harm — the "crimes without victims" argument. As older conceptions of homosexuality, sodomy, and pornography have altered, it is maintained with increasing frequency that the law has no place in the bedroom, that, in general, victimless crime should be either legalized or treated much differently than has been the traditional pattern.[53]

In a sense the above-mentioned position is not so much a doctrine for dealing with a social problem as a move to redefine a form of behaviour so that it is not regarded as a social problem at

---

53. There has been a great deal of discussion of this topic in recent years. See the argument summarized in Edwin M. Schur, *Crimes Without Victims*, Englewood Cliffs, N.J.: Prentice-Hall, 1965. In terms of "over-criminalization," see Sanford Kadish, "The Crisis of Over-Criminalization," *The Annals*, 374, 1967, pp. 157-170; and Herbert L. Packer, *The Limits of the Criminal Sanction*, Stanford: Stanford University Press, 1968.

all.[54] But there is another variant of the doctrine of reduced intervention which clearly recognizes the existence of a problematic situation yet recommends less activity as a means to its reduction. Such a recommendation can be made when it is felt that the prevailing forms of intervention do more harm than good. A prominent example of such a doctrine arose in economics in the late 1700's. The doctrine of laissez faire, to be discussed in greater detail in Chapter 2, arose in reaction to the economic system of mercantilism, an approach advocating a tightly regulated market.[55] Advocates of laissez faire proposed to advance prosperity beyond the potential of mercantilism by prescribing a *hands-off policy* on the part of the government toward economic affairs. Modern economies no longer operate according to laissez faire principles — although some continue to give it lip-service — but the doctrine undoubtedly remains the most prominent example historically of the strategy of intervention reduction.[56]

Recently a doctrine of intervention reduction has been generated by the labeling theorists (to be discussed in Chapter 3) in terms of the treatment of mental illness and juvenile delinquency. According to this perspective, the labeling of someone as delinquent or mentally ill tends to solidify and perpetuate the very condition which the agency involved is attempting to change. Schur's recent book on "radical non-intervention" makes the case quite clearly for leaving adolescents alone wherever possible.[57] From a somewhat different perspective Wilkins comes to the same conclusion respecting drug laws.[58] In the case of mental disorder Scheff argues that much of it is a

54. See Henshel and Henshel, *op. cit.*, for an extensive discussion of the importance of society's shifting definition of what constitutes a social problem.
55. See E.F. Hecksher, *Mercantilism* (translated by Meyer Shapiro), London: Allen and Unwin, 1935.
56. Some prominent contemporary economists continue to advocate many precepts which have a close affinity to laissez faire economics. The most prominent examples are the Friedmanists, the followers of the economic theories of Milton Friedman.
57. Edwin M. Schur, *Radical Non-Intervention: Rethinking the Delinquency Problem*, Englewood Cliffs, N.J.: Prentice-Hall, 1973.
58. Leslie T. Wilkins, *Social Deviance*, Englewood Cliffs, N.J.: Prentice-Hall, 1965, pp. 85-94.

transient phenomenon which, however, tends to become stabilized after the imposition of the label.[59] It has been argued that the medical model of mental "illness" encourages psychiatrists to impose the label excessively in marginal cases because in regular medical practice it is better to err on the side of treatment when the physician is in doubt. In all of these cases a policy of reduced intervention (or, in some cases, deinstitutionalization) by official governmental agencies is now being advocated.

Finally, there is one strategy for dealing with social problems aimed at preventing even the *earliest instances* of a problem from arising. The *preventive strategy* relies on the foreknowledge that if certain proposed social developments are allowed to take place, deleterious outcomes are likely to result. Hence the developments are never allowed to happen. On a crude level such a strategy is employed continually and has been throughout history. Every time a legislature considers a bill, for instance, it can reject it if problems arising from its passage can be foreseen.[60] More to the point are developments in society as a whole which can be prohibited in order to prevent new problems. Where amelioration of conditions or denial of opportunity aim at the *minimization of existing problems* by preventing further occurrences, the preventive strategy aims at *precluding their emergence altogether*.

To consider a single example, the United States recently banned the overflight of supersonic transport (SST) aircraft above its borders at speeds that break through the sonic barrier. This was accomplished before any commercial use of SST aircraft had commenced, although not before military aircraft had demonstrated the nature of the potential problem posed by daily sonic booms. This step has been correctly evaluated as a major break with a tradition which, permitting technological development to occur as it might, only regulated the development *after* its appearance. Proponents of the new law maintained that once investment in development had been made, the arguments against wasting the hundreds of millions of dollars involved

59. Thomas Scheff, *Being Mentally Ill*, Chicago: Aldine, 1966.
60. See this point made in Adolf Feingold, "Technology Assessment: A Systematic Study of Side-Effects of Technology," *The Canadian Forum*, February, 1974, pp. 10-11.

would in reality preclude any truly effective policing. So the prohibition had in effect to be initiated beforehand, as it was.

Subsequent to the success of this attack, legislation has recently established an Office of Technology Assessment in the American government. Early in 1975 the Canadian government sponsored an exploratory conference on "Technology Assessment and the Limits of Growth" in Ottawa. Before new technologies are introduced, their likely consequences can, hopefully, be studied and evaluated in order to explore the advisability of allowing them to take place. To date, this proposal—so radically at odds with traditional Western values — remains relatively untested.

The strategy of prevention, which aims at preventing a particular problem from ever appearing, should not be confused with policies that aim at minimizing future occurrences of an existing problem—for instance the doctrine of incapacitation. In a sense, intervention doctrines and strategies can be grouped in a primitive classification that distinguishes those reactions that are essentially preventive (of additional outbreaks) from those that are essentially remedial, aimed at repairing or minimizing damage from a particular occurrence. Prevention, in the strict sense we have just been considering, is only one of a number of strategies that attempt to limit future occurrences.[61]

Essentially Preventive	*Essentially Restorative*
deterrence	retribution
incapacitation	restitution
removal of opportunity	expiation
amelioration of conditions	moral regeneration
prevention	relief
reduced intervention	

(rehabilitation)
(social reorganization)
(value substitution)

61. Yet another terminological usage consists of dividing preventive measures into "primary prevention" (what we call amelioration of conditions) and "secondary prevention," consisting of early diagnosis of individual problem cases and appropriate remedial action (what we call rehabilitation). See Dorothy Anderson and Lenora McClean, eds., *Identifying Suicide Potential*, New York: Behavioral Publications, 1969. There is no universal agreement on terminology.

In this simple typology the strategies of rehabilitation, social reorganization, and value substitution possess a dual status or capability.[62]

THINKING ABOUT THE STRATEGIES

It should be emphasized at this point that one must distinguish between explicit doctrines and concealed motives, as well as between doctrine and consequence. The possibility of some covert motivation behind an expressly stated doctrine is easily recognizable. Revenge, for instance, is only an overt feature in relatively early doctrines, but quite possibly it has been a factor in later punitive formulations as well. Sadism may actually be operative in what is apparently the honourable (righteous, stern, unbending) administration of punishment.[63] Many of the ostensibly "control-oriented" features of contemporary penal institutions are actually punitive. This is often recognized by a guard force, which can raise or lower the disruptiveness of its control measures as a means of keeping the inmates in line without appearing to be vindictive. Frequent strip searches, for instance, can actually be a form of mass punishment even while they are justified as necessary for control. On the other hand, feelings of pity for harshly treated deviants are also motives which underlie doctrines with radically different surface justifications. At least some of the effort to substitute rehabilitation for punishment, or to show that certain offenders are not really responsible for their actions, springs as much from such concealed motivations of pity as from desire for scientific truth or "greater protection of the public."[64]

62. For other schemes which classify strategies of intervention, see Jessie Bernard, Social Problems at Midcentury, New York: Dryden Press, 1957, p. 157; and Bernard Rosenberg, et al., eds., Mass Society in Crisis, New York: Macmillan, 1964, p. 564. See also Daniel Glaser, Social Deviance, Chicago: Markham, 1971, Chapter 5.

63. The concept of sadism undoubtedly aids today in the detection of what may have been guessed on occasion in earlier times but without sufficiently clear understanding. The label most definitely serves what Blumer has called a sensitizing function.

64. One prominent early sociologist noted that "in all probability the sentimental philanthropic impulse has done more than the scientific impulse to bring sociology into existence." Albion W. Small, General Sociology, Chicago: University of Chicago Press, 1905, p. 36.

Just as there are differences between explicit doctrine and private motivations, there can be disparities between *doctrine and reality*, or between the measures advocated and the actions actually taken. We will reserve until Chapter 4 discussion of whether doctrines and strategies actually alleviate the social problems at which they are directed, but it can be seen at once that the Quaker practices directed toward rehabilitation were as punitive in their way as the direct physical punishment they superseded. For that matter, real rehabilitation might be psychologically punishing to a person (most conversions are), whereas in debates the rehabilitative orientation is usually *contrasted* with the punitive.[65] Numerous examples show that the disparity between the doctrine and the reality are sometimes very great indeed.[66] Thus analysis and classification of strategies, useful though it is in recognizing the variety of ways man has attempted to deal with his social problems, only hints at underlying motives and at the actual results of applying the approaches in practice.

It should also be pointed out that a listing of the basic strategies does not detail the possible variations within each, nor more than hint at the often bewildering number of combinations of strategies that have been proposed for specific problems. It is by no means the case that all disagreement occurs between advocates of different strategies. Some strategies contain *within* their confines divergent approaches which call forth strong feelings of preference. One example should suffice to show that conflict can take place within a single strategy.

Scholars have traditionally held that a child's early upbringing largely determines how he will conduct himself in adult life. The Freudian mythos, by dressing this viewpoint in modern theory, invariably buttressed the importance of early socialization in contemporary thought. To be sure, sociologists have accepted a concept of "adult socialization" but not at the expense of the general feeling regarding the importance of socialization in childhood. Yet, as Wrong and others have pointed out,

65. See Herbert L. Packer, *op. cit.*
66. As one set of linguistic indications: reformatories do not seem to reform; rehabilitation centres do not seem to rehabilitate; and correctional institutions do not seem to correct.

the evidence for the supremacy of early socialization in determining later behaviour is certainly not sufficient to account for
the unthinking endorsement which this belief is given in modern sociology.[67]

One's conception of the relative importance (for present-day
behaviour) of socialization in childhood versus day by day experience factors in the later life of the individual clearly influences the choice of measures to alleviate certain social problems. For instance, in the recent "war on poverty" in the United
States, some sociologists favoured helping the "unreachable
poor" through vastly increased job opportunities—concentrating on adults—while others wanted to concentrate on breaking
up the intergenerational transmission of what they called a
"culture of poverty" — concentrating on child socialization.[68] The strategy chosen by a given theorist was partly an
outgrowth of the presumed importance, relatively speaking, of
childhood socialization and adult experiences in breaking people out of the poverty cycle.[69] Yet it should be noticed that both
approaches are examples of the *single strategy* of amelioration of
conditions. This fact has not prevented the generation of tension, even considerable animosity, between advocates of the two
concrete approaches.[70]

In this chapter we have attempted to set forth the various
fundamental approaches to the resolution of social problems
which have been employed or advocated at different periods.
One of the most significant questions is, of course, the reasons
why particular cultures choose one means over another, why

67. Dennis H. Wrong, "The Oversocialized Conception of Man in Modern
Sociology," *American Sociological Review*, 26, 1961, pp. 183-193. This point is
also expressed by the critics of the "culture of poverty" notion.
68. A variant of the former approach is the negative income tax (or income
maintenance) programme discussed as an experiment in Chapter 4.
69. See Zahava D. Blum and Peter H. Rossi, "Images of the Poor," in *On Understanding Poverty*, edited by Daniel P. Moynihan, New York: Basic Books, 1969.
For an attempt at assessment of the two approaches see Louis Kriesberg, *Mothers
in Poverty*, Chicago: Aldine, 1970.
70. See, for example, William Ryan, *op. cit.*, and E.B. Leacock, ed., *The Culture of
Poverty: A Critique*, New York: Simon and Schuster, 1971. The idea that the
"culture of poverty" approach necessarily amounts to blaming the victim (and

specific historical periods have favoured particular strategies. The next three chapters deal in various ways with the facets of this problem.

---

hence to excusing repressive measures of inaction) can be challenged. See as a counter-example G. Walsh, *Indians in Transition*, Toronto: McClelland & Stewart, 1971. The concept of a culture of poverty originated in Oscar Lewis, *La Vida*, New York: Random House, 1966.

2 Objections to Intervention

As one surveys the history of reactions to social problems, a long-term trend toward *expansion* of intervention — a trend continuing in this century — becomes unmistakable. Many reasons have been given for this expansion. In part it stems from the emergence of the social problems concept itself, in part from a re-evaluation of the duties of government—its extension into areas formerly touched only by sporadic private philanthropy. Today, when virtually all governments claim to be servants of the people, it is difficult to recapture what a radical idea this once seemed—how perverse, even difficult to understand, this interpretation was in times when a sovereign state was openly considered the private personal property of its monarch. It is also true that governmental services are expanding today partly because there are vested interests whose livelihood would otherwise be eliminated or curtailed—the specialists in social problems who will be surveyed in a later chapter. In addition, it is probable that such problems as poverty were not attacked because, prior to the industrial revolution mass impoverishment as we think of it today was truly unavoidable. In this chapter we shall examine a particular set of reasons for the recent expansion of intervention: the decline or, in some cases, complete collapse of several *fatalistic viewpoints*.

We shall concentrate here on certain major developments in the history of ideas, with a selective emphasis on ideas of the recent past. Attention will be focused on ideas of greatest relevance to intervention. We shall inspect ideas which see the persistence of social problems as God's will, others which affirm the natural inferiority of certain races and the unalterability of human nature, and conceptions of inexorable social "laws" which rule out meaningful change. These ideas have at various times formed potent conceptual obstacles to intervention. The importance of ideas of progress will also be stressed in a separate section.

INTERPRETING GOD'S WILL

The oldest disputes on the consequences of intervention have a theological foundation. Religious interpretations of social problems have been declining in importance, but a significant vestige remains and they continue to exert substantial influence on some sensitive issues. We can roughly divide the influence of religious orientations into two components: explicit doctrines and implicit views of the world. We shall look at the doctrinal aspects first.

Basing their theory on what they believe to be revealed knowledge from scriptural sources, some religious groups maintain that certain interventions to resolve social problems are contrary to God's will. These theologically-based assertions, which used to be quite common, argue in effect that certain types of changes in the society are sacrilegious—that is, offensive in the sight of God.

The division of social matters into those in which it is legitimate for the rulers to meddle and those in which it is not (the sacred and the secular, God and Caesar) has been a common feature across a great many otherwise dissimilar cultures. Thus, for example, in the High Middle Ages the prevailing division of society into three classes (clergy, nobility, and serf) was sanctified as the way ordained by heaven, following the Trinity of Father, Son, and Holy Ghost. Any thought of tampering with this divine scheme of society was regarded as blasphemy. But on other matters, deemed secular affairs, it was agreed that mortal men could make social adjustments without committing sacrilege.[1] Especially since the Renaissance the number of social

---

1. This is not to imply that religious leaders have not themselves made new arrangements of society. Ecclesiastical courts were once as powerful as those of kings, and papal encyclicals were equally powerful.

arrangements considered open for alteration has steadily expanded at the expense of the sacrosanct, unalterable areas.[2] But this expansion has been a matter of degree.[3] It is still quite possible today to find people who insist that intervention on some issues violates divine commandments and will subject a people to the wrath of God. The sanctity of the family, for instance, of woman's place, and of various forms of marriage and procreation or birth control are discerned in sacred text, and the proscription of numerous activities is equally seen as not subject to argument. These proscriptions become relevant to our discussion when they conflict with proposed resolutions to social problems or when the pattern endorsed by a religion (such as paternalism) comes to be seen as a social problem in itself.

To anyone socialized in Western culture the following ideas have a familiar, if perhaps faintly archaic, ring. Man was put on this earth to suffer; original sin must be recompensed; each soul must go through its trial; because of his burden of free will, man must be exposed to temptation. Such ideas do not prohibit specific forms of intervention, but they do contain certain fatalistic overtones.[4] As a part of the *Geist* or spirit of traditional Christianity they imply that suffering is to be expected. Implicitly they impart an aura of sinfulness in interposing against the God-given condition of man. "Born in throes, 'tis fit that man should live in pains and die in pangs."[5] Even more than the

2. Howard Becker has developed the term "sacred society" to refer to cultures characterized by extreme reluctance to change the prevailing arrangements. See also comments in Chapter 5 on the increased rationalization of society.

3. For an example from a more recent period consider S.F. Wise on the reaction of conservative clergy in Upper Canada to the new political ideas of the American and French Revolutions. See his "Sermon Literature and Canadian Intellectual History," in *Canadian History Before Confederation*, edited by J.M. Bumstead, Georgetown, Ont.: Irwin-Dorsey, 1972.

4. See Ritchie P. Lowry, *Social Problems*, Lexington, Mass.: D.C. Heath & Co., 1974. Lowry argues that these religious orientations were reflected in the early stages of social science in what he calls the "natural theory" of social problems. Freudians and social Darwinists argued that social problems were "the natural, inevitable, unavoidable and expected result of *man's evil nature*" (p. 246). They felt that social problems were "an unavoidable part of man's life" (p. 251).

5. Herman Melville, *Moby Dick*, New York: Rinehart, 1959 (1851), p. 427. For some insightful contrasts between the religious orientations of English Canadian Protestants and French Canadian Catholics see W. Kirkconnell, "Religion and Philosophy: An English Canadian Point of View," in *Canadian Dualism: Studies in French-English Relations*, edited by Mason Wade, Toronto: University of Toronto Press, 1960.

specific prohibitions mentioned earlier these patterns of Christian feeling and tone are in decline.[6]

One religious orientation has virtually disappeared: the idea of poverty and suffering as glorious in God's eyes. To be sure, there are survivals of this idea in language and literature, but the intense feeling of earlier centuries that poverty and suffering are ennobling is conspicuously absent.[7] Again manifestations of this idea sound familiar: Suffering on earth is to be rewarded in heaven; care not for the man's body but for his eternal soul; "Lay not up treasures upon this earth, but . . . "; vows of poverty among orders of the clergy; poverty as virtuous; mortification of the flesh; worldly goods as a source of evil. Such thoughts were accorded the greatest attention and respect through centuries of Christian history.[8]

In the age of religious commitment intervention was directed toward saving the individual's or group's spiritual soul, as opposed to dealing with social problems as we think of them today. ("What is a man profited if he shall gain the whole world and lose his own soul?") The established church went to great lengths to save the souls in its keeping. However punitively this commitment was enforced, social reaction was based ultimately on the belief that the most important pitfall—eternal damnation —was being avoided. In periods of religious dissent the social problems which occupied the attention of concerned men were those relating to religious schisms and heresies, not, as today, the existence of poverty and inequitous distribution of income.

The "tranquilizing" aspect of religion is certainly not unique to Christianity but has been observed in the content of other religions as well. One prominent and frequently cited example

6. In addition to formal church doctrine, folk fatalism has often been overladen with religious overtones. As a Russian peasant supposedly said during a plague, "If God had intended for us to drink boiled water, He would have heated the Neva." It seems likely that in such cases religion is merely a convenient vehicle for expressing conservative resistance to change.

7. A certain ambivalence toward poverty can be detected in the attitudes of earlier times. Poverty was ennobling if self-inflicted and in the service of God. Poverty on the part of the serf, on the other hand, of the man born to it, was merely his miserable lot. It was debasing.

8. In speaking of a Christian worldview in the singular, we are abstracting certain frequently found components, but it is clear that there are profound differences between faiths within Christianity, especially Protestant-Catholic differences.

is Hinduism and the Indian caste system. In theory, there are rigid class lines in traditional Hindu culture that cannot be crossed. Social mobility from class to class is virtually absent, either during a person's life or between generations.[9] The interesting question is how a caste system such as this can be maintained with minimal unrest. The answer is contained in the Hindu belief not only in immortality but in eternal existence on earth—the myth of reincarnation in which the soul moves from one body to another after death. A central feature of reincarnation is the belief that the caste of the body that one's soul next inhabits depends on the faithfulness of one's performance of caste duties (dharma) in the present body. Thus we get social-mobility-through-reincarnation, and unrest is minimized.

The significance of these religious orientations in the study of social problems is that they form conceptual obstacles to intervention. There is little wonder that for radical critics such as Marx—as well, it might be added, as for other skeptical writers of his day—religion was the "opiate of the people."[10] Intentionally or not, a religious, other-worldly orientation tended to keep underprivileged people from rebelling against their harsh lot while on earth. It prevented them from recognizing what many today consider their true class interests.

Given these positions manifest or latent in religious doctrines, it is tempting to say that the increased secularization of modern society, the decline in intensity of religious belief, may have much to do with the increase in intervention. But matters may not be quite so simple, for the twentieth century church has developed (or possibly returned to) a "social gospel."[11] As Allen put it,

> The sacred gospel rested on the premise that Christianity was a social religion, concerned . . . with the quality of human relations on this earth. Put in more dramatic terms, it was a

---

9. As Srinivas has shown, the system in actual fact is by no means this tight and probably never was. This does not substantially affect the adequacy of the analysis however.
10. See as other examples Nietzsche's *Beyond Good and Evil*; Mark Twain's *Letters from the Earth*.
11. C.H. Hopkins, *The Rise of the Social Gospel in American Protestantism, 1865-1915*, New Haven: Yale University Press, 1967.

> *call for men to find the meaning of their lives in seeking . . . the Kingdom of God in the very fabric of society.*[12]

Most denominations of organized religion are now far more concerned with alleviating misery on earth than with saving souls from the torments of Hell. To be sure, both interests have always been manifest, but the balance has shifted decisively. Some members of the clergy are now, in fact, leaders of activist causes and apostles of intervention — sometimes considerably more so than their parishioners.[13]

The emergence of the social gospel leads one to wonder whether the church *led* society in each age (fostering the status quo, for example, in the High Middle Ages and encouraging some forms of interventionism today) or whether the emphases of the church have merely *reflected* the dominant orientation of each period. (Or, might it be possible that the church led the other institutions of society during the Middle Ages and follows these institutions today?) What, in short, was the "direction" of causality? This is, of course, an example of the classical issue of the relative importance of ideas versus social structure and social conditions in determining history. It is one of those questions which is of the utmost importance, which has fascinated great minds for generations, yet is virtually impossible to demonstrate conclusively one way or the other.

The principal bases for denying the feasibility of intervention have gradually shifted from religious to secular grounds. As science has gained in public esteem, the grounds for the supposed unalterability of social problems have become less a matter of divinely inspired literature and more and more a matter based on supposedly "scientific" assumptions about the unalterability of "human nature" or the inevitability of a pattern of history. It is to these secular orientations that we shall now turn our attention.

---

12. A.R. Allen, *The Social Passion: Religion and Social Reform in Canada, 1914-1928,* Toronto: University of Toronto Press, 1971, p. 4.
13. Gary T. Marx, "Religion: Opiate or Inspiration of Civil Rights Militancy?" in his *Protest and Prejudice,* New York: Harper & Row, 1967, pp. 94-105. In addition to modern movements, *reinterpreted* religious doctrines have served historically as focal points for peasant uprisings. See Norman Cohn, *The Pursuit of the Millennium,* rev. ed., Cambridge: Oxford University Press, 1970.

CONCERNING HUMAN EQUALITY

The prevailing view of the nature of man that is held by a society, or perhaps the view held by its dominant members, is of the greatest importance for determining (a) the acceptability of intervention—that is, its apparent feasibility—and (b) the forms such intervention will assume.[14] It is time now to look at the relation between models of man and the apparent feasibility of intervention. This section will consider specifically the long-standing conflict between advocates of *heredity* and advocates of *environment* ("nature and nurture") in terms of which factor has the greater importance in shaping human behaviour. The position accepted on this issue by a culture, as well as its views on human alterability, have profound implications for intervention decisions, as we shall see.

In many historical periods, belief in the *inheritance* of "character," of ability, and of what we now call personality was absolute, virtually unquestioned. In fact, throughout history, up to very recent times, the hereditary or "blood" argument has been strongly favoured over that of the environment and socialization — nature over nurture. As recently as the turn of the century such views were still predominant. Thus in criminology, for example, the great Italian theorist Lombroso advanced an hereditarian theory of crime around 1866. The criminal, according to Lombroso, was a genetic "throwback"; he was atavistic.[15] A few biological advocates survive in criminology even today; around 1900 it was the prevailing view.[16]

The belief in the inheritance of ability encompassed not only individuals (for example, the superiority of royal blood) but

---

14. See John Kunkel and Michael Garrick, "Models of Man in Sociological Analysis," *Social Science Quarterly*, 50, June, 1969, pp. 136-152.

15. Cesare Lombroso, *L'uomo Deliquente*, (expanded version), Torino: Bocca, 1896.

16. For an illustration of a biological theory of crime, we turn to Robert Dugdale's famous work, *The Jukes: A Study in Crime, Pauperism, Disease, and Heredity*, New York: 1877. Some of the "tentative" conclusions reached were: "Illegitimacy as such does not invariably entail viciousness or criminality in descendants; crime is correlated with the crossing of a vicious blood with a more vigorous outside strain; pauperism is correlated with the close inbreeding of a vicious and weakened strain." (from the Introduction by F.H. Giddings.) I am indebted to Gwineth Andrews for this example.

extended to include entire races. Certain races, it seemed, were naturally inferior. Everyone agreed that it was too bad, but there was nothing that could be done about it. Intervention to improve the lot of the lower races was not only foolish but pernicious. Not only would such efforts lead directly to the miseries of resistance, revolt, revolution, and reprisals, but all would be for naught because the inferior people *could not* do what the "superior races" did.[17] The Blacks, for instance, simply could not survive outside of slavery.

The progression of the Black is most interesting. When Blacks were first brought to the New World, there were some writers who seriously maintained that they were incapable of learning a European tongue. While some felt that the Blacks should be converted to the Christian faith, others found this virtually sacrilegious. Then it became clear that Blacks could never be taught to read or write. Today a few writers maintain that Blacks are unsuited for scientific or scholarly work.[18]

Similarly the "savage races" simply could not be incorporated into the social mainstream — they were incapable of being "civilized". Thus, cultures which happened to be inferior in powder and shot were dominated and, in some cases, extinguished at the leisure of the industrialized Western World—not only in North and South America but in Africa, the Pacific Island chains, and the steppes of Central Asia.[19] Colonial exploitation for economic and military objectives was an inevitable by-product of the combination of real military superiority and beliefs in racial superiority.

It should be recognized that the concept of race that was advanced in earlier times was far more extensive than that held by physical anthropologists today. Experts today reject the idea

17. A short history of the origins of racism is found in Ashley Montagu, *The Idea of Race*, Lincoln: University of Nebraska Press, 1965.
18. It should be recognized that racism was more than racial prejudice; it was a formal doctrine presented by such intellectuals as de Gobineau. For a survey of the older disputes on race and intelligence, see Pitirim A. Sorokin, *Contemporary Sociological Theories Through the First Quarter of the Twentieth Century*, New York: Harper Torchbooks, 1928. For a modern text see David R. Hughes and Evelyn Kallen, *The Anatomy of Racism: Canadian Dimensions*, Montreal: Harvest House, 1974.
19. See A. Grenfell Price, *White Settlers and Native Peoples*, Westport, Conn.: Greenwood Press, 1972 (original, 1950).

of fixed races, although recognizing that frequencies of heritable traits such as skin colour differ greatly between populations. Earlier, the concept was extended to include any intermarrying group. Thus there was supposedly an Italian race, a French race, and so forth, in the most literal sense.[20] There was also a lower-class race — again, speaking quite literally. Such groups were considered to be races not only because their members truly did marry among themselves, and did have numerous distinctive eccentricities of behaviour, but also because it was thought that these behaviour patterns were *inherent* — genetically determined. If Germans were stolid and Italians excitable, for example, it was because of their heredity, not their culture and unbringing. It was recognized that an Albanian brought up from infancy in Britain would speak English, but it was thought that he would still be prone to all of the cultural features attributed to the Albanians because they were "in his blood."

It is easy to see how such beliefs could enjoy prominence — indeed, they were very difficult to overthrow. Certain peoples did tend to marry only among themselves (more so in former times than today because the sanctions for crossing traditional lines were much more severe); they did tend to manifest unique beliefs and forms of behaviour (what today would be called their cultural pattern and "national character"); and, in addition, there are *some* physical characteristics that are clearly, and truly, inherited. How easy to conclude, then, that the *behavioural* traits detected were hereditary. With respect to social classes, there was no intermarriage, and there were extremely severe sanctions for members of one class who exhibited behaviour considered appropriate to another.[21] Small wonder that it was all seen as linked to heredity. Again, it appeared there were "natural," biologically determined roles for women (supportive, tender, emotional) and for men (cynical, clear-headed, aggressive).[22] In fact, severe sanctions existed for females assuming male roles and vice versa.

20. For the confusion of ethnic and religious differences with race on the Canadian scene, see Mason Wade, *The French Canadians, 1760-1967*, Toronto: Macmillan Co. of Canada, 1967, esp. pp. 276-330.

21. R.S. Neale, *Class and Ideology in the Nineteenth Century*, London: Routledge and Kegan Paul, 1972.

22. See Duncan Crow, *The Victorian Woman*, London: Allen and Unwin, 1971.

It might be a mistake to attribute the pervasiveness of such beliefs solely to their obvious usefulness for the dominant groups — although of course they are useful to an aristocracy. The classical counter to racist beliefs is the seemingly obvious point that a Chinese boy growing up in Toronto of Jewish parents displays far more interest in hockey and his Bar Mitzvah than in the analects of Confucious (or the writings of Mao). This is obvious today, but in a time of strict racial separatism and intense concern with "purity" of blood lines such natural experiments had little opportunity to develop—were, in fact, repressed severely. An objective description of results could hardly be made under such conditions.[23] In their absence a racial theory of culture did answer most of the questions posed of it.

Obviously, a belief in inferior peoples, classes, sexes, and individuals had a dramatic effect on efforts to alleviate social problems. Certain forms of amelioration were not so much proscribed as, apparently, ridiculous. One did not waste education on the uneducable—hence women long remained without formal schooling. Within living memory similar arguments were raised in the American South respecting Blacks. So too when the Nazis revived ideas of racial superiority, they wasted no efforts on the "sub-human," the *Untermensch*, people such as the Slavs, fit only to be "hewers of wood and drawers of water."[24] Similarly if someone was a "born criminal," or even a member of a "criminal class," there was no use in trying to change him.[25] Knowing that such were the beliefs of previous eras — beliefs held until quite recently, in fact—we can understand better the lack of effort toward resolution of what would be considered horrible social problems today.

As if this confusion were not sufficient, in the late 1800's a new ideological supplement to hereditarianism appeared. So-

23. When a child *was* born of parents from two so-called "races," a form of self-fulfilling prophecy came into effect: he was tolerated and accorded opportunities at a level somewhere in between the dominant culture's view of the proper "place" or "station" of his two parents. At times this self-fulfilling prophecy extended to a whole new class — as with the mestizoes (mixed-bloods) in many parts of Latin America.
24. For racial theories and concentration camp existence see Bruno Bettelheim, *The Informed Heart*, Glencoe, Ill.: Free Press, 1960.
25. J. Lange, *Crime as Destiny*, New York: Boni, 1930.

cial Darwinism extrapolated Darwin's evolutionary law of survival of the fittest from its biological origin into the sociocultural arena.[26] If it was natural for there to be conflict and domination between biological species, and if this was apparently all for the best, perhaps it was so as well for cultures. If the members of certain cultures were virtually destroyed like vermin, this too was all for the best because the fittest cultures *deserved* to survive for the long-run development of the human race.[27] It was, as has been remarked by more recent observers, a very odd confusion of evolution with progress, and hence of science and morality, but it had a persuasive scientific ring and it convinced many men for several generations.[28] For many writers of the day, social welfarism would result only in the survival of the less fit and hence lower the overall quality of the human race. They preferred instead to advocate eugenics (the selective breeding of "better" human stock) as a means of progress. The eugenics movement was very popular in the late nineteenth and early twentieth centuries.[29]

Social Darwinism fit quite nicely with the then-prominent doctrines of classical economics, especially with Adam Smith's vision of the ideal governmental policy as one of minimal interference.[30] The fittest industries and individuals would survive in the conflict of the marketplace, and such non-interference (and non-regulation) of commerce would result in the greatest possible economic good. On the basis of this economic doctrine, strictly interpreted, the British government

26. See Chapter 19 of Howard Becker and Harry Barnes, *Social Thought from Lore to Science*, 3rd ed., Volume II, New York: Dover Publications, 1961 (original, 1938).
27. This of course assumes that the fittest do survive. Some writers have maintained that in human society this is not the case even for the crudest meaning of "fittest." In war, for instance, the extremely unfit may be exempted.
28. A classical discussion of the general influence of Social Darwinism is contained in Appendix Two of Gunnar Myrdal, *An American Dilemma*, New York: Harper, 1944.
29. For a Canadian eugenics work see Morris Siegal, *Constructive Eugenics and Rational Marriage*, Toronto: Macmillan, 1934. Immigration policy was also viewed as a tool to keep up the "stock" of a country's population. John Porter has a nice discussion of the notions of leading Empire Loyalists circa 1920. See John Porter, *The Vertical Mosaic*, Toronto: University of Toronto Press, 1965.
30. Classical economics will be discussed later in the chapter.

refused to intervene in the Irish potato famine until—incredible as it seems—about a million persons in Ireland had succumbed to starvation and related disease.

> Years of partial failure of the Irish potato crop were followed in 1846 by total failure. Because many of the Irish peasants lived almost entirely on a diet of potatoes . . . the result was disastrous. The actions of the British government, torn between the harsh doctrine of Political Economy and whatever humanitarian feelings existed in the breasts of its members, were inadequate to meet the crisis.[31]

Between 1841 and 1851, the population of Ireland declined, by death and emigration, from around 8,000,000 to about 6,500,000.[32] We see here the nadir of nineteenth-century élitism, racism (yes, the Irish were an inferior "race"), and economism.[33] But in spite of such horrors, or perhaps in part because of them, the climate of intellectual opinion was gradually shifting.

Was it indeed heredity which accounted for the leadership ability of a class, or was it the social training the class received? Were the characteristics of the Italians, as an example, a result of group ("racial") heredity or of common patterns of socialization? From an early base among the French (especially the encyclopedists), the environmentalist viewpoint gradually gained strength in the late nineteenth century as new facts and theories were assimilated. Ethnic patterns, criminal activities, sexual roles, class mannerisms, all came to be viewed as predominantly learned (that is, culturally induced) behaviour.

More sympathetic (and realistic) treatments of primitive cultures were produced by anthropologists who, around the turn of the century, began to insist on doing their own fieldwork instead

---

31. Kenneth Duncan, "Irish Famine Immigration and the Social Structure of the Canadian West," *Canadian Review of Sociology and Anthropology*, Special Edition on Aspects of Canadian Society, 1974, p. 142.

32. R.D. Edwards and W.T. Desmond, eds., *The Great Famine*, 2nd ed., New York: Russell and Russell, 1975. See also Cecil Woodham-Smith, *The Great Hunger*, New York: Harper & Row, 1963.

33. The Irish case is the most obvious with respect to the influence of the doctrines discussed, but similar fates overtook the Indian and Eskimo, with resulting decimation of their populations. See for one example, Farley Mowat, *The People of the Deer*, Toronto: Little, Brown, 1952.

of relying on reports of missionaries, explorers, or soldiers.[34] The educated sector slowly recognized that world history included more — much more — than Greece, Rome, the Renaissance, and western Europe. Contact with sophisticated non-Western forms of thought led gradually from ethnocentric beliefs about the "white man's burden" to a position of cultural relativity.[35] Cultural (and ethical) relativity had roots in much earlier periods, but the writings of the anthropologists and antiquarians (students of classical civilizations) did much to popularize the position among intellectuals. The sophisticated study of race by physical anthropologists and others began to tear down the superstructure of hereditarianism and racism.[36]

Throughout most of human history, hereditarians have been dominant. The situation is reversed today, yet even now we find common verbal expressions which reflect the actual belief of earlier eras in hereditarian dominance: the "born leader," the "born criminal," "blood will out," or "tell." Modern genetics can document true inheritance of *behaviour* only in specific, isolated conditions: in some forms of schizophrenia and in sex chromosome abnormality linked with violent crime.[37] That the lessons about heredity took considerable time to be absorbed was made terribly clear by the primitive racial doctrines of the Nazis, still clinging in the nineteen-forties to nineteenth- century beliefs about the genetic superiority of the Nordic "race" and the sub-human character of Jews and Slavs.

THE ALTERABILITY OF HUMAN NATURE

The question of the *malleability of human nature*, that is, the extent to which there are perhaps some cultural forms which are more "natural" or more congenial to man than others, has in-

34. Robert H. Lowie, *A History of Ethnological Theory*, New York: Holt, 1937.
35. See this position discussed in more detail in Chapter 3.
36. For an excellent summation, while the battle was still in progress, see Sorokin, *op. cit.* For the distinction between ethnic group and race see Ashley Montagu, *Man's Most Dangerous Myth*, New York: Columbia University Press, 1942.
37. See David Rosenthal, *Genetic Theory and Abnormal Behavior*, New York: McGraw-Hill, 1970; and Roger N. Johnson, *Aggression in Man and Animals*, Philadelphia: Saunders, 1972, especially pp. 87-91.

terested thinkers for thousands of years. In contrast to what seems, historically, to be the more common belief, the intellectual *Zeitgeist* of today endorses a view of man as almost infinitely alterable, infinitely moldable.[38]This vision or "model" of man is rarely made explicit today; the best overt discussions endorsing extreme conceptions of malleability can be found in the anthropological literature of an earlier era, for example, Ruth Benedict's *Patterns of Culture*.[39] The viewpoint is all-pervasive in sociological and anthropological literature today.[40]

In part, the responsiveness of modern man to this view of himself is a function of the increasing rapidity of cultural change. So long as a person's culture changes little over his life-span, it is relatively easy to believe in a "natural" way that things should be. When he sees vast changes take place in his own lifetime, this belief becomes increasingly difficult to maintain. Toffler has vividly documented the increased rapidity of technological and social change.[41] Then too, the ease with which film and the electronic media can bring the farthest reaches of the earth into everyday experience must also heighten awareness of the variety of human cultures.

It is important that a belief in the malleability of human nature is a *congenial* view for persons or groups interested in amelioration of social problems. If human nature is readily changeable, the obstacles to social reconstruction are far less serious. For this reason there may be a strain toward this viewpoint within socially conscious fields such as sociology. In the Soviet Union of the 1930's the doctrinaire belief in the emergence of a "new Soviet man" became so intense that biological science was twisted so as to "demonstrate" great human malleability. The

38. The view received great stimulation from the decline of instinct theory in the first decades of the century. For a modern overview, see Frank Beach, "The Descent of Instinct," *Pyschological Review*, 62, 1955, pp. 401-410.
39. New York: Mentor, 1934.
40. See Paul Hollander, "Sociology, Selective Determinism, and the Rise of Expectations," *The American Sociologist*, 8, November, 1973, pp. 147-153. For a rare exception see Pierre Van den Berghe, "Bringing Beasts Back In: Toward a Biosocial Theory of Aggression," *American Sociological Review*, 39, December, 1974, pp. 777-788. In anthropology, Lionel Tiger and Robin Fox are reviving some ideas about genetically-based predispositions of Homo sapiens.
41. Alvin Toffler, *Future Shock*, New York: Bantam Books, 1970, Chs. 1 and 2.

scientifically discredited doctrine of the biological (genetic) inheritance of *socially acquired characteristics* became an officially endorsed dogma with the full force of the Soviet scientific director, Lysenko, behind it. Professors who refused to accept the doctrine were dismissed from their posts. "Lysenkoism" seemed to promise that man could be reformed (that is, the biology of man transformed) at a much faster rate than conventional biological theories predicted, but of course all of this was predicated on the false premise that culture could influence the genes.[42] In the end the doctrine was abandoned after setting soviet biology back for decades. But this controversy illustrates graphically the manner in which the wish may become father to the doctrine with respect to conceptions of human changeability.[43]

If one believes in alterable human nature, it has direct consequences for the struggle against social problems. The range and scope of social reconstruction is vastly expanded; the constraints become less serious. One may dream, as did some early sociologists, of forming new religions as part of the reconstruction of society. Conversely, a belief in the existence of a "natural" way for mankind to be—either God-given or based on an interpretation of nature—diminishes confidence in efforts at social and cultural reconstruction.

This faith in the plasticity of man is held by virtually all modern intellectuals and is highly interesting from several standpoints.[44] It is at odds with most of the great minds of the

42. D. Joravsky's article on Lysenko is one of the best available short summaries of this period of soviet biology. See his "The Lysenko Affair," *Scientific American*, 207, November, 1962, pp. 41-49. See also Zhores Medvedev, *The Rise and Fall of T.D. Lysenko*, New York: Columbia University Press, 1969.

43. Interspersed through the questions of heredity versus environment and human malleability has been the strength of socialization (or education, as it was formerly regarded). Can socialization of the child guarantee the nature of the adult man, as the early Jesuits claimed? Psychoanalytic theory and other theories of personality would agree with this idea. But see Denis Wrong's "The Oversocialized Conception of Man in Modern Sociology," *American Sociological Review*, 26, 1961, pp. 183-193, which notes the importance of situation, culture, and social structure (relative to child training) in the production of adult behaviour patterns.

44. Infinite plasticity of man and his culture does not necessarily mean that human beings are easily pliable in the short run. Amitai Etzioni has argued that persuading individuals is not a very effective way to solve social problems, in

past, from Plato to Tolstoy, yet is accepted today virtually without question. To quote the modern Polish intellectual, Milosz,

> *All the concepts men live by are a product of the historic formation in which they find themselves. Fluidity and constant change are the characteristics of phenomena. And man is so plastic a being that one can even conceive of the day when a thoroughly self-respecting citizen will crawl about on all fours . . . as a sign of conformity to the order he lives in.* [45]

This specific illustration notwithstanding, the general faith in malleability may be one of the few foci for optimism left in Western thought. [46]

SOCIAL "LAWS" AND SOCIAL REALITY

There is another line of thought which denies man the ability to intervene effectively on some, perhaps most, of his problematic conditions. This objection maintains that the existence of some social "law" poses an insurmountable barrier to the solution of a social problem. This differs from our analysis of the nature of man since it is now the social structure which is apparently unbending, rather than the "quality" of the individual human.

In one sense the examination of social "laws" (or "strong tendencies," as they would probably be called today) is part of the business of the social scientist. Such examination impinges directly on our topic of intervention when the "law" in question

---

comparison with altering the social structure. But the very conceivability of indefinite alterations in the latter reveals his underlying faith in human adjustability. See "Human Beings are not Very Easy to Change After All," *Saturday Review,* June 3, 1972, pp. 45-47.

45. Czeslaw Milosz, *The Captive Mind,* New York: Vintage Books, 1955, pp. 27-28. For an overdrawn but useful review of some recent counter tendencies, see Tom Alexander, "The Social Engineers Retreat under Fire," *Fortune,* October, 1972.

46. See the section on ideas of progress later in this chapter. For an excellent discussion of "the problem of human nature" see the Coda of Herbert Muller's *The Children of Frankenstein: A Primer on Modern Technology and Human Values,* Bloomington: Indiana University Press, 1971.

predicts that certain efforts to remove a social problem will not succeed. Most of the examples of such inherently obstructing "laws" predate the twentieth century. Let us examine a straightforward example: Ricardo's iron law of wages. Popular during the heyday of classical economics, the so-called iron law claimed that wages *must* in the long run remain just above the subsistence level for workers.[47] If in the short run wages rose higher, then more workers would live to, and through, their reproductive ages; larger families would result; and because of better conditions more children would survive. The result? An excessive number of workers (supply) for the jobs to be filled (demand), resulting in a return to lower wages. On the other hand, if wages dropped below the subsistence level, more workers would die before producing children, and fewer of the children that were born would survive to working age, thereby producing a scarcity of labour in relation to demand. Wages would rise under these conditions. Hence, wages in the long run would remain at subsistence level. An iron law had been established which all sorts of good intentions for the workers could not overcome. What is more, when examined carefully, the law showed that efforts to improve the workers' lot would not only fail, but would fail after producing greater misery than would otherwise have taken place. Not for nothing was economics known as the dismal science.

The iron law of wages had the virtue of being explicable in short order—a virtue which was also a vice in terms of repressing social reform. Its defect, of course, is that it is not an inexorable economic law at all, merely a relationship which only holds true under highly specific conditions. If, for example, the national population and/or foreign trade was increasing, then an increase in income, resulting in more workers available for work, would not necessarily lower the wages again because more jobs would also be available. The so-called law makes a simply staggering number of assumptions which are not spelled out—relations of income to family size and to number of surviving children, the absence of worker organizations and combinations, or of

---

47. See Pierro Sraffa, ed., *Works and Correspondence of David Ricardo*, Cambridge: Cambridge University Press, 1951.

minimum wage laws and unemployment payments, just to
name a few. The defects of this little scheme are today pitifully
obvious, but to earlier industrial England the "law" seemed
quite impressive.

The importance of such "laws" stems not from their validity
but from the fact that, as men *believed* them to be true, reformers
were precluded from taking certain measures.[48] To paraphrase
W.I. Thomas's famous dictum, situations believed to be real
were real in their consequences. Obviously a belief in an "iron
law" will affect social intervention into the problems of the day,
and even the conception of what *is* a social problem. Whatever
men regard as unavoidable or inexorable tends not to be considered a social problem, however unpleasant it may be. Of course
the validity of the law is an entirely separate question.

As Piven and Cloward have noted, rarely has self-interest and
social theory so neatly coincided as it did in the early nineteenth
century.[49] We have already noticed this remarkable congruity
with respect to the popular ideas of racial inferiority. These
ideas in turn were buttressed by sophisticated theories of the
"prelogical character" of the primitive mind.[50] Another popular
idea of the period was that sociocultural development passed
through a specific number of "stages" before reaching the apex
of civilization—invariably situated in western Europe. Not only
did such value-laden beliefs deny cultural relativity by presuming that some cultures were "better" or "higher" than others,
and that this could be infallibly known, they also proposed a
single invariable sequence of stages (differing somewhat between theorists) which all cultures had to follow in their "development." This conception of *unilinear cultural evolution*, in
which there was a single path along which all cultures had to

48. As an example, Michels formulated a famous "iron law of oligarchy" which,
whatever its intrinsic merits, undoubtedly had side effects in terms of justifying
oligarchical trends.
49. Frances Piven and Richard Cloward, *Regulating the Poor: The Functions of
Public Welfare*, New York: Pantheon Books, 1971. Richard Hofstadter has noted
that the capitalist Carnegie became the personal benefactor of Herbert Spencer,
the theorist of Social Darwinism.
50. See Lucien Lévi-Bruhl, *Primitive Mentality*, London: Allen and Unwin,
1923. For an attack on this belief see Bronislaw Malinowski, *Magic, Science, and
Religion*, Glencoe, Ill.: Free Press, 1948. For a modern review of the controversy
see William Kay, *Moral Development*, rev. ed., London: Allen and Unwin, 1970,
especially Chapter 3.

progress, implied that cultures could not skip or leap "stages"; each supposedly had to move through every level in turn before it could approximate the most "advanced" countries. Again, efforts toward social reform were stymied by such theories.[51]

The iron law of wages was but a single segment of a larger body of doctrine that has come to be known as *laissez faire economics*. Developed by the classical economists — Adam Smith, Ricardo, Malthus, John Stuart Mill—followers of laissez faire (from the French, roughly "let it be") argued that maximum economic good would come from allowing unrestrained competition in the marketplace with an absolute minimum of governmental interference. Only the law of contracts and, of course, laws insuring the safety of citizens in their property and their person, were considered legitimate functions of government. In his immensely influential book, *The Wealth of Nations*, Adam Smith maintained that out of this unregulated chaos would come the greatest obtainable economic benefit—produced, in his famous phrase, as though led by an "invisible hand."[52] Promulgated in an era where it was widely believed that "that government is best that governs least," followers of the classical economists came to abhor such "socialistic" proposals of their day as a government-run postal system, or public education. They would have been speechless before such unimaginable phenomena as auto safety regulations or pure food and drug laws.[53] Not everyone was prosperous in Adam Smith's England,

51. For the doctrine of unilinear evolution see Marvin Harris, *The Rise of Anthropological Theory*, New York: Thomas Y. Crowell Co., 1968. Although this old model is far too restrictive, there is evidence that at least some cultural components regularly precede others. See Linton Freeman and Robert F. Winch, "Societal Complexity: An Empirical Test of a Typology of Societies," *American Journal of Sociology*, 62, March, 1957, pp. 461-466.
52. Adam Smith, *An Inquiry into the Nature and Causes of the Wealth of Nations*, New York: P.F. Collier, 1909 (originally published 1776), p. 351. It should be pointed out that brief summaries unavoidably neglect Smith's subtleties and intellectual range, which can be seen in both *The Wealth of Nations* and his *Theory of Moral Sentiments*.
53. The single universal exception — true for every major country in the Western world — was governmental stimulation of railroad building. For the Canadian case see Pierre Berton, *The Last Spike*, Toronto: McClelland & Stewart, 1971. Government sponsorship and central planning were somewhat more prevalent in Canada during this period than elsewhere. See Harold Innis, "Government Ownership and the Canadian Scene," in Innis, *Essays in Canadian Economic History,* Toronto: University of Toronto Press, 1956, pp. 78-96.

but then not everyone *could* be prosperous: let it be. The significance of laissez faire and related views for our purposes is quite simple: insofar as men believed in these doctrines, efforts to advance economic reform were thwarted.

FAITH IN PROGRESS

We turn now to an idea whose impact on intervention is rather more complex than those subjects examined before: the idea of progress, which refers to a generalized forecast about the future improvement of the condition of humanity as a whole. Although there are always individuals who think their own future will be better, the idea of progress is not universal across human cultures by any means. Instead, the idea of progress contrasts with an equally common idea of a decline from a "Golden Age" in the past. There are a great many variations of the latter theme. At times it seems as if all classical mythologies have one. The "Fall" is, of course, the familiar Biblical version. The early Greeks believed in an initial golden race, succeeded by a race of silver, a race of brass, and finally the present iron race. Even within the last, "as the generations pass, they grow worse; sons are always inferior to their fathers."[54] The idea of progress, of course, points toward the proximate future instead of to the past for an age of glory and happiness.[55]

The sociology of knowledge (that branch of sociology that studies the social basis of ideas) can give us some insight into the factors at work in the development of an idea of progress. In some eras the rate of technological and cultural change is sufficiently slow that it is almost imperceptible in a single life time. Under such conditions expectations about the future are difficult to predict. But when improvement or decline become more noticeable, when marked changes within a single life-span

---

54. Edith Hamilton, *Mythology,* New York: Mentor, 1940, p. 69. See also James George Frazer, *Folklore in the Old Testament,* New York: Tudor, 1923. Parenthetically, it is a belief in *secular* or worldly progress that is our interest here, not a belief in a coming apocalypse.

55. For the various interpretations of history in terms of human happiness, (lineal, cyclical, spiraliform, etc.) see Georges Sorel, *The Illusions of Progress,* Berkeley: University of California Press, 1972 (originally 1908).

can be observed, then consistent optimism or pessimism is expected.[56] When this is linked with a plausible rationale for *why* progress or decline should occur, it can lead to dramatically intense beliefs.

In the period known to intellectual history as the Age of Enlightenment (1600-1800), a strong belief in progress, based on faith in the supremacy of man's reason, arose.[57] The scientific revolution was gathering momentum; the period saw the successes of Copernican and Galilean astronomy as well as the capstone of early physics — the development of Newtonian mechanics.[58] It was during this time that the great philosopher-mathematician Descartes declared, in what seems today an unbelievably naive, optimistic assertion, that all scientific knowledge could be discovered in a single lifetime. The writers of the period were in virtual awe of the intellectual accomplishments which had been achieved so recently in the sciences and humanities. Extrapolating into the future they foresaw endless improvement. Not only the thinkers but the ordinary people too were beginning to believe in progress; it was becoming a matter of common sense.

The Enlightenment has sometimes been termed the "Age of Reason" by historians of social thought, not because the age was so reasonable in the conduct of human affairs, but because there was such great faith in the powers of reason.[59] (The unreasoning side of the human psyche was yet to be unveiled by Freud and others.) The idea of progress found such proponents in this period as the Marquis de Condorcet who, in 1794, wrote his *Outline of an Historical Picture of the Progress of the Human Mind*. Characteristically, we find these lines: "nature has assigned no limit to the perfecting of the human faculties, that the

56. See discussion in Toffler, *op. cit.*
57. For faith in progress during the classical civilizations of antiquity, see the first several chapters of Robert A. Nisbet, *Social Change and History: Aspects of the Western Theory of Development*, Cambridge: Oxford University Press, 1969.
58. See Thomas Kuhn, *The Copernican Revolution: Planetary Astronomy in the Development of Western Thought*, Cambridge, Mass.: Harvard University Press, 1957.
59. See H.G. Nicholson, *The Age of Reason, The 18th Century*, New York: Doubleday, 1961.

perfectibility of man is truly infinite.''[60] Sociology itself was born amid optimism and dreams of indefinite human progress.[61] Such faith in progress, coupled with a belief in man's power of reason, led to great confidence in social experimentation—for example, to the French and American Revolutions. Only in such an era could one encounter a Condorcet, sentenced to the guillotine during the Terror, still optimistic to the end about the French Revolution and human rationality.

In the nineteenth century faith in reason diminished, but faith in general progress continued unabated. Technological advances were everywhere at hand. Conquest of several diseases took place. After the Napoleonic era there were long periods without major wars between European powers. Intellectually, utopian writings were prominent and numerous utopian communities were founded.[62] The early nineteenth century also saw the birth of what was called scientific positivism and its proposed extension to the study of human affairs.

But there was, meanwhile, a steadily declining faith in man's inherent rationality. Starting in the early decades of the nineteenth century among the more conservative, élitist thinkers (for example, Edmund Burke and Joseph de Maistre), the decline spread in the latter half of the century. Fear of the masses became prominent in a great proportion of the writers of the time, with repeated references to what were called the "dangerous classes." New scientific theories of man's irrationality were proposed—Tarde's emphasis on suggestability, Le Bon's group mind, Freud's unconscious. In the early twentieth century new intellectual movements such as phenomenology and the sociology of knowledge championed the relativity of all knowledge and perception.[63]

The First World War exerted a stunning, dramatic effect on the

60. As quoted in Becker and Barnes, *op. cit.*, p. 474. See also the discussion in Chapter 13 of their book.
61. See for this intellectual movement Frank Manuel, *The Prophets of Paris*, Cambridge, Mass.: Harvard University Press, 1962.
62. The confusing of evolution with progress at this time has already been discussed briefly. For a more extensive treatment see the first section of Leslie Sklair, *The Sociology of Progress*, London: Routledge and Kegan Paul, 1971.
63. See these intellectual trends surveyed in Gunter Remmling, *Road to Suspicion: A Study of Modern Mentality and the Sociology of Knowledge*, New York: Appleton Century-Crofts, 1967.

intellectual view of things. Its impact would be difficult to exaggerate.[64] Europeans, it seemed, were savages after all. Reports of atrocities were rampant. The scale of death and misery was unprecedented, the involvement of noncombatants ubiquitous. Attempts to reestablish a sense of normalcy and tranquility followed the war's end, but they were shattered by a worldwide depression in the 1930's. The inability of man to control his fate seemed clear enough; the Age of Disillusionment had begun. Oswald Spengler's *Decline of the West* was symptomatic of the intellectual malaise of the time.[65]

The First World War also led directly to the triumph of Bolshevism in Russia and to renewed fear of the "masses" elsewhere in the world. But there also came to be a trend toward uncritical optimism about the Soviet Union. Around 1930 there was a widespread feeling among the Western intellectuals that the bourgeois civilization was doomed, and some of the best—Gide, Malraux, Koestler, Silone, Haldane, Strachey, to mention only a few—turned their hopes towards the U.S.S.R. They were disappointed to a man. Although the love affair with the Soviet Union died in the late 1930's with the purge trials and Stalin's pact with Hitler, serious disenchantment with the West continued amidst the intellectual community. The period of the thirties marks the start of a transition from faith in progress within the system, via evolution, to what Killian calls "revolutionary optimism"—faith in progress through *radical transformation*.

The 1930's brought Hitler and his chanting followers. The intellectual world watched the collapse of representative democracy in country after country with morbid fascination. Propaganda reached a new peak of shrillness and sophistication. World War II was the most destructive war in history; the immunity of noncombatants was now virtually nil, and belief in man's essential *irrationality* was now dominant.

---

64. See W. Warren, *Good Times: The Belief in Progress from Darwin to Marcuse*, Bloomington: Indiana University Press, 1972. Also note Barbara Tuchman's *The Guns of August*, New York: Macmillan, 1972 — meaning August, 1914, the outbreak of the First World War.
65. Published in 1922, the English translation appeared in 1932, New York: Knopf.

Yet, with the defeat of the Axis powers, a climate of optimism again arose — temporarily. The United Nations, the last great institution founded on the idea of man's essential rationality, was slowly but inexorably nullified by the exigencies of the Cold War. After a lengthy period of guarded optimism, corresponding rather closely with the economic rebirth of Europe and rising standards of living in North America, the intellectual mood again changed in the mid-1960's. This was a period of protest and strong dissent. And yet, it carried a measure of hope — a revolutionary optimism that foresaw progress possible through basic structural reorganization.

It is difficult to characterize Western intellectuals today other than to say that now, more than ever before, they sense an urgent need for drastic change and yet despair of either bringing it about or seeing it occur naturally. Having long ago lost their faith in God, they are losing faith in themselves and human action.[66] The sense of progress is dead among the intelligentsia, and seems, by both objective polling and impressionistic reporting, to be declining with the man on the street as well.[67] No utopias are found in contemporary Western writing (although they still occur in Soviet literature).[68]

As the theorist Polak has shown, forecasts of progress or decline can have complex, seemingly contradictory effects. Popular belief in inevitable progress can lead to a ready acceptance of new innovations as part of the grand pattern of the future. We find such a welcome for new technology occurring in the United States in the early twentieth century. But faith in progress can also lead to complacency. Pessimism about the

66. See Bernard James, The Death of Progress, New York: Knopf, 1973.
67. Many European observers have noticed a decline in American optimism. The trend seems even stronger in Britain, with waves of persons wishing to emigrate, and Japan in the early 1970's would truly seem the best subject for discussing a dramatic decline in optimism.
68. See Chad Walsh, From Utopia to Nightmare, New York: Harper & Row, 1962; and Isaac Asimov, "Introduction," in Soviet Science Fiction, edited by Isaac Asimov, New York: Collier, 1962, pp. 7-13. Interestingly, utopias are once again being attempted in the West in the form of countercultural communes. (See Kenneth Westhues, Society's Shadow: Studies in the Sociology of Countercultures, Toronto: McGraw-Hill Ryerson, 1972; Ron E. Roberts, The New Communes, Englewood Cliffs, N.J.: Prentice-Hall, 1971.) But these efforts are largely without intellectual assistance from the intelligentsia.

future can also have contradictory effects. It can lead to despair, lethargy, and alienation, or it can galvanize men to activity. The effects are difficult to trace because the *efficacy* of human efforts to change the future is also an issue. Pessimism coupled with a belief in the potency of one's actions can call forth heroic effort; pessimism coupled with lack of faith in counteractions can lead to passivity.[69] We see again the significance of beliefs about the efficacy of intervention.

As Killian notes, sociological literature on social problems is virtually unique among modern intellectual efforts in that it contains as an optimistic undercurrent the view that all problems are in principle solvable — be the solution through the revolution of the radical sociologist ("revolutionary optimism") or the gradual reform of the liberal sociologist. Most other contemporary analyses, as he notes, have become far more pessimistic.[70] That sociological writings on social problems should still give heed to a "happy ending" is neither splendid nor shameful; it is intensely interesting.[71] This is because, in an important way, the mood of the serious literature of a period affects the feasibility of intervention in that period.

SUMMARY AND NEW ISSUES

When one reviews the conceptual obstacles to intervention de-

---

69. See an excellent analysis of these factors in Wendell Bell and James A. Mau, "Images of the Future: Theory and Research Strategy," in *Theoretical Sociology,* edited by J. Mckinney and E. Tiryakian, New York: Appleton Century-Crofts, 1970. See also Richard L. Henshel, *On the Future of Social Prediction,* Indianapolis: Bobbs-Merrill, 1976, especially parts III and IV.
70. Lewis M. Killian, "Optimism and Pessimism in Sociological Analysis," *The American Sociologist,* 6, 1971, pp. 281-286. For the predominantly pessimistic content of contemporary writing, see extensive documentation in Fred Polak, *The Image of the Future,* Amsterdam: Elsevier, 1973 (orginal: 1952).
71. On the subject of sociological optimism, see also Hollander, *op. cit.,* especially pp. 150-151. Although these observers seem essentially correct, it should not be supposed that sociological writing is *invariably* optimistic. As examples of works which suggest that some major problems have no solution, see David Armor, "The Evidence on Busing," *The Public Interest,* 28, Summer, 1972, pp. 90-126; Kingsley Davis, "Population Policy: Will Current Programs Succeed?" *Science,* 158, Nov. 10, 1967, pp. 730-739; Garrett Hardin, "The Tragedy of the Commons," *Science,* 162, December, 1968, pp. 1243-1248; and Gwynn Nettler, *Social Concerns,* Toronto: McGraw-Hill Ryerson, 1976.

scribed in this chapter, it is clear that many are in decline, and some have virtually disappeared. The conviction that suffering is part of God's will, a reflection of original sin, plays no real part in social policy, however much it may still be endorsed by certain groups. Racism is by no means dead; yet when one surveys its pervasiveness in earlier times, it is clearly on the wane. Biological élitism and sexism have become separated from racism; both are on the defensive and in decline.

It is in the contemporary lack of optimism or trust in progress that we find the greatest intellectual obstacles to intervention today. Among intellectuals there exists a growing distrust of bureaucratic solutions. Recognition is increasing of the cyclical nature of reforms, of the evils of careerism and opportunism — subjects to be discussed in the chapter on expertise. Long ago Michels formulated what he called the iron law of oligarchy in organizations.[72] In this view, no matter how democratic a labour organization or political party is when it begins, there are structural factors inherent in all large organizations that make control by the mass membership almost impossible for extended periods of time.[73] Perhaps the only remaining "laws" which seem to mandate the failure of intervention are those which mandate the *humanistic failure of bureaucracies in general* — only coincidentally including those bureaucracies set up for social reform.

Finally, a new form of prohibitive law has come into existence. In place of the sheer prohibitions found, for example, in the old iron law of wages, we find what might be called "*choice laws*," which state that one sometimes cannot increase one good without simultaneously decreasing another, or decrease one evil without strengthening one to which it is linked. Thus it is often claimed in contemporary economics that an economy cannot have full employment without suffering inflation. Un-

72. Robert Michels, *Political Parties*, Glencoe, Ill.: Free Press, 1949. First published in Germany in 1911.
73. For a test of this theory see S.M. Lipset, *et al.*, *Union Democracy*, Glencoe, Ill.: Free Press, 1956. It was to combat such tendencies that radical student organizations in the 1960's resurrected the idea of "participatory democracy." See the S.D.S. "Port Huron Statement" of that period.

like iron prohibitions, one can, to an extent, pick one's evil, but one cannot maximize both goals at once.[74]

To take another example, some historians have argued that although it is common to regard the Middle Ages negatively because of the ignorance, poverty, and physical misery which prevailed, there was a certain psychic tranquility which arose from the orderliness of existence. Psychic tranquility may be at a very low ebb today. One probably cannot have "progress" in its modern form without destroying this, and so again we have a choice of obtainable benefits. As Hollander puts it, "sociology (and the other social sciences) if honestly pursued, cannot but conclude with the dispiriting finding that . . . not all highly valued ends are compatible."[75]

These choice-law assertions provide exceptions to Killian's point, discussed earlier, that a tendency exists in sociological writing to regard all social problems as solvable. The validity of the assertions is one issue; another issue is the effects of such relationships on the struggle against social problems; and yet a third is the consequences of *believing* such relationships to hold even if they do not.[76]

A similar assertion with much the same consequences is found when an acknowledged evil is said to be inextricably mixed with or caused by the same agents which promote certain good or beneficial features of society. The difficulty here, of course, is that, to do away with the bad, one must also destroy the good. Indeed we are at times informed that it is naive, or pre-scientific, to believe that evil always flows from evil.[77] The

74. As Karl Popper has pointed out, there are numerous parallels in the physical sciences and in technology. Thus, for example, engineers will speak of "trade-offs" between stability and speed in the design of ships where, once again, one cannot maximize both desiderata at the same time.

75. Hollander, *op. cit.*, p. 152.

76. Popper maintains that the discovery of "impossible relations" is one of the most important tasks of the social sciences. See his *Conjectures and Refutations*, New York: Basic Books, 1963. He may be right; we merely point out the consequences for social action of holding such beliefs.

77. One argument to this effect is provided by Edward Shils. Speaking of "civil politics" (his ideal), he feels for instance that it "requires an understanding of the complexity of virtue, that no virtue stands alone, that every virtuous act costs something in terms of other virtuous acts, that virtues are intertwined with evil. . ." Edward Shils, *The Intellectuals and the Powers and Other Essays*, Chicago: University of Chicago Press, 1972, p. 62.

same innovative individualism in a culture which leads to scientific advance may, for instance, be one cause of criminal activity; to diminish the latter, we must resign ourselves to less of the former. This form of argument can be seen in Bell's "Crime as an American Way of Life."[78] In sociology this argument is often expressed as the view that one cannot eliminate certain social problems without simultaneously destroying desirable social features. Such relationships bring us close to the idea that efforts to eliminate social problems can have very different, entirely unanticipated consequences.

78. The significance of Bell's work is discussed in David Matza, *Becoming Deviant*, Englewood Cliffs, N.J.: Prentice-Hall, 1969, pp. 73-80. See also Arthur K. Davis, "Social Theory and Social Problems," *Philosophy and Phenomenological Research*, 18, December, 1957, pp. 190-208, especially pp. 200-201.

3 Unanticipated Consequences: A Conservative and Radical Notion

The insight that purposeful social action can have unanticipated results, and that these results may be highly deleterious, has an ancient and venerable history. A valuable article in the 1930's, "The Unanticipated Consequences of Purposive Social Action," examined the classical problem in some detail.[1] Clearly the possibility is of more than passing concern to anyone interested in the solution of social problems, since a solution—neglecting "spontaneous" improvement from chance factors—will require some sort of active intervention. If the programme is vulnerable to untoward outcomes, it is important to detect these possibilities beforehand.

Instances of unanticipated consequences are legion, as are the studies which have been made of them. Some seem marginal to the study of social problems. For example, we learn from the unforeseen consequences of introducing rabbits into Australia to respect ecological factors, but there is seemingly little of relevance to social issues.

Considerably more relevant are the effects of technological innovations, which have at times produced unexpected social consequences of considerable importance. Some of these inno-

1. Robert K. Merton, "The Unanticipated Consequences of Purposive Social Action," *American Sociological Review*, 1, December, 1936, pp. 894-904. Merton lists numerous precursors of his article in the modern period. One precursor is Jamieson Hurry, who wrote in 1917: "He who desires to give permanent and effective help in remedying social ills must consider not only the immediate result of his action but also the remote and collateral issues. For this both historical study and philosophic circumspection are necessary." The quote is from *Poverty and Its Vicious Circles*, London: J. & A. Churchill, 1917.

vations have been rather thoroughly studied. Many years ago, for instance, Ogburn made a detailed analysis of the social impact of the airplane.[2] More recently, studies of the introduction and diffusion of the automobile have documented important social consequences. Old patterns of dating and courtship were radically altered; parents lost considerable control over their adolescent offspring; geographical mobility of the population increased enormously; entirely new recreational patterns emerged—these are just a few of the more significant unanticipated alterations brought about by the automobile.[3]

Recently there has been a call to regulate and review emerging technology in terms of its side-effects—insofar as these can be anticipated.[4] With respect to the impact of technology our society is characterized by extreme laissez faire. While we have extensive planning for change at the production level—in order to introduce new products and produce old ones more efficiently—we have virtually no planning for change at the "consequence level." As Servan-Schreiber, the French commentator, notes in The American Challenge, we have attained a new plateau of expertise in research and development and the marketing of new innovations. But until recently we have never worried officially about the consequences of our technologism.[5] One of the most drastic consequences of technology may be the current world food and population crisis, insofar as it has resulted from the unprecedented success in conquering disease, especially infant mortality, over the past one hundred years.

Finally, there are some unanticipated consequences which, because they are the result of *social* alterations, have a direct and immediate relevance to social problems. A familiar example is

2. William F. Ogburn, The Social Effects of Aviation, Boston: Houghton Mifflin, 1946.
3. On another major invention see Sidney H. Aronson, "The Sociology of the Telephone," International Journal of Comparative Sociology, 12, 1971, pp. 153-167.
4. For a brief review see Adolf Feingold, "Technology Assessment: A Systematic Study of Side-Effects of Technology," Canadian Forum, February, 1974, pp. 10-11. See also the discussion in Chapter 1 of the prevention of the supersonic transport.
5. Numerous "sleepers" with potentially serious social consequences have received relatively little attention. For one example see Richard L. Henshel, "Ability to Alter Skin Color: Some Implications for American Society," American Journal of Sociology, 76, January, 1971, pp. 734-742.

the provision in the Canadian Immigration Act which permits the family of an immigrant to acquire immigrant status with virtually no restriction. Intending the provision as a humanitarian measure, the act's drafters did not foresee the possibility of *chain migration*. Once a single member of a foreign community gains immigrant status, extended family networks can provide eligibility for a train of further immigrants with very little control by the government of Canada.

Perhaps the ideal example of unanticipated consequences is the American experience with prohibition, the complete banning of alcoholic beverages in the 1920's. The "noble experiment" killed numerous drinkers of tainted liquor, reduced millions to the nominal status of law-breakers, increased corruption and contempt for the law, and — most significantly — created ideal conditions for the growth of organized crime. All of these results were totally unanticipated by the moral entrepreneurs of prohibition, who simply wanted to do away with Devil Drink.[6] Eventually the United States reluctantly passed an amendment to its Constitution repealing the earlier amendment which had outlawed alcoholic beverages. Prohibition taught the bitter lesson that depriving half of a nation's population of something it wants results in an increase, not in morality, but in lawlessness.

Analytically there are four possible types of unintended consequences to be considered.

1. Reforms may turn out *better* than expected because there was an unrecognized deleterious feature about the old condition in addition to that which was noticed. When the old arrangement is destroyed, both problems are removed. It is also possible that

2. Reforms may turn out *better* than expected because there was an unnoticed beneficial feature about the reform itself (in addition to taking care of the recognized evil). But, on the other hand,

3. Reform may turn out *worse* than expected because there was an unnoticed or unappreciated good feature about the old arrangement. When it is destroyed to get rid of the problem, the good feature is lost as well. Finally,

---

6. The causes of the movement are more complex than its single aim. See James H. Timberlake, *Prohibition and the Progressive Movement: 1900-1920*, Cambridge, Mass.: Harvard University Press, 1966.

4. Reform may also turn out *worse* than expected because there was an unnoticed deleterious feature about the reform itself.[7]

Before proceeding further we had best pause momentarily to consider the terms "better" and "worse" in the categories above. These are not terms ordinarily used in sociological analysis. But it is precisely in the realm of intervention, and in the designation of a condition as a social problem in the first place, that value judgments are unavoidable. One cannot speak of "problems" without implying a bad condition nor of intervention (or reform, or solution, or remedy) without implying good.[8] We can speak of better and worse, good and bad provided we recognize that these terms refer to the values of *specific cultures* or possibly to powerful elements within them, not to some universally valid standard.[9] The concept of *ethical relativity*, in which no ethical system or set of values can be shown to be superior to any other, is largely an outgrowth of cultural relativity, a twentieth century philosophical development which denies the superiority of any culture.[10] The terms good and bad must also be in reference to a particular audience because there may be value conflict within a single culture. Finally the terms must refer to a particular period in that culture's history, inasmuch as values can be reversed over long spans of time in the same culture. Every age redefines its social problems.[11]

---

7. A fifth type of unanticipated consequence — the situation in which a reform has no effect at all — will be surveyed in Chapter 4.
8. It was for this reason that sociology, in a period of exaggerated concern with its status as a science, downgraded the very study of social problems.
9. For an extensive discussion see Chapter 1 of Richard L. Henshel and Anne-Marie Henshel, *Perspectives on Social Problems*, Don Mills, Ont.: Longman Canada, 1973.
10. The classical works on this subject were done by Melville J. Herskovits. His scattered writings have been collected in M.J. Herskovits, *Cultural Relativism: Perspectives in Cultural Pluralism*, edited by Frances Herskovits, New York: Random House, 1972. See in contrast the attempts to devise some universally valid scheme of ethics. Older efforts are summarized in C. Kluckholn, "Cultural Relativity," *A Dictionary of the Social Sciences*, edited by J. Gould and W. Kolb, New York: Free Press, 1964, pp. 160-162. See also more recent efforts by V. Kavolis, *Comparative Perspectives on Social Problems*, Boston: Little, Brown, 1969; and Barrington Moore, Jr., *Reflections on the Causes of Human Misery*, Boston: Beacon Press, 1970, Chapter 1.
11. See Herbert Blumer, "Social Problems as Collective Behavior," *Social Problems*, 18, 1971, pp. 298-306.

Whether an event is judged good or ill depends on one's place in the social structure as well as proximity to the event. Let us consider a single example: the effects of the Black Death on the structure of feudalism. When this epidemic of bubonic plague swept across Europe in the fourteenth century, it killed almost one-third of the population of the continent. With this great disaster came a severe shortage of labour in the following years. As a result, many of the feudal rules which bound the serf to the land of his master were relaxed in order to give some measure of flexibility to the distribution of labourers. To the nobles the entire affair was a disaster—the plague, the labour shortage, and the remedy. To the serfs the remedy did not seem disastrous, but still they undoubtedly regarded the Black Death as infinitely more catastrophic than the slackening of their traditional obligations might have seemed beneficial. Today, however, we recognize that this shift in labour restrictions was an important factor in the ultimate downfall of the tenacious system of feudalism; hence we are tempted to regard the whole affair as good in the balance in spite of the deaths and suffering.

Let us examine the four types of unanticipated consequences. In two cases (numbers 1 and 3) it is an unobserved aspect of the prevailing status quo which is the source of planning breakdown. For the other two cases there is an unappreciated aspect of the intervention itself (the reform).[12] For each source of breakdown there is the possibility that the undetected feature is "good," and the possibility that it is "bad." These values can become transformed, however, for if a reform gets rid of a good feature of the old system, the end result is bad. We wind up with two outcomes better than expected and two outcomes worse than expected. It is the latter that attract attention, and rightly so, for people plan intervention to improve conditions. If, by chance, conditions improve more than expected, there are no

---

12. Merton (*op. cit.*, p. 897) reminds us that the problem of causal imputation is as applicable to the examination of unanticipated consequences as it is elsewhere in sociology. How is it known that it was the problem condition or the remedy which produced the unexpected effect? The answers (very partial, always tentative) are to be found in works that treat causal inference in detail, but the precaution is a good one to bear in mind throughout the chapter. We shall examine this problem briefly in Chapter 4.

repercussions, except perhaps for speculation that the measures might have been applied sooner. But if the conditions improve *less* than expected, this poses practical problems. And it is entirely possible that a reform will not only produce less benefit than expected but produce such harmful side-effects that people would be better off without the reform—the acknowledged case with prohibition and many other cases. No wonder that more interest is devoted to the two outcomes that are worse than anticipated: these are developments which it is important to avoid.[13]

MANIFEST AND LATENT FUNCTIONS

One branch of sociological inquiry fits closely with such concerns, although, ironically, interest in it has declined in a period when interest in intervention has increased. *Functionalism* is one of the most basic orientations within sociology. We shall make no attempt to cover all of the manifold questions and issues which have developed around functionalism;[14] the only requirement here is to explore those aspects which are relevant to intervention. Functionalism in social science has a long and multifaceted history. Initially developed in biology, it was adapted to social phenomena by British anthropologists and independently by the French sociologist Durkheim. It was subsequently systematized in one form by Robert Merton and later transformed by Talcott Parsons into yet another basic model. We shall concentrate here on Mertonian functionalism.

The key word "function" in functionalism is not employed in

13. When studying a specific problem, sociologists must ask themselves what will happen if *nothing* is done? What will be the social and economic costs if nothing is done? Is there a chance of spontaneous improvement? See Bernard Rosenberg, *et al.*, eds., *Mass Society in Crisis*, New York: Macmillan, 1964, p. 567. See also the discussion of reduced intervention as a strategy in Chapter 1.

14. See for this the special issue of *The Annals*: "Functionalism in the Social Sciences," edited by Don Martindale, February, 1965. Also Bernard Barber, "Structural-Functional Analysis: Some Problems and Misunderstandings," *American Sociological Review*, 21, April, 1956, pp. 129-135; and Arthur Stinchcombe, *Constructing Social Theories*, New York: Harcourt, Brace & World, 1968. For the variety of meanings of the perspective, see "Function," in J. Gould and W. Kolb, *op. cit.*, pp. 277-279.

the sense of a mathematical function but in a utilitarian sense. When it is asked what the function of something is, the answer is given in terms of what the thing *does* — in its consequence.[15] "The function of the heart is to pump the blood."[16] "The function of the public school system is to educate the young in the various forms of accumulated knowledge." Naturally a given sociocultural phenomenon can have more than a single function. Thus a second function of the public school system might be to teach practical skills needed in the surrounding society. Some of the functions may be marginal to the system under consideration—purely accidental and incidental. A heart produces thumping sounds, but it seems strange to say that this is a function of the heart. A school system keeps children off the street, but again it seems odd to call that a function of the school system—or does it?[17] Finally, there are unrecognized but important things that some systems do. A less-recognized but significant function of the public school system, for instance, is to indoctrinate children in the dominant values of the culture.

These last functions — products of some system which are unrecognized by the participants—are a special class of particular interest. They are termed *latent functions* (unrecognized), in contrast to the *manifest* (recognized) *functions* of the system.[18] One example should suffice. The Hopi Indians traditionally performed a sacred dance ritual to bring rain for their crops. People gathered from scattered locations at the time of the rain dance. The manifest function was, of course, to bring rain. The latent, unrecognized function of the dance ceremony was to assemble people together, renew ties, reestablish group bonds and feelings of solidarity. What is important is that if one took the Hopi at their word, asked them what the dance was for, one could come to the erroneous conclusion that the dance actually

15. We shall avoid the word "purpose" since it seems to imply an awareness which may be absent and use "consequence" instead.
16. This example is indicative of the biological origins of the functionalist perspective.
17. See for a recognition of this function Gwynn Nettler, *Explaining Crime*, New York: McGraw-Hill, 1974, pp. 174-175.
18. Robert K. Merton, *Social Theory and Social Structure*, rev. ed., Glencoe, Ill.: Free Press, 1957.

served no real purpose since it did not really bring rain. One might therefore suppose that the dance could be eliminated with no adverse consequences. But the dance did bring tribespeople together; its latent function was, by all reports, rather important in the life of the tribe — certainly more important than the manifest function. The idea of a latent function underscores one of the chief virtues of the functional approach: its emphasis upon the *interrelatedness* of supposedly distinct segments of society.

In the language of functionalism, the rain dance is said to be "functional" for social cohesion. In general, one item is *functional* (or eufunctional) for another if it promotes or supports, creates or maintains the other. If it weakens or destroys the second item, it is said to be *dysfunctional* for it. Naturally, a given item can be functional for one thing and dysfunctional for something else. And to say that an item is functional does not mean it is "good," unless what it supports is considered good.[19]

Unanticipated consequences can result from the existence of latent functions in the problematic condition itself, in the corrective action, or both. In the example just given, the breakdown of Hopi tribal solidarity might be a result of abolishing supposedly useless ceremonials. Let us look at a classical example of intervention that went astray because of a failure to search for the latent as well as manifest functions of social arrangements.

Colonial administrators once abolished the practice of polyandry (one woman having several husbands) in favour of strict monogamy among a remote tribe that practised female infanticide (the killing of selected female babies). The administrators looked only at the manifest function of polyandry—that is, at the reason for it as given by the native people—which was that it satisfied ritual and sacred custom. Had they considered

19. By noting that "functional" and "dysfunctional" refer solely to the effect of one item on another, and by rejecting conventional morality in noting that some supposedly evil things had good latent consequences, the functionalists were wont to speak of their method as being *value free*. This claim eventually precipitated a great deal of trouble for the school as it became increasingly obvious that biases were indeed showing through. See the discussion on conservatism later in this chapter and Melvin Tumin, "The Functionalist Approach to Social Problems," *Social Problems*, 12, Spring, 1965, pp. 379-388.

instead the latent function of such a marriage-form in a society where the supply of males greatly outnumbered the supply of females, they might have foreseen the tensions and problems for both sexes produced by their arbitrary fiat.

The above illustration should not be taken as endorsement of polyandry; the point is that there are farsighted and shortsighted ways to achieve the same objective. It is little wonder that British anthropologists ultimately obtained a strong hearing from the Colonial Office after the latter experienced repeated disaster and unnecessary hostility.[20] These early functionalists developed their ideas in close association with colonial administration, and they developed a conservative bias as an unavoidable by-product of their brand of functional analysis.

The early functionalists tended, quite correctly, to see numerous hidden uses in existing customs and social arrangements of little apparent utility. But the potential value of this insight was truncated by a failure of conceptualization. Having detected the unnoticed uses of existing arrangements, they became wedded to the status quo; any proposal for alteration to remove some problematic aspect met with the objection that a very important latent function was served by the prevailing system. If the prevailing conditions were to be altered, this beneficial component would also be lost since the two were inextricably linked. We shall consider the validity of this position momentarily.

Functional analysis has continued to play a largely conservative role by demonstrating either the undesirability or apparent impossibility of proposed alterations. Indeed, Alvin Gouldner has called functionalism the "wise man's conservativism." In order to demonstrate the functionalist approach, we shall consider two case studies. One describes some unforeseen vices of a true meritocracy; the other argues the apparent impossibility of a viable classless society.

---

20. The example just provided had important historical repercussions, but it was by no means unique or isolated. Colonial administrations and administrators of Indian affairs experienced repeated disasters and unintended consequences, many stemming from their failure to understand the workings of the cultures they "managed." See, for example, F.G. Vallee, "The Emerging Northern Mosaic," in *Canadian Society: Pluralism, Change, and Conflict*, edited by R.J. Ossenberg, Scarborough, Ont.: Prentice-Hall, 1971.

In 1959 Michael Young published a seminal book called *The Rise of the Meritocracy, 1870-2033*.[21] It is an absorbing "history" book, supposedly written in 2034, tracing the development of a fair, equitable employment system in Britain up to that time. Young starts with nineteenth-century Britain (large parts of his book are actual history), a society in which one's birthright meant considerably more than native talent in determining one's final position in society. Tracing Britain's history, he shows how this system slowly gave way to a mixed one in which individual merit assumed an ever larger role, at the expense of class of origin. But even today the measures of competence are far from perfect — some mediocrities rise, some gifted persons are excluded. Where Young begins to speculate is when, extrapolating from the present, he describes the development of *perfect* intelligence and competency tests — virtually flawless examinations which reduced the proportion of errors to zero. When these tests were given free rein in selecting persons for the better positions, Britain developed — in Young's future history — into a true meritocracy, a rule by the best.

At first glance this seems ideal, and indeed it is certainly a far better system than one which allocates position by the accident of birth. But Young's truly original contribution comes from his insightful analysis into the *drawbacks* of such a system. To begin with, the people in lower echelons no longer could excuse their place by reference to the inequities of selection: everyone had been given a truly equal chance, and if some had not "made it," it was because they *really were inferior* with respect to the criteria measured. So long as there had been obvious flaws in selection, the acceptance of a lower level position had not been psychologically damaging. Now it was.

A rationale at last existed for differential privilege since the people at the top really were better. Their time really was more valuable and should not be wasted on trivia; hence servants seemed the logical answer. Since the lower class truly could not understand complex ideas very well, it seemed justifiable not to inform them of many things. Indeed, for their own happiness, it seemed best that they be manipulated. In one pathetic scene

---

21. Published by Random House (New York).

Young describes labour-management meetings being ritually continued but with labour represented now by truly incompetent people.

Perhaps worst of all, Young paints a picture of the first society in which revolution is impossible. (He ends the book with a revolution anyway, but it is rather unconvincing.) In all previous societies, enough inequities in the selection process existed to ensure that talented people (perhaps many of them) were trapped at the bottom. These persons could form the cadre, the backbone and the brain, for a rebellion.[22] But in the meritocracy, we encounter for the first time a repressed class with *no potential*. The efforts are made, but without insight, strategy, or adequate planning they are doomed to failure — Young's last-page sop to the sentimental reader notwithstanding.

In his book, Young has carefully examined a particular social ideal, equality of opportunity, carried it to its logical culmination, and demonstrated how in the absence of other standards of decency it could become a nightmare. The book itself is a magnificent *tour de force*, but for our purposes it is interesting because it shows, first, unanticipated consequences from the perfection of certain reforms, and it does so by way of showing us the *latent functions of imperfect selection*. Imperfect selection furnishes people who do not "make it" with an excuse for their final status, restricts the reasons the people at the top can give to justify special privileges, and continually provides talented personnel for the roles of labour leader and, if need be, revolutionary general. Does this mean we must forever rest content with an imperfect system? Not necessarily: Young concedes that under certain patterns of values a meritocracy might be acceptable. But his analysis does make the task of creating ideal opportunity structures harder, and that is good because one suspects it is also more realistic.[23]

Perhaps one way out of the dilemma would be a meritocracy in an egalitarian, classless society — one with no differential in

22. Readers might wish to look at a theory of the "circulation of élites" through cycles of revolution. See V. Pareto, *The Mind and Society*, New York: Harcourt, Brace, 1935 (originally published in Florence in 1916).
23. See this dilemma of Young's work affirmed in Barrington Moore, Jr., *op. cit.*, p. 64.

the rights and perquisites of different positions in society. Those with talent would be in charge, but would have absolutely no privileges nor even extra prestige. Could this be achieved? In the late 1940's a prolonged debate arose in sociology over the sheer possibility of such a classless, egalitarian society. The functionalists, Davis and Moore, began the debate with an article denying the possibility of a viable society without stratification.[24] To summarize the argument briefly: they started by noting that some of the essential occupations in modern society were mentally taxing; some were unpleasant in a culturally-defined sense; and some required long periods of preparation. Since people would ordinarily avoid these occupations, which were apparently essential to societal functioning, the question posed by Davis and Moore was how societies obtained the necessary personnel to fill them. If these tasks were to be performed, said Davis and Moore, they must be associated with higher rewards to compensate for the costs incurred. Since even a differential allocation of honour without financial gain constitutes a form of stratification, they concluded that a workable society without stratification was an impossibility. Differential rewards were, they said, a functional requisite of every viable society.

In actuality there are two approaches that have been used historically for unpleasant occupations: *coercive service* (for example, the military draft or, in earlier periods, mandatory service in road building), and *differential rewards* of some sort — either prestige, honour, or monetary gain. Davis and Moore did not consider the former — an irony since World War II was still in progress when they were writing. Modern society is slowly purging itself of the coercive route, even in roles where it was used in the past, and some essential tasks simply do not lend themselves to the coercive alternative. It is a practical impossi-

24. Kingsley Davis and Wilbert E. Moore, "Some Principles of Stratification," *American Sociological Review*, 10, 1945, pp. 242-249. Their argument did *not* endorse social classes (meaning enduring strata in which rank is passed on by birth). For a recent test confirming a small part of their theory, see Mark Abrahamson, "Functionalism and the Functional Theory of Stratification: An Empirical Assessment," *American Journal of Sociology*, 78, March, 1973, pp. 1236-1246.

bility, for instance, to force someone to become a nuclear physicist or a heart surgeon.

The Davis and Moore thesis provoked extensive controversy,[25] some of which was rather irrelevant. Davis and Moore had not tried to justify the *prevailing* stratification system, nor had they justified social classes or denied the virtues of social mobility and equality of opportunity. One important point in criticism, however, was made by Richard Schwartz.[26] According to Schwartz, a stratification-free society was not an impossibility at all — it was merely our values which made such a system virtually unthinkable. We could, for instance, have a system in which people *rotated* from one occupation to the next, and everyone took his turn at the less pleasant tasks. If it were pointed out that such a system would be grossly, terribly inefficient, Schwartz would agree, but that was quite different from saying that such a society was impossible. Instead it was our *other values*, such as the importance of efficiency, which stood in its way, not some functional necessity. For that matter, the requirements of various positions could be modified to render them more equal in terms of their desirability.

This analysis of the feasibility of an egalitarian society illustrates a particular form of functional analysis in which one begins by abstracting certain *functional prerequisites* which every society must have in order to continue.[27] For example, every society must provide some means for the socialization of the young, for producing the necessities of life, such as food and shelter, etc. Societies are wonderfully diverse, and it stands to reason that any effort to find universal necessities (the kind without which a society would collapse) must be very carefully undertaken. Even then, conclusions may be difficult to draw, as we have just seen. Filling occupational positions through re-

25. Melvin M. Tumin, "'Some Principles of Stratification': A Critical Analysis," *American Sociological Review*, 18, 1953, pp. 387-394. See also the debate continued on pp. 394-397 and 672-673, and in 1955, 20, pp. 419-423.
26. Richard Schwartz, "Functional Alternatives to Inequality," *American Sociological Review*, 20, August, 1955, pp. 424-430.
27. See D.F. Aberle, *et al.*, "The Functional Prerequisites of a Society," *Ethics*, 60, 1950, pp. 100-113. See also Marion J. Levy, Jr., *The Structure of Society*, Princeton, N.J.: Princeton University Press, 1952.

wards turned out to be only *one* way of satisfying the functional requirement that persons must fill difficult positions. That there turned out to be at least one other way to meet this requirement is illustrative of a general principle of functionalism: the existence of alternative ways to meet most needs, what are called *functional alternatives.*[28]

Let us recall the discussion of the early functionalists, who tended to favour the status quo because they saw everywhere hidden uses (latent functions) in apparently useless or problematic phenomena. What they failed to realize, or acknowledge, was that *there are usually several ways to accomplish a given function.* If the Hopi abolish their rain dance, it will not destroy tribal unity as long as another, similiar mechanism can be substituted. These substitutes—alternate ways to accomplish the same desired result — are called functional alternatives; recognition of their existence has tended to reduce or eliminate the built-in conservatism of early functionalism while retaining its value in anticipating the consequences of intervention.[29]

There are several reasons why functionalism has been termed conservative—some less fair than others. One insightful reason has been set forth by Matza, with regard to the work of functionalists in the area of deviance — or, we might add, social problems.

What did functionalists actually write about deviant phenomena? Overwhelmingly, they stressed the functions — not dysfunctions — of deviant forms. The dysfunctions were hastily acknowledged in a first paragraph. The actual analysis ignored them, took them for granted ... (because) the

---

28. It should be noted that the search for functional requirements has been pursued for social systems other than whole societies, and for goals other than the mere survival of the system.

29. One other flaw of some early functionalists was their refusal to see that some elements of a culture may have no function at all, manifest or latent. Their emphasis on the interrelatedness of supposedly disparate parts of a culture — itself a largely beneficial insight — precluded any recognition of the persistence of cultural "survivals" that had no remaining functions. See on this William R. Catton, Jr., *From Animistic to Naturalistic Sociology,* New York: McGraw-Hill, 1966, pp. 59-60. Lack of recognition of survivals and functional alternatives leads eventually to making whatever is into a necessity.

dysfunctions (of deviance) were manifest. *Their reiteration was deemed neither a contribution to knowledge nor a sign of acuity. The important and remembered contributions to functionalist theory always contained an element of surprise—the functions of inequality, of ignorance, of deviance, of crime, of prostitution, of the political boss, of organized gambling . . . To the recitation or publication of manifest functions, the obvious response is yawning acknowledgement. Thus the actual work of most functionalists (when dealing with deviance — R.L.H.) focused on the latent contributions of previously maligned phenomena to society. . . . It is precisely on this account that the functionalists have been persistently criticized as conservative.* [30]

Matza is certainly correct in asserting that most actual analysis of deviance from the functionalist viewpoint has concentrated on locating unexpected (latent) benefits from supposedly unpleasant activities. And he is correct in maintaining that some of the functional arguments advanced have been conservative. Thus discussions of the unforeseen positive consequences of the traditional political "ward boss" might be considered conservative. So might discussions of the positive functions of social inequality, or the dysfunctions of total equality of opportunity, mentioned earlier. But some cases are ambiguous in terms of political orientation. Is a discussion of the positive functions of tobacco smoking conservative? [31] What can be said of the positive functions of lying? [32] Ludwig's book on lying is insightful and informative, but is it liberal (radical) or conservative (reactionary)? It is difficult to say.

Finally there are some functional analyses which, while confirming Matza's point about concentrating on latent functions,

30. David Matza, *Becoming Deviant*, Englewood Cliffs, N.J.: Prentice-Hall, 1969, p. 55. On the surprise aspect of functionalism, see also Murray S. Davis, "That's Interesting! . . . ,"*Philosophy of the Social Sciences*, 1, 1971, pp. 309-344, especially pp. 319-320.
31. See "Beneficial Effects of Tobacco" in Chapter 13 of *Smoking and Health*, Report of the Advisory Committee to the Surgeon General, Washington: U.S. Government Printing Office, 1964.
32. Arnold M. Ludwig, *The Importance of Lying*, Springfield, Ill.: Charles C. Thomas, 1965.

have anything but conservative implications. Lewis Coser's famous book, *The Functions of Social Conflict*, lists several features of social conflict — for example, the providing of a measure of power to otherwise powerless groups — which are beneficial from a liberal or radical standpoint.[33] Coser's presidential address to the Society for the Study of Social Problems had the same radical implications.[34] An article by Herbert Gans on the positive functions that poverty provides for the affluent in society also has radical implications.[35] And we shall shortly devote a whole section to the *labeling school*, a radical critique of existing criminal justice and mental health establishments which is based essentially on the latent functions of trials and hearings.[36] Finally, Herbert Marcuse, a key figure of radical sociology, has himself performed a functional analysis (albeit without using the terminology of functionalism) in his effort to show that radicals should not grant tolerance to institutions whose values they strongly oppose.[37]

Functionalism is used typically to explain the persistence or stability of systems (for example, why they sometimes return to their earlier conditions).[38] Of course this ties in with its supposed conservative bias. But functionalism's most essential conception is of the interrrelatedness of aspects of society, and

33. Lewis A. Coser, *The Functions of Social Conflict*, New York: Free Press, 1966. See also Coser, "Some Social Functions of Violence," *The Annals*, 304, March, 1966, pp. 8-18.

34. Lewis A. Coser, "Unanticipated Conservative Consequences of Liberal Theorizing," *Social Problems*, 16, Winter, 1969, pp. 263-272.

35. Herbert J. Gans, "The Positive Functions of Poverty," *American Journal of Sociology*, 78, September, 1972, pp. 275-289.

36. Other liberal discussions of the latent functions / unanticipated consequences of present-day criminal justice can be seen in the sociological input to the LeDain Commission on the use of drugs in Canada. In one section, "The Unintended Consequences of Punitive Legislation," the subtitles list: the increase in theft, the failure to deter the drug user, the encouragement of organized crime, estrangement of the police, and estrangement of youth. See LeDain, *et al.*, *Interim Report of the Commission of Inquiry into the Non-Medical Use of Drugs*, Ottawa: Queen's Printer, 1970.

37. Herbert Marcuse, "Repressive Tolerance," in *Political Elites in a Democracy*, edited by P. Bachrach, New York: Atherton, 1971.

38. See this form of explanation outlined in Stinchcombe, *op. cit.*, pp. 84-98. For the argument that functionalism has extreme difficulty accounting for revolutionary change in a society, see J. Rex, *Key Problems of Sociological Theory*, London: Routledge and Kegan Paul, 1961.

under certain circumstances this conception can explain change as well as persistence. Thus if we assume that one cultural component is changed via intervention, the functions of the reform or of the detested condition can explain the emergence of changes in other parts of the society — that is, unanticipated consequences.

One final comment: functionalism, as well as being a theoretical framework, is a *style of thought*. Once one begins functional analysis, it opens a vast new range of insights into social dynamics. But it is only a style of thought, not a foolproof process or method. There is no way to ensure that we have located *all* latent functions, no automatic generating device to guarantee this. The approach depends, in the last analysis, on insight and theory. As Kingsley Davis once pointed out in a rather obscure way, one need not be a functionalist, or even know the term, to use the functional mode of analysis.[39]

Functional analysis is linked to the previous chapter on conceptual obstacles to intervention. Obviously, we may not realize until too late a positive aspect of the "problem" we are trying to get rid of, or a negative aspect of the "remedy" we apply. Such were the deep convictions, fiercely held, of many writers of the nineteenth century who opposed governmental intervention as dangerous meddling in areas in which little was known. Herbert Spencer provided numerous concrete illustrations of suffering caused by misguided legislative decrees.[40] So too did a legion of lesser writers. Unforeseen consequences, in short, can be disastrous.

Perhaps the best response to exclusive concentration on the ills of misguided intervention has been given by a modern-day interventionist, B.F. Skinner. Skinner sees little logic in the

39. One major subject within functionalism that we have ignored is the effort to provide explanations of the *existence* of a sociocultural item by reference to the function it provides. This seemingly backwards "teleological" explanation (i.e., explaining the existence of an earlier event by its effect on some later event, or outcome, which supposedly "caused" it) has been the subject of seemingly endless debate. The topic will be ignored here because it is not central to our investigation of unanticipated consequences, but no one can take up functionalism for long without encountering it. See Ronald P. Dore, "Function and Cause," *American Sociological Review*, 26, December, 1961, pp. 843-853; Stinchcombe, *ibid*.

40. Herbert Spencer, *The Man Versus the State*, London: 1884.

arguments of laissez faire advocates. To be sure, intervention may go astray, but what of it? Do we then place our confidence in blind accident? "It is hard to justify the trust which is placed in accident...there is no virtue in accident. *The unplanned also goes wrong.*"[41] Skinner is pointing to what might be called the unanticipated consequences of inaction, of doing nothing. Obviously, once again, such consequences can be either better or worse than what was expected. The place to look for unanticipated consequences of inaction — especially negative consequences — is in Marxian, and Weberian, analysis.

INTERNAL CONTRADICTIONS:

MARXIAN AND WEBERIAN CONCEPTIONS

Functionalism is one basic approach to unanticipated consequences. Its value for this purpose lies in its ability to sensitize us to the results of *altering* the status quo in some fashion — in our own terms, the results of intervention to resolve a social problem. Another basic mode of analysis in sociology provides a way to anticipate the unexpected consequences of *continuing* with the present system. In this approach, one searches for "strains" in the existing structure of society, for "internal contradictions" between various components of this complex structure. It is from these internal discontinuities, rather than from external forces, that the most basic forms of social change are seen as taking place. The internal mechanisms of change are termed *dialectical processes,* and the form of analysis is called dialectics.[42] The student of internal contradictions looks, for example, to the internal dynamics of the Roman Empire for clues to its decline and fall, not to the barbarians at the gates. Change, in short, is largely generated from *within* the system and is ubiquitous: change is assumed to be the basic reality, if we may speak loosely. The dialectical approach sees unanticipated con-

---

41. B.F. Skinner, *Beyond Freedom and Dignity,* New York: Knopf, 1971, p. 161.
42. In this chapter we examine the dialectical approach as a view of historical processes. It can also be a theory of physical processes and/or a theory of knowledge. See for the latter Joan Huber Rytina and Charles P. Loomis, "Marxist Dialectic and Pragmatism: Power as Knowledge," *American Sociological Review,* 35, April, 1970, pp. 308-318.

sequences stemming from the unfolding or "natural" development of the old system, that is from continuities, not from purposeful breaks with it. The latter is the contribution of functional
analysis.

The best known advocates of the dialectical approach are of
course the followers of Karl Marx, but, as we shall see, the
perspective has also been pursued by many others who fall
outside of his overall framework.[43]Marx borrowed the idea of
the dialectical process from the philosopher Hegel. According
to one rendition of Hegelian dialectics, the historical process
may be understood in terms of a repeating cycle (or, better, a
spiral): thesis begets antithesis; the two conflict but ultimately
mix to create a synthesis, which forms the thesis of the next
cycle. Marx accepted Hegel's view of historical change as due to
an inner unfolding within a given system. But where Hegel had
employed the dialectic to explain the development and
emergence of key *ideas* in history, Marx was predominantly a
materialist, in the sense of regarding ideas as mere
"epiphenomena." Although Marx himself often abandoned
materialism, he was responsible for turning the dialectic on
what later followers regarded uncritically as the basic causal
mechanism of history, economic forces. Some of his own writing, and especially the writings of his followers, is explicitly
that of economic determinism. In these writings Marxists saw
economic relations determining not only other aspects of social
structure (for example, the family), but also the culture and,
ultimately, even the sophisticated ideas of each era, which the
wise men of the day thought of as independently generated.[44]
Economics, in turn, was governed by its own dialectical processes and internal contradictions. Each economic system
(feudalism, mercantilism, capitalism) contained within itself
the "seeds of its own destruction."

Given the presence of internal contradictions, many Marxists

43. Also, Marx employed on some occasions a form of analysis which might be
considered a variant of functionalism. See Stinchcombe, *op. cit.,* pp. 93-98.
44. Marx was a prolific writer, and the early Marx does not always agree with the
later Marx. There are many times in which Marx abandons the theme of
economic determinism, and scholars argue over the primacy of this theme in his
thought.

accepted the thesis that each economic system in the history of the world has been successively doomed to ultimate self-destruction and replacement by the next economic order. The new order itself contains internal contradictions, which become more pronounced and apparent as the system matures. The perspective is both deterministic and unilinear, in the sense discussed in the previous chapter. Significantly, it is not external attacks on the established system which lead to its downfall (except, perhaps, when it is already crumbling), nor is it intervention into recognized problems. It is rather the continuation, the "unfolding" or "becoming", of its own internal development which is the system's undoing. The unanticipated consequences stem in fact from the *successes* of the system as it attains a "higher order" of development.

Marx foresaw, for example, the ultimate destruction of capitalism through its very successes, through its essential nature. In one analysis he forecast that the increasing complexity of capitalism would eventually require the training and education of workers, but this in its turn would give them the tools and potential to revolt against the capitalist system. In a subsequent refinement, Lenin predicted that the capitalist system, requiring control over client states, would arm the working class in order to secure its goals of empire. The workers, thus educated and armed, would then be in a position to overthrow the very order which had provided the means.[45]

In another analysis Marx saw power being concentrated into fewer and fewer hands because the natural order of development of capitalism is toward a condition of monopoly or oligopoly control. As the process continues, more and more former entrepreneurs are forced out of business through economic crises, squeezed out through the very dynamics of capitalism into the ranks of the proletariat. Economic crises intensify, and after each the residue of bourgeoisie shrinks ever smaller and the proletariat base expands. Thus by its natural tendency to move toward its more "advanced" form (monopoly), capitalism sows the seeds of its ultimate downfall. This was one of many internal contradictions Marx saw in the capitalist system.[46]

45. I thank Peter Archibald for this example.
46. See Karl Marx, *Capital*, Volume 1, New York: E.P. Dutton & Co., 1930.

The particular process just described has been subjected to repeated and telling criticism. In fairness, it should be recalled that this particular theory is well over one hundred years old. There is an unfortunate tendency to read only the original Marxian formulations; when they are rejected, the dialectic itself is rejected, and the contributions and alterations of Polanyi, Schumpeter, and more recent writers are ignored.[47] In any case, it is not so much the accuracy of a specific illustration which is of interest as the general framework of analysis. The idea of internal contradictions, sometimes rephrased as internal "tensions" or structural "strains," has ultimately become a key conception in the hands of *non-Marxian* sociologists.[48]

Although many Marxists have done so, there is no compelling reason to assume that ideas exert no causal influence in history, or to refrain from using on them the concept of internal strains. Max Weber considered the spread of ideas to be a key causal force in history, and at one point he became interested in what his widow, Marianne Weber, called "the tragedy of the idea." To paraphrase Marx, certain historical ideas may contain within themselves the seeds of their own destruction.[49]

Weber's study of what he called the Protestant ethic had convinced him that the complex of religious ideas of early Protestantism was one of the causes for the emergence of capitalism in the economic sphere.[50] According to his interpretation, the set of ideas embodied in some early Protestant doctrines — salvation of the elect, predestination, "stewards of God" — led believers to another complex of ideas and behaviour with respect to hard work, time budgeting, and self-sacrifice, which in turn produced great accumulations of wealth on both the per-

47. See David Sallach, "What is Sociological Theory?" *The American Sociologist,* 8, August, 1973, pp. 134-139.
48. See, for example, Wilbert E. Moore, *Social Change,* Englewood Cliffs, N.J.: Prentice-Hall, 1963.
49. For Weber, the relationship seemed stronger still: Marianne Weber concludes that for him, "the idea, in the end, *always and everywhere* works against its original meaning and thus destroys itself." Quoted in Louis Schneider, *Sociological Approach to Religion,* New York: Wiley, 1970, p. 104, italics added. See on this point also Werner Stark, "Max Weber and the Heterogony of Purposes," *Social Research,* 34, Summer, 1967, pp. 249-264.
50. Max Weber, *The Protestant Ethic and the Spirit of Capitalism,* New York: Scribner's, 1930.

sonal and community level. This drove him to speculate further on whether early Protestantism's very successes led to its ultimate downfall. Far from the former religious glorification of poverty, wealth was now welcomed by the early Protestants as a sign that they were among the chosen. Ultimately, however, the wealth and material well-being they had accumulated exerted a corrosive effect on the puritanical aspects of their religion and way of life. According to Weber, Protestant asceticism brought about its own demise. The very success of the idea led to its ultimate deterioration — hence, the tragedy of the idea. Weber saw not just capitalism but the *worst aspects* of "victorious capitalism" springing from and ultimately destroying an antithetical religious doctrine. "The early Puritan aimed at salvation; he had no interest in wealth *per se*; the modern capitalist, his direct descendant, has no interest in anything but wealth *per se*; he has forgotten about salvation. The early Puritan revered the Ten Commandments, but the modern capitalist dances around the Golden calf."[51]

Although Weber himself did not do so, Schneider demonstrates how easily the analysis fits Marxian methodology: "Protestant asceticism, featuring industry, thrift, and frugality, works for the 'good,' for the greater glory of God, but then it produces the 'bad,' in the form of temptation to abandon asceticism. The temptation is created by the wealth that asceticism itself brings about. It is a characteristic dialectical element in this that the very emergence of the 'good'. . . contains within itself, as it were, its opposite, the emergence of the 'bad' lapse of asceticism: a phenomenon harbors its own 'contradiction'."[52]

Weber's thesis concerning Protestantism and capitalism has been subjected to searching criticism.[53] But it is the extension of the dialectic into the realm of ideas which is of central concern here. Weber also observed the "tragedy" at work in the growing emphasis on reason, because increasing rationalization of society leads to bureaucratization and to the stifling of the very impulses which reason hopes to promote.[54] Horkheimer and Adorno, in their *Dialectic of* [the] *Enlightenment*, are quite ex-

51. Stark, *op. cit.*, p. 253.
52. Schneider, *op. cit.*, p. 112.
53. See the several challenges surveyed in H.R. Trevor-Roper, "Religion, the Reformation and Social Change," *Historical Studies*, 4, 1963, pp. 18-44.

plicit in applying the concept of self-destructiveness to the ideas of the Enlightenment period. Merton's examination of early science[55] suggests another instance: Puritan desires to appreciate God's works in all their glory and wisdom led to the stimulation of early scientific study of nature, but in the end the very findings of science undermined the doctrinal foundations of religion. Barrington Moore gives yet another illustration through his analysis of the ultimate consequences of the application of direct democracy. From his historical appraisal, he concludes that "direct democracy *generates* revolutionary terror, its own nemesis."[56]

We see in Marx and in the above-mentioned aspect of Weber a concern with unanticipated consequences, with outcomes which are the opposite of what the actors intend or desire. The idea that systems may contain inherent strains or "contradictions" which in the long run cause their demise, although perhaps not so all-embracing as some Marxists have assumed, is a terribly important analytic contribution.

Functionalism and dialectics seem to many to be entirely antithetical.[57] They operate under different methodologies, deal with different problems, and, perhaps more importantly, have attracted scholars of fundamentally divergent political philosophies. Functionalists have emphasized the degree to which society is held together by consensus on values, while dialecticians have emphasized the conflict and coercion within society. Yet both have much to offer to the serious student of social problems, and both have much to say on the matter of unanticipated consequences.[58]

In the following sections we will look at a specific type of unintended consequence. The labeling of individuals as deviants by agencies designed to change them may actually tend to

54. See Stark, op. cit., pp. 261-262.
55. Robert K. Merton, *Science, Technology and Society in Seventeenth Century England*, New York: Howard Fertig, 1970.
56. Barrington Moore, Jr., op. cit., p. 66, italics added.
57. See, as one expression of this standard view, Alvin W. Gouldner, *The Coming Crisis of Western Sociology*, New York: Basic Books, 1970.
58. For an extensive discussion of functionalism and the dialectic, see Guy Rocher, *A General Introduction to Sociology: A Theoretical Perspective*, Toronto: Macmillan Co. of Canada, 1972. This is in reality more a theory text than an introduction to sociology for beginners.

stabilize and perpetuate their unappreciated behaviour. This situation can be approached functionally by considering labeling as a latent function of the bureaucratic decision-making process.

LABELING: A "CASE STUDY" OF UNANTICIPATED CONSEQUENCES[59]

Inasmuch as contemporary sociologists tend to be more critical of existing social arrangements than they were in the past, it is perhaps only natural that social control agencies (the police, the courts, corrections, mental hospitals, welfare agencies) are now sometimes seen as inadvertently worsening some of the very problems they attempt to control. This emphasis upon latent, deleterious consequences produced by formal agencies of control has been accompanied by the development of a reaction theory, or, as it is more commonly termed, a theory of *labeling*. Labeling by official agencies produces an unanticipated consequence that has been subjected to searching inquiry.

In earlier theoretical approaches, the agencies of social control have been seen primarily as reducing the magnitude of social problems or, at worst, as having no effect at all. By contrast, the labeling theorists believe that, inadvertently, public agencies designed to alleviate social problems have become, in a very real sense, a part of the problem themselves, through their capacity to impose stigma of various sorts on the persons under their purview. Lemert, one of the earliest labeling theorists, noted that traditional sociology placed heavy reliance on the idea that deviance leads to social control. But he came to believe that the reverse direction — that social control inadvertently leads to more deviance — was the "potentially richer premise."[60] In the more extreme statements of labeling theory, actions of the agencies of social control are seen as the main, or even the only, source of the very problems they supposedly

59. Portions of this and the following section are taken, with permission, from Henshel and Henshel, 1973, *op. cit.*, and from Richard L. Henshel and Robert A. Silverman, eds., *Perception in Criminology*, New York: Columbia University Press, 1975.

60. Edwin M. Lemert, *Human Deviance, Social Problems, and Social Control*, Englewood Cliffs, N.J.: Prentice-Hall, 1967, p. 5.

combat. The affinity of the labeling perspective to the idea of unanticipated consequences already seems clear.

Kai Erikson presents the perspective in this way: "Even the worst miscreant in society conforms most of the time, if only in the sense that he uses the correct silver at dinner, stops obediently at traffic lights, or in a hundred other ways respects the ordinary conventions of his group."[61] There are, therefore, two levels of analysis in the definitions of deviance: what is a deviant act, and who is a deviant person? "When the community nominates someone to the deviant class, then, it is sifting a few important details out of the stream of behavior (the "deviant") has emitted and is in effect declaring that these details reflect the kind of person he 'really' is."[62]

Any agency with official power to impose a label on a person can bring about marked changes in that person's life — not only through altering his experiences via prison or hospitalization, but also by changing his self-image, the impressions that important others have of him, and his future employment opportunities. The labeling theorists would argue that in many cases an agency takes a marginal individual, one who is not entirely committed to any position, closes off certain paths to him, and by various devices forces him to accept its designation. By so doing, his deviant tendencies may well be heightened instead of reduced. The unintended consequence of the label is that it perpetuates or accentuates what it is supposed to attack. The subject may come to see himself precisely as the agency sees him (for example, "I am a dangerous criminal"), accept the given label (with its own psychological rewards), and become that much more intractable. The emphasis in labeling theory is thus upon "*secondary deviation*" — behaviour produced by society's reaction to an initial deviation, which is termed the "*primary deviation*."[63]

61. Kai T. Erikson, *Wayward Puritans*, New York: Wiley, 1966, p. 6.
62. *Ibid.*, p. 7.
63. It is thus the secondary deviation which is the unanticipated consequence of the imposition of a label. Possibly the clearest case of the vicious feedback that may result is the homeless alcoholic. See P.J. Giffen, "The Revolving Door: A Functional Interpretation," *Canadian Review of Sociology and Anthropology*, 3, 1966, pp. 154-166.

THE LABELING PROCESS IN GREATER DETAIL

Let us examine the process of labeling more closely. The manifest function of the official imposition of a label in criminal trials and insanity hearings is to arrive at a determination (or verdict) of an individual's status so that appropriate actions can be taken. But some other things happen as well. These are the latent functions of trials and hearings, possibly unrecognized by the parties involved but critical in the labeling perspective.

In the beginning, it is perception on the part of the public or the police that an individual has committed a deviant act which leads to his labeling as "sick" or criminal.[64] Often the objective reality of a situation becomes clear too late to overcome the effects of such labeling. Even if a trial finds an individual innocent, and even if, speaking objectively, he did not commit the offence, much psychological harm may be done by the arrest, pre-trial confinement, and the judicial procedure itself, and the harm may be permanent.

Even before an individual offender is apprehended, indeed even if he is never apprehended, the effects of *potential* labeling and sanctioning can be detected. Matza has given us an excellent treatment of this.[65] After performing a forbidden act, the person is bedeviled, haunted internally. The bedevilment begins to turn him away from his previous outlooks toward greater acceptance of a deviant career. He also begins to feel transparent in the company of conventional people, afraid that he may slip, so it is easier to consort with fellow deviants among whom he need not fear disclosure. Thus performing a proscribed act already causes changes in personality and affiliation, even without or before apprehension.

Suddenly the arm of the state reaches out for some party,

64. Richard Schwartz and Jerome Skolnick, "Two Studies of Legal Stigma," *Social Problems*, 10, 1962, pp. 133-142, is a well-known empirical investigation of the consequences of legal sanctions which simultaneously illuminates the role of public perception of the offender in such consequences. There is also an exchange of opinions between the authors and H. Lawrence Ross in *Social Problems*, Spring, 1963, pp. 390-392, which readers might find important.
65. David Matza, *op. cit.* Matza's contributions here are marred by a seeming inability to use an old, conventional word whenever a new one can be invented. Nonetheless his analysis merits the translation required of the reader.

guilty or innocent, mentally "ill" or not. Usually everything happens with bewildering swiftness; the person is distracted, distraught, and in a highly suggestible condition. Even before a final determination of his case is reached, he finds people he knows altering their behaviour toward him. The day of the hearing (or trial) arrives. Here, every aspect of bureaucracy is brought to bear to ensure, in the mind of the individual, the significance of the acquisition of a label.[66] Emphasis is placed on the seriousness of the consequences, and therefore the impartiality of the hearing is stressed.[67] There is an aura of sanctity, of the majesty of officialdom, of a sharp cleavage between the innocent and the guilty, the sane and the insane. And then the label is imposed. Small wonder that a lasting impression is made in this traumatic situation.

Let us assume first that the labeled person undergoes no period of hospitalization or incarceration. Even without these experiences he encounters potent change mechanisms which can lead to alterations in his personality and behaviour. Labeling theory relies heavily on George Herbert Mead's classic conception that the self (self-image, for our purposes) arises out of social interaction.[68] As Ichheiser puts it,

> The images we hold of other people are not only mirrors which reflect, whether correctly or not, their personalities, but they are also dynamic factors which control the behavior of those people ... it is often the personality itself which has to adjust to its distorted reflection in the "mirror."[69] .

66. See for insights, Harold Garfinkel, "Conditions of Successful Degradation Ceremonies," *American Journal of Sociology*, 61, March, 1956, pp. 420-424.
67. But impartiality may be largely mythical. Thomas Szasz locates the vested interests at work in supposedly impartial hearings on insanity. See his *Psychiatric Justice*, New York: Basic Books, 1966.
68. For Mead see John W. Petras, "George Herbert Mead's Theory of Self: A Study in the Origin and Convergence of Ideas," *Canadian Review of Sociology and Anthropology*, 10, 1973, pp. 145-159.
69. Gustav Ichheiser, *Appearances and Realities*, San Francisco: Jossey-Bass, 1970, p. 54. See also James Hackler, "Predictors of Deviant Behaviour: Norms Versus the Perceived Anticipations of Others," *Canadian Review of Sociology and Anthropology*, 5, 1968, pp. 92-106.

An individual who feels that he has been labeled, that society (or at least the offended majority) will henceforth react to him negatively, no matter what his subsequent behaviour, may begin to internalize the components of the role that parallels the stereotype and thus move from primary to secondary deviance.[70] Old associates, including his most significant others (family, work peers, etc.), alter their conception of him. His reference group adjusts and changes its attitude toward him. Usually, of course, he is welcomed by new associates as well as rejected by old ones, and this exerts a considerable influence upon a person already in a highly anxious state. From his new associates he may learn appropriate rationalizations ("neutralizations") of his stigma.

Of course imprisonment or hospitalization intensifies all of these trends. The institution introduces the labeled individual to new peers, all of whom are similarly stigmatized. Different life experiences materialize in the institutional setting. The individual may acquire new, illicit skills to replace legitimate ones.[71] Afterward there are economic consequences: changed employment opportunities, perhaps dismissal from one's previous job, life-style changes mandated by financial conditions. It may be difficult, if not impossible, to obtain loans, bonding, or licences.

The labeling process with mental illness is at once more profound and more intricate. Since no one has been able to express the viewpoint quite as well as Scheff, we shall let him describe it in his own words.[72] First he defines "residual rule-breaking."

70. Mary Owen Cameron, *The Booster and the Snitch*, Glencoe, Ill.: Free Press, 1964, pp. 159-164, takes up the self-perception aspect of labeling, discussing the mechanisms by which shoplifters who do not have an impression of themselves as deviants may begin to acquire such a self-image. Readers intrigued by the analysis in Cameron might also wish to examine Leroy Gould, "Who Defines Delinquency?" *Social Problems*, 16, Winter, 1969, pp. 325-336, on the development of self-perceived delinquency from official labeling.

71. See an excellent treatment of these issues in Gresham Sykes, *Society of Captives*, Princeton, N.J.: Princeton University Press, 1965.

72. Subsequent quotations are from Thomas J. Scheff, *Being Mentally Ill: A Sociological Theory*, Chicago: Aldine, 1966. Page numbers at the end of each cited section refer to this book.

> *The culture... provides a vocabulary of terms for categorizing many norm violations: crime, perversion, drunkenness, and bad manners are familiar examples. Each of these terms is derived from the types of norm broken, and ultimately, from the* type of behavior involved. *After exhausting these categories, however, there is always a residue of the most diverse kinds of violations, for which the culture provides no explicit label... (A)lthough there is great cultural variation in what is defined as decent or real, each culture tends to reify its definition of decency and reality, and so provides no way of handling violations of its expectations in these areas. The typical norm governing decency or reality, therefore, literally "goes without saying."... For the convenience of the society in construing those instances of* unnameable *rule-breaking... these violations may be lumped together into a* residual *category... in our society, mental illness. In this discussion, the diverse kinds of rule-breaking for which our society provides no explicit label, and which, therefore, sometimes lead to the labeling of the violator as mentally ill, will be considered to be technically residual rule breaking. (p. 34, italics added).*

In short, when people do the inexplicable, it may be labeled "mental illness." It may be inexplicable only to the observers, not inexplicable in itself, but its weirdness to a number of observers may be sufficient to set a process in motion which ultimately provides its own confirmation and justification. How that may happen is Scheff's next point.

> *It is customary in psychiatric research to seek a single generic source or at best a small number of sources for mental illness. The redefinition of psychiatric symptoms as residual deviance immediately suggests, however, that there should be an unlimited number of sources of deviance. The first proposition is therefore:*
> *Residual rule-breaking arises from fundamentally diverse sources. (pp. 39-40)*
> *Relative to the rate of treated mental illness, the rate of unrecorded residual rule-breaking is extremely high. There is*

evidence that gross violations of rules are often not noticed or, if noticed, rationalized as eccentricity. Apparently, many persons who are extremely withdrawn, or who "fly off the handle" for extended periods of time, who imagine fantastic events, or who hear voices or see visions, are not labeled as insane either by themselves or others. Their rule-breaking, rather, is unrecognized, ignored, or rationalized. This pattern of inattention and rationalization will be called "denial." (pp. 47-48)

What is the extent of residual rule-breaking that is "denied" by others?

Since the Plunkett and Gordon review was published, two elaborate studies of symptom prevalence have appeared, one in Manhattan, the other in Nova Scotia. In the Midtown Manhattan study it is reported that 80 per cent of the sample currently had at least one psychiatric symptom. Probably more comparable to the earlier studies is their rating of "impaired because of psychiatric illness," which was applied to 23.4 per cent of the population. In the Stirling County [Nova Scotia] studies, the estimate of current prevalence is 57 per cent, with 20 per cent classified as "Psychiatric Disorder with Significant Impairment." (p. 48)

If there is that much "mental illness," how is it handled?

Most residual rule-breaking is "denied" and is of transitory significance.... For this type of rule-breaking, which is amorphous and uncrystallized, Lemert used the term "primary deviation." (p. 51)

What happens in the cases of persons for whom residual deviance is not denied?

If residual rule-breaking is highly prevalent among ostensibly "normal" persons and is usually transitory, as suggested by the last two propositions, what accounts for the small percentage of residual rule-breakers who go on to deviant

careers? To put the question another way, under what conditions is residual rule-breaking stabilized? The conventional
hypothesis is that the answer lies in the rule-breaker himself.
The hypothesis suggested here is that the most important
single factor (but not the only factor) in the stabilization of
residual rule-breaking is the societal reaction. (pp. 53-54,
emphasis added)

It was stated that the usual reaction to residual rule-
breaking is denial, and that in these cases most rule-breaking
is transitory. The societal reaction to rule-breaking is not
always denial, however. In a small proportion of cases the
reaction goes the other way, exaggerating and at times distort-
ing the extent and degree of the violation. This pattern of
exaggeration . . . we will call "labeling." (p. 81, italics added.)

How might labeling perpetrate the very problem it is supposed
to remove?

Labeled deviants may be rewarded for playing the
stereotyped deviant role. Ordinarily, patients who display
"insight" are rewarded by psychiatrists and other personnel.
That is, patients who manage to find evidence of their "illness" in their past and present behavior, confirming the medical and societal diagnosis, receive benefits. This pattern of
behavior is a special case of a more general pattern that has
been called the "apostolic function" by Balint, in which the
physician and others inadvertently cause the patient to display symptoms of the illness the physician thinks the patient
has. (p. 84)

Labeled deviants are punished when they attempt to return to conventional roles. The second process operative is
the systematic blockage of entry to non-deviant roles once the
label has been publicly applied. Thus the former mental patient, although he is urged to rehabilitate himself in the community, usually finds himself discriminated against in seeking to return to his old status, and on trying to find a new one
in the occupational, marital, social and other spheres.
(p. 87)

In the crisis occurring when a residual rule-breaker is pub-

lically labeled, the deviant is highly suggestible, and may accept the proffered role of the insane as the only alternative. When gross rule-breaking is publicly recognized and made an issue, the rule-breaker may be profoundly confused, anxious, and ashamed. In this crisis it seems reasonable to assume that the rule-breaker will be suggestible to the cues that he gets from the reactions of others toward him. (p. 88)

The preceding ... hypotheses form the basis for the final causal hypothesis.

Among residual rule-breakers, labeling is the single most important cause of [lengthy] careers of residual deviance. (pp. 92-93)

A classical dictum by W.I. Thomas lays the foundation for a discussion of the linkage between labeling, stereotypy, and the self-fulfilling prophecy. Recognizing the possibility of error in men's perceptions, Thomas emphasized the importance of the error by noting that "situations defined as real are real in their consequences." Although this acknowledges the reality of effects from mistaken ideas, it was left to another to point out the possibility that these effects might actually include making the originally wrong idea come true.

The concept of a self-fulfilling prophecy originated in a famous article by Robert Merton in 1948.[73] He defined it to be a prophecy which, although false at the time it was made, became true as a result of having been pronounced. The simplest example is that of the bank run, where rumors spread about a bank's insolvency causing depositors to besiege the bank frantically, withdrawing their own deposits. Even if the bank were reasonably sound, it would not ordinarily carry enough funds to meet the demands of all of its depositors at the same time. Thus if a false prediction of bank failure is believed by enough people, their own actions can in fact make the prediction come true; it will fail because of their frantic actions. Instances of self-fulfilling prophecies abound in the social world.[74]

---

73. Robert K. Merton, "The Self-Fulfilling Prophecy," *Antioch Review*, 8, Summer, 1948, pp. 193-210.
74. Richard L. Henshel and Leslie W. Kennedy, "Self-Altering Prophecies: Consequences for the Feasibility of Social Prediction," *General Systems*, 18 (annual), 1973, pp. 119-126.

The labeling process is a form of self-fulfilling prophecy.[75] The prediction is made that, if allowed to act freely, a particular person will act in a deviant way. To prevent this he is forced to undergo certain experiences that in fact tend to solidify these deviant tendencies. At last the other actors in the drama look in upon what they have themselves helped to create, and pronounce it, not surprisingly, in line with their expectations. This is one way in which stereotypes can be made self-confirming — and indeed self-perpetuating — if we explore just a bit more closely.

The self-fulfilling prophecy is closely linked in its labeling aspect with Walter Lippman's concept of the *stereotype*.[76] A stereotype, it will be recalled, is a preconceived, standardized, group-shared idea about a supposedly inherent quality of some other group of persons. Mental pictures of Jews as greedy, Indians as stupid, Italians as excitable — these are examples of stereotypes. Stereotypes can become self-confirming in one sense through the direct exercise of *power*: if an employee, for example, thinks that he will survive in his job only by *enacting* the stereotype expected of him, he will do so and thereby create self-confirmation of the stereotype, and its self-perpetuation as well. (The mechanism is well documented by case studies of Blacks in the American South.) But we are more interested in the self-confirmation and perpetuation of a stereotype in the context of labeling. Here, power is employed as well, but the process is more complex. Let us follow it in the labeling process for criminals and delinquents.[77]

In the selection of those minor offenders to be arrested and convicted, two important forms of *discretion* come into play: in the decision to arrest and in the decision to imprison. As has often been noted, it is manifestly impossible for a legislature to

75. Jock Young carefully considers the self-fulfilling aspects of labeling. See his "The Police as Amplifiers of Deviancy . . . ," in *Images of Deviance*, edited by Stanley Cohen, Harmondsworth: Penguin, 1971, pp. 27-52.
76. Walter Lippman, *The Public Philosophy*, Boston: Little, Brown, 1955. In "Public Stereotypes of Deviants," J.L. Simmons states that "stereotyping . . . is an inherent aspect of perception and cognition." *Social Problems*, 13, 1965, pp. 223-232. He analyzes both the correlates of a tendency to stereotype and the consequences of public stereotyping.
77. A good case can also be made for the self-confirmation of a stereotype in mental labeling. See Scheff, *op. cit.*, Chapter 3.

set down rules for law enforcement officials which can cover the infinity of discrete situations encountered in practice. Many occasions exist in which a policeman must use his own judgement in deciding whether or not to make an arrest. This is most often the case for relatively minor or marginal offenses, in which the statutory language is intentionally vague. In contrast to the relative precision with which such a serious crime as rape is defined, laws regarding loitering, disturbing the peace, public nuisance, drunk and disorderly conduct, or interference with a peace officer on official duty are necessarily less specific, having to cover a broad range of concrete instances in multi-dimensional situations. For such offenses, what is termed *police discretion* is quite apparent. The official must decide whether the offender should be ignored, lectured, sent home in a taxi, "remanded" to his parents, or arrested. The man on the spot must be allowed considerable latitude because of the heterogeneity of situations in which a given law may apply.

Difficulties, therefore, arise and minor offenses are frequently handled in a discriminatory way. No one doubts that the police arrest murderers in a systematic fashion, regardless of social class, but what of drunks? The man drunk in his Cadillac in a fashionable section of town is guided to a taxi; the grizzled old man on skid row is hustled into the drunk tank because it is assumed that he does not have a home. We need not depend on casual observation to confirm this trend: observers have accompanied police on their rounds and have systematically recorded bias on the decision to arrest.[78] Much the same factors come into play with police discretion as with judicial and jury discretion (to be discussed momentarily)—old, white, female, and middle- or upper-class persons are less likely to be taken into custody. Additional factors are also at work here:[79] the locale of apprehension, the time of day, whether the policeman thinks a

78. The most extensive study is Wayne R. LaFave, *Arrest: The Decision to Take a Suspect into Custody*, Boston: Little, Brown, 1964.
79. *Ibid.*

conviction will "stick" and, most importantly, the demeanour of the suspect.[80]

We have discussed police discretion as a source of preferential treatment, but there is another covert process within the criminal justice system which must be examined: the differential *sentencing* of offenders on the basis of *personal attributes* that are apparently unrelated to either the crime or to rehabilitation. These attributes include the race of the offender, sex, age, and social class. The one positive thing about such discrimination is that it is relatively easy to document. Essentially, one compares sentence lengths (or proportion of sentences suspended) for persons with differing characteristics who commit the same offense. As the sentence and the offense are in each case matters of official record, all that remains is to ascertain the attribute under consideration. With such attributes as sex there is usually no difficulty, the name ordinarily being sufficient.[81]

Such analyses of sentencing have been done. The most famous early study considered the effects of race of the offender. In a survey in the American South, Blacks were found to be sentenced to prison disproportionately and given longer terms for the same offenses than were whites.[82] Similar analyses have been conducted on other attributes, indicating for instance that younger adults (except for adolescents) are more likely to receive stiff sentences than older persons, working-class persons more so than persons from higher socio-economic strata, boys from broken homes more than boys from homes intact. In Florida, where a judge may withhold the label of "convicted" if a guilty person is placed on probation, this favour was found more frequently among persons who were white, well educated,

---

80. Irving Piliavin and Scott Briar, "Police Encounters with Juveniles," *American Journal of Sociology*, 70, September, 1964, pp. 206-214.
81. The real offense is sometimes disguised by reductions of the charge which at times accompany "pretrial bargaining," though, if anything, this may well reduce the evidence of bias.
82. Henry A. Bullock, "Significance of the Racial Factor in the Length of Prison Sentence," *Journal of Criminal Law, Criminology and Police Science*, 52, 1961, pp. 411-417.

without prior record, young, and defended by a private attorney.[83] One of the most recent studies finds Canadian men more likely to receive prison sentences than women for a given offense.[84] Indians fare poorly vis-à-vis whites.[85]

While the establishment of the patterns is important, interpretation of their meaning is equally essential. The kindest face which can be put on such prejudicial treatment is to speculate that the judges are doing precisely what they were mandated to do—applying sanctions in terms of the perceived "needs" of the offender. It might just happen that judges feel that boys from broken homes are more likely to benefit from custody than are boys from homes with both parents. (Such a conclusion would in itself be of questionable integrity unless some supporting evidence were forthcoming.) But, with the possible exception of the aforementioned boys, it seems very doubtful that judges base their practices on the overt grounds that such criteria as race, sex, age, class are of predictive value in determining the *rehabilitative or preventative worth* of a sentence of a given severity.[86] Therefore, in order to explain differential treatment based on certain attributes, we must fall back onto less admirable explanations, on covertly held ideas about blacks and whites, males and females, executives and labourers. The vast majority of judges are white, upper-middle-class (or upper-class), old, and male. In all but the last they are themselves in the favoured category in terms of sentencing. Those holding an "interest theory" of class (read: self-interest or vested interest) may wish to explain this relation on rather obvious grounds. The truth, however, seems to be that the judges are themselves largely unaware of these trends and feel that they examine each

83. Theodore G. Chiricos, *et al.*, "Inequality in the Imposition of a Criminal Label," *Social Problems*, 19, 1972, pp. 553-572.
84. Douglas F. Cousineau and Jean Veevers, "Incarceration as a Response to Crime: The Utilization of Canadian Prisons," *Canadian Journal of Criminology and Corrections*, 14, 1972, pp. 10-36. This is confirmed by the American experience, which also finds women given shorter sentences. See Elmer H. Johnson, *Crime, Correction and Society*, rev. ed., Homewood, Ill.: Dorsey Press, 1968.
85. See Harold Cardinal, *The Unjust Society*, Edmonton: Hurtig, 1969.
86. See John Hogarth, *Sentencing as a Human Process*, Toronto: University of Toronto Press, 1971; and Edward Green, *Judicial Attitudes in Sentencing*, London: Macmillan, 1961.

case on its own merits. Their behaviour might be better regarded as exemplifying their stereotype with respect to the kind of person they are dealing with.

Certainly, judges see before them many more workers than executives, young adults than old, men than women, and — either in proportion to their ratios in the total population or even in absolute numbers — more Blacks and Indians than whites. And this may in turn lead them to draw certain conclusions about these attributes.[87] When an atypical offender appears before a judge (as, ideally, an old, white, upper-class lady — already we say "lady"), the tendency is to perceive such a person as basically non-criminal, reformable. When a young, unemployed, Indian or black male appears, however, exactly the opposite is likely to occur. It is not so much that the judge consciously reflects upon the person's attributes but that the attributes provide cues which trigger a particular frame of mind. As the psychologists might say, the judge is "perceptually ready" to see certain qualities, good or bad, in the person.[88]

What is true of judges must also occur with juries, although in subtly different ways. A jury member, of course, is not typically upper-middle-class and old. His perceptual biases may be altogether different from those of the judge; he may be more or he may be less inclined to appraise the defendant on the basis of specific attributes. But juries too have their preconceptions, for jurisdictions in which the juries sentence rather than the judge also manifest differentials based on attribute rather than offense.

Even in the absence of an arrest, it is clear that stereotype of the public by law officers results in differential treatment, sometimes in an extreme form. Inasmuch as their perception of an individual leads to actions on their part which may result in the subjects becoming violent or abusive, it may be said that the police often engage in a self-fulfilling prophecy.[89] In fairness, it

---

87. There are biases already at work, in these differences, as discussed earlier.
88. Jerome S. Bruner, "On Perceptual Readiness," in *Current Perspectives in Social Psychology,* edited by E.P. Hollander and Raymond G. Hunt, New York: Oxford University Press, 1963, pp. 42-47.
89. See in this connection John P. Clark, "Isolation of the Police: A Comparison of British and American Situations," *Journal of Criminal Law, Criminology, and Police Science,* 56, 1965, pp. 307-319; and *Due-Process Safeguards and Canadian Criminal Justice: A One-Month Inquiry,* Toronto: Canadian Civil Liberties Education Trust, 1972 (no author listed).

must be added that certain members of the public also have preconceptions of the police, which lead them to perform actions in the encounter that drive the police to more drastic steps.

Stereotyping of the suspect occurs at every stage in the criminal justice process — at the initial encounter, the decision to arrest, the arrival at the verdict, and the severity of the sentence. (It is probably at work, too, in parole decisions.) Popular stereotypes, or in some cases, full-fledged ideologies, result in preferential treatment of certain categories (whites, females, the aged, the well-to-do), irrespective of the offense. Official statistics on the characteristics of offenders (for example, the proportion of convicts who are blacks, Indians, males, or juveniles) are distorted by these mechanisms, so that some categories will be over-represented — perhaps markedly so.[90] *Insofar as such statistics form the basis for selective enforcement, they are to that extent self-fulfilling.* If, for example, statistics show a high proportion of Indians among convicted criminals, and if policemen are more or less aware of the statistics, they will be watching Indians more closely, will be more likely to apprehend an Indian criminal than a white criminal, and their manner may "trigger" more illegal reactions from Indians than from whites. As more Indians are brought in, the perception of criminality among Indians becomes self-confirming.

PRESENT STATUS AND IMPLICATIONS OF THE LABELING VIEWPOINT

Historically, Frank Tannenbaum's *Crime and the Community*, written in 1938, is often cited as the original work in labeling theory. In one section, "The Dramatization of Evil," Tannenbaum explicates concisely the nature of the labeling process and its potentially damaging consequences. The first direct treatment of the strategic distinction between primary and secondary deviation is found in work by Edwin Lemert in 1951. However, it was Howard Becker who popularized the viewpoint in 1963

---

90. There are many mechanisms besides stereotype which lead to the statistical over-representation of certain groups. Financial inequities lead to differences in the competence of attorneys and the feasibility of appeals. Court procedures may be totally baffling to uneducated defendants. The court language may be unintelligible to Indians or Eskimos, or to recent immigrants.

with a book entitled, appropriately, *Outsiders*.[91] Other early writings include those of Erikson and Kitsuse.[92] Since then, numerous contributors have advanced the perspective, including Aaron Cicourel and Thomas Scheff.[93]

Beginning with Scheff, several attempts have been made to place the labeling perspective into a systematic framework.[94] The labeling perspective has by now been used to analyze such diverse topics as political deviance, mental illness, juvenile rehabilitation, and the police.[95] It has even been coupled with systems analysis.[96]

Critics of labeling have come from many quarters. Gibbs, an early critic, emphasized the vagueness and lack of direction of the perspective. He challenged Becker's apparent intention to distinguish whether a behaviour was deviant by reference to the societal reaction to it.[97] Both Gibbs and Schur noted a tendency for extreme advocates of the labeling perspective virtually to deny the existence of *primary* deviation.[98] Schur also condemned the lack of systematization of the perspective, a failing that Scheff does much to overcome in the area of mental label-

91. Edwin M. Lemert, *Social Pathology*, New York: McGraw-Hill, 1951. (The book is definitely mistitled.) Howard S. Becker, *Outsiders: Studies in the Sociology of Deviance*, New York: Free Press, 1963.

92. Kai T. Erikson, "Notes on the Sociology of Deviance," *Social Problems*, 9, Spring, 1962, pp. 307-314. John I. Kitsuse, "Societal Reaction to Deviant Behavior: Problems of Theory and Method," *Social Problems*, 9, Winter, 1962, pp. 247-256.

93. Other lists of contributors to labeling theory are contained in Matza, *op. cit.*, p. 144, and Robert K. Merton and Robert Nisbet, eds., *Contemporary Social Problems*, 3rd ed., New York: Harcourt, Brace & World, 1971, p. 826.

94. See Thomas Scheff, *op. cit.*; Edwin M. Schur, "Reactions to Deviance: A Critical Assessment," *American Journal of Sociology*, 75, 1969, pp. 309-322; and Schur's *Labeling Deviant Behavior: Its Sociological Implications*, New York: Harper & Row, 1971.

95. See, in the above sequence, Paul Schervish, "The Labeling Perspective: Its Bias and Potential in the Study of Political Deviance," *The American Sociologist*, 8, May, 1973, pp. 47-57; Scheff, *op. cit.*; Edwin M. Schur, *Radical Nonintervention*, Englewood Cliffs, N.J.: Prentice-Hall, 1973; and Jock Young, *op. cit.*

96. Leslie T. Wilkins, *Social Deviance*, Englewood Cliffs, N.J.: Prentice-Hall, 1965, pp. 85-100.

97. Jack P. Gibbs, "Conceptions of Deviant Behavior: The Old and the New," *Pacific Sociological Review*, 9, 1966, pp. 9-14.

98. Schur, 1969, *op. cit.* See the final chapter of Becker's new (1973) edition of *Outsiders* (*op. cit.*) for a discussion of this problem.

ing. But Schur also found great value in labeling's sensitizing aspect. Milton Mankoff criticizes existing theory on a number of grounds, maintaining that the school underestimates the psychological and social factors that caused the initial deviance and ignores those factors that cause some persons to stop the behaviour even after being labeled.[99] He also points out that the labeling school has failed to analyze the strength and severity of the reaction necessary to have "successful" labeling. For instance, if one has enough money or power, one may be able to overcome the effects of the label. Thorsell and Klemke argue that theory suggests a possible *deterrent* effect from labeling, as well as the commonly cited reinforcement of deviance.[100] They offer tentative guidelines as to which outcome should be expected in specific cases. Other sophisticated theoretical critiques have been made by Glaser, Nettler, and Sagarin.[101]

Some of the objections are empirical: does everything really work the way the school maintains? In addition to some theoretical criticisms of his own, Walter Gove examined empirically the role of various agents in mental labeling; he found that experts have by far the greatest say in commitments to mental hospitals and that they reject about two-thirds of public requests.[102] Lee Robins investigated what happens to deviant children when they have grown up, finding in general that labeling did not seem to embark them on a mental illness "career" extending into adulthood.[103]

These theoretical and empirical critiques have by no means destroyed the viability of the basic conception, as the critics themselves would be among the first to admit, but they have constrained the initial enthusiasm and some of the imperialistic

99. Milton Mankoff, "Societal Reaction and Career Deviance: A Critical Analysis," *Sociological Quarterly*, 12, Spring, 1971, pp. 204-218.
100. Bernard Thorsell and Lloyd Klemke, "The Labeling Process: Reinforcement and Deterrent?" *Law and Society Review*, 6, February, 1972, pp. 393-403.
101. Daniel Glaser, *Social Deviance*, Chicago: Markham, 1971; Gwynn Nettler, 1974, *op. cit.*, pp. 202-212; Edward Sagarin, *Deviants and Deviance*, New York: Praeger, 1975.
102. Walter R. Gove, "Societal Reaction as an Explanation of Mental Illness: An Evaluation," *American Sociological Review*, 35, 1971, pp. 873-884.
103. Lee Robins, *Deviant Children Grown Up*, Baltimore: Williams and Wilkins, 1966.

claims of the advocates. The development of labeling or reaction theory is by no means completed.[104] As mentioned earlier, there is a trend toward more systematic formulations as well as greater empirical scrutiny of the claims.

Labeling in contemporary sociology has come to have many of the qualities of a social movement,[105] and because certain *additional* assumptions are often made by advocates, it has become the centre of attention and controversy in current studies of social problems.[106] Since it is known that few individuals are actually labeled out of a vast number who break the rules, it has been claimed that the enforcement of moral rules is essentially a *political act*.[107] This is not an inherently necessary aspect of labeling theory, but it is one often assumed by its supporters. It is also central to the perspective to maintain that the very defining of certain behaviours as a social problem in the first place is a political, or at least ideological, activity rather than one of community consensus.[108] After the definition of a social problem has been made, a decision is reached about the "nature" of a particular person with respect to this problem, and thus a second definition (a label) is affirmed. "The deviant, in short, is made by society in two senses: first, that society makes the rules which he has broken, and secondly, that society 'enforces' them and makes a public declaration announcing that the rules have been broken."[109]

Labeling theory is important for our analysis because it demonstrates that the concept of unanticipated consequences cannot be placed exclusively in either the arsenal of the progressive

104. For an attempt to explain the dearth of material on labeling in the Canadian scene, see John Hagan, "The Labeling Perspective: The Delinquent and the Police," *Canadian Journal of Criminology and Corrections*, 14, 1972, pp. 150-162.

105. See Matza, *op. cit.*, pp. 158-159.

106. For an early exploration of the possible consequences of labeling theory, see James Hackler, "An 'Underdog' Approach to Correctional Research," *Canadian Journal of Criminology and Corrections*, 9, 1967, pp. 27-36.

107. See especially the first 18 pages of Becker, *op. cit.*

108. This view is adopted in Henshel and Henshel, *op. cit.* and discussed at length.

109. Alvin W. Gouldner, "The Sociologist as Partisan: Sociology and the Welfare State," reprinted in *The Sociology of Sociology*, edited by Larry T. Reynolds and Janice M. Reynolds, New York: McKay, 1970, p. 221.

or the conservative. In some instances, an awareness of unexpected outcomes assists defenders of the status quo by shutting off superficially plausible reforms. But in the present section an awareness of the unanticipated consequences of official labeling points to the deleterious nature of *existing* social mechanisms, to a pressing need for their reexamination, and possibly toward their alteration.[110]

Although the theory of labeling is important, we noted earlier the negative evidence that has come forward about certain aspects. This brings to mind the more basic question that can be raised about all claims to unanticipated consequences: how do we know they are so? In some cases, such as prohibition, the *prima facie* evidence seems clear enough, but for other allegations we would like to see empirical proof beyond plausible-sounding assertions. Traveling backward to Chapter 1, we wonder whether some strategies can be proven more effective than others, going beyond the pervasiveness of glib oratory and into the realm of concrete demonstrations. In other words, we want to *evaluate* intervention, so we need to look into how this might be done.

---

110. Other analyses discussed earlier in the chapter, for instance Coser's analysis of the functions of social conflict, also furnish examples of progressive or radical arguments under a functionalist framework.

4 Evaluation Research and Intervention Decisions

Let us consider a set of very basic questions. What are the effects of a specific instance of intervention? Has it worked? Has it worked as well as planned, or better? For instance, is there a decrease in mental illness, in income disparity, in criminality, after programmes have been applied during the preceding years? Or, if the size of the problem has not diminished, might it otherwise have grown even larger without the programme? Is the programme worth the economic and social costs of implementation? Does an alternative method work better? Is it preferable to do nothing? Surely the originators of a given programme had the alleviation of some social problem in mind when they began. Therefore, at some subsequent time it should be asked whether the programme meets the expectations under which it was established. It is reasonable to demand at least tentative answers to such questions, notwithstanding the difficulties involved in answering them. Attempts to provide the answers, to ascertain the effects of planned intervention, are termed *evaluation research*.

The questions above appear to be so basic that it may be shocking to learn that, until recently, they were rarely investigated in any systematic fashion, and that even today their pursuit is more the exception than the rule. Yet such is indeed the case; we shall examine some of the reasons for this strange state of affairs later in the chapter.

At the outset it should be realized that there is a primary issue:

what is meant when it is said that the benefits do or do not outweigh the costs? Ignoring for the moment the difficult question of how this can be investigated, we address the even more primitive question: benefits for whom? costs for whom?[1] Obviously better street lighting is not a gain for the "mugger"; police dogs that can detect marihuana are a bane for the smoker. But even if we ignore the user of proscribed goods or services, or the offender in a criminal action, we should ask whether there is *any* intervention in which the costs and gains are the same for everyone. The taxpayers may be outraged at the cost of changes; certain groups will almost certainly benefit more than others; some groups may be inconvenienced by a measure which does them no good at all. One need not adopt an extreme conflict perspective — seeing social conflict at the root of all major change — to recognize that there is no problem, and no remedy, in which costs and gains are the same for everyone. (Consider: there are DDT manufacturers and there are ecologists; highway planners and landowners; marihuana cultivators and law enforcement agencies — the list is endless.) There is, therefore, a need to specify the relevant group in order to evaluate meaningfully the costs and gains of a new intervention: "costs" and "gains" *to whom*? Any discussion of costs and gains must refer to the values of some particular audience.

The difficulty this problem produces cannot be denied. The usual response is to ignore the issue and tacitly adopt a "consensus model" of society for the duration of the evaluation. That is, the possibility of extreme divergence of values is simply not considered. The difficulty as just presented is perhaps exaggerated in one sense: monetary components sometimes form a major portion of the balance of costs and gains, and it is in the nature of monetary measures that they do afford an unusually high degree of comparability over different sectors of the population. Again, however, this is only a matter of degree, for there are still the obvious discrepancies between population sectors with varying incomes. An impoverished community, for exam-

---

1. Before proceeding further, it should be noted that "costs" as used in this chapter include negative consequences of a non-monetary nature as well as the more traditional financial meaning.

ple, may be more interested in the jobs a new plant will provide than in the damage it will do to the environment. A more prosperous community, given the same options, might choose environmental protection.

Although this conceptual difficulty cannot be ignored, the virtues of performing evaluation are very great indeed. Even if one disregards the struggles which precede intervention, there are, inevitably, hardships associated with its implementation — monetary costs, certain freedoms circumscribed, opportunities relinquished. Naturally one wishes to know, in everyday language, if it is all "worth it."Without ignoring the diversity of values, then, it still seems worthwhile to be able to say what a given programme is accomplishing.

In spite of the apparent obvious value of the systematic study of intervention, it is at once disturbing and fascinating to know that until very recently this type of study was rarely done, and even more rarely done in a manner which would permit meaningful conclusions to be drawn. In part this failure has been a reflection of a widespread lack of understanding of the essential elements of experimentation, and lack of recognition that the experimental approach could be applied to the appraisal of social reforms. Although this book is not a text on research methods, the consideration is of such vital importance for the evaluation of social intervention that a limited discussion of procedures of research — as they apply to social reform measures — is appropriate.[2]

This chapter takes up the issue of evaluation, beginning with a brief description of research design. The first section explicates

2. The treatment given this complex subject here is necessarily very cursory. For extended discussions see Claire Selltiz, *et al.*, *Research Methods in Social Relations*, rev. ed., New York: Holt, Rinehart & Winston, 1959; Hubert M. Blalock, Jr., *Social Statistics*, New York: McGraw-Hill, 1960. On a more advanced level see Donald T. Campbell, "Factors Relevant to the Validity of Experiments in Social Settings," *Psychological Bulletin*, July, 1957, pp. 297-312; Robert A. Scott and Arnold Shore, "Sociology and Policy Analysis," *American Sociologist*, 9, 1974, pp. 51-59; and Hubert M. Blalock, Jr., *Causal Inferences in Nonexperimental Research*, Chapel Hill, North Carolina: University of North Carolina Press, 1964. An excellent discussion of experimental design is found in Bernard Phillips, *Social Research; Strategy and Tactics*, 2d. ed., New York: Macmillan, 1971.

the ideal approach to evaluation of intervention, for the most part ignoring practical and political difficulties. The next section considers the theoretical weaknesses of the approach, dealing with conceptual and procedural problems such as inadequate measurement. There follows a section on politically-based difficulties, taking into account the bureaucratic structure of most forms of intervention, the stake that people have in the outcome, ethical dilemmas of research, and related considerations. Finally, the feasibility of evaluation research for private and/or radical forms of intervention is considered in the closing section. Those readers already familiar with the basics of experimental design may wish to turn to the later sections.

EXPERIMENTS AND REFORMS: SOME BASIC ASPECTS OF PROCEDURE

Most sociologists agree that an experiment (in the technically correct sense of the word) is, whenever possible, the best way to evaluate intervention. Classical experimental design was first systematized by John Stuart Mill. He wished to set forth the "designs" (logical procedures for manipulating events and data) which enable us to ascertain the causal relationship between one variable and another: does variable x produce a change in variable y? (Does, for example, the creation of a child guidance centre improve the children's mental health?) Although methodologists have altered Mill's methods, and have realized that answers are always tentative, his basic objective remains. If possible, we also want to learn how much x produces how much change in y, and we should like to know whether there is a third variable, z, whose presence alters the influence of x on y.[3] For our purposes, the independent variable, x, is always the *planned intervention.*

We begin with two simple designs, the "after-only" and the "before and after." Understanding the weaknesses of these two designs — which are still employed all too frequently — will be

---

3. This is perhaps the point to note that the attribution of causality is one of the thorniest issues in the philosophy of science. For an excellent advanced treatment, there is a chapter on the subject in Jack P. Gibbs, *Sociological Theory Construction*, Hinsdale, Ill.: Dryden Press, 1972.

useful in grasping the ideas behind more adequate designs.

If we start with the procedure known as the "after-only" design, we make a comparison of the dependent variable, y, in those cases where intervention (x) has been employed (collectively these cases are called the experimental group) with the status of y in those cases where it has not (collectively called the control group). If major differences between the two groups in the prevalence or magnitude of y are noted, it is presumed that this difference was caused by the introduction of the intervention, x, since this occurred in only one of the groups. But, because all of the observations of y take place after x has been introduced — that is, because there were no "before-measures" — the cases in the two groups could have been different at the very start. This is especially possible in social intervention where, often, the most drastic cases receive attention first. One can "prove" with this design that going to a hospital causes death, since the death rate of people in hospitals is so much higher than the death rate of those outside. But, of course, this argument ignores the fact that the people who became patients (by entering the hospital) were different from the general population *before* hospitalization (x) was "applied." Unless one can be sure that the two groups were comparable before x was applied, the after-only design is therefore not the best approach. Although before-measures are simply not possible in some kinds of inquiry (research on the social effects of disasters, for example, where you cannot tell in advance where the disaster will strike), they should be possible in most cases of planned intervention.

In the *"before-after"* design — another less than satisfactory approach — we have measures of y both before and after intervention, but either the treatment is applied to all cases or no systematic attention is given to the remaining "controls." In this design the extent or magnitude of differences in y before and after the application of x determines whether we believe x exerts an effect on y. (A familiar illustration is the fat-person advertisement.) But a simple before-after difference in y cannot rule out the possibilities of what are called history or maturation effects on y, effects which have nothing to do with x. For instance, a psychiatrist might appear to demonstrate an improvement in his patients, but there might have been "spontaneous remission" of symptoms even without his treatment. Mental health may appear to have responded to the treatment, but might have improved without it.[4] Perhaps it would have improved *more* without it! Who can say from this procedure? With no control group one can "prove" that drinking milk causes death — since all subjects on milk eventually will die. (Before they drank the milk [x], they were alive; afterward, they all eventually died.) Those without milk will die also, but we have no way to establish this without a control group.

Therefore, for an improved test of the effects of x, we need four measurements of the dependent variable y. *We compare the before-after differences in the experimental group with the before-after differences in the control group.* (See below, right.)

After-only design		Before-after design	Before and after with control group		
Exper. Gp.	Contr. Gp.	Exper. Gp.	Exper. Gp.		Contr. Gp.
		Before-measure y_1	Before-measure	y_1	y_3
Test period x	—	Test period x	Test period	x	—
After-measure y_1	y_2	After-measure y_2	After-measure	y_2	y_4

It is essential to ensure that the two groups are as strictly comparable as possible in all respects *except* for the presence of the experimental programme (the independent variable x) in the experimental group. But since all individuals (and all collectivities) are in fact different, the means of attaining this objective is a most serious issue. Two basic strategies are used: randomization and matching.

Random assignment is a procedure which takes the available persons in the population and allots them on a strictly random

---

4. We shall consider later a problem of ethics in the creation of control groups that are denied treatment.

basis to either the experimental or control groups.[5] Thus neither the subjects themselves nor the investigator have any say about which group a person is assigned to. The advantage of this procedure is that, if we have a large enough number of cases in each group, the extraneous variables (factors other than x) that might influence y will be equally distributed between both groups. Only x, therefore, is present in one group and not the other.

Matching is a process of pairing individuals in the experimental group with others in the control group who possess the same or highly similar characteristics. When random assignment cannot be accomplished, this is another way of controlling for the effects of extraneous variables on y. Since the matched pairs are equivalent on all characteristics except x, which only the party in the experimental group receives, any consistent differences in y between the two parties must be a result of the administration of x.

Of the two procedures, random assignment is the preferable approach since it automatically takes care of *all* extraneous variables whereas matching can only take care of those extraneous variables explicitly noticed. However, there are cases in which for one reason or another random assignment is simply not possible. In such cases matching can be of considerable value.[6]

Most evaluation research has been done in situations which were poorly designed at the outset. Random assignment, for instance, could have been introduced in a far greater proportion of programmes than it actually was. The unfortunate tendency has been to either apply new treatments only to the worst "problem cases" or only to the "best" cases that seem most capable of making effective use of the treatment (for instance, scholarships). Although these approaches seem to make sense in the short run, they play havoc with any attempt to do serious evaluation research thereafter since there was no random assignment,

---

5. It should be noted that at times it is not *individuals* who are randomly assigned but larger collectivities such as classrooms, factories, etc. In all cases the logic is the same.
6. It is also true that matching and random assignment are at times used in combination; the reasons for this procedure need not be considered here.

and obviously the experimental and control groups are anything but comparable. This also illustrates the importance of *planning for evaluation research from the onset*, for after certain key decisions have been made in the planning stage, the value of any subsequent evaluation research is more or less fixed. Programmes frequently neglect random assignment, or omit the control group altogether, or fail to collect before-measures. In such cases it may still be possible to accomplish some evaluation through sophisticated statistical techniques, but the results will be less conclusive, and in some cases analysis will simply be impossible.

Perhaps a single example of a well-designed experimental programme will be helpful. (There are not very many examples, after all.) Lamar T. Empey and Jerome Rabow conducted an elaborate programme of delinquency rehabilitation in the early 1960's. Known as the Provo experiment, it profited from the evaluation pitfalls of earlier delinquency programmes by setting up a tight experimental procedure.[7] As a delinquent youth came before the judge for sentencing, the judge literally opened a sealed envelope to determine whether the youth would be sent to Provo or to the traditional training-school alternative. (Of course this required the cooperation of the judiciary.) The method provided such excellent randomization that no before-measures were necessary: it could be assumed that over a large number of cases the initial levels of y (let us call it delinquency tendency) were equivalent in both groups. One set of boys then experienced Provo and the other the traditional treatment. Afterwards, the success rates of the two groups were compared on several criteria, with some criteria showing a success for Provo and some merely showing the experimental group level equivalent to the control group level.[8]

The Provo experiment can be contrasted to older intervention measures (and, alas, to many new ones as well) which were set up initially in such a way that no meaningful conclusion can be reached regarding effectiveness. Let us continue with delin-

---

7. Lamar T. Empey and Jerome Rabow, "The Provo Experiment in Delinquency Rehabilitation," *American Sociological Review*, 26, 1961, pp. 679-695.
8. This synopsis oversimplifies the analysis in several respects. There was a long succession of boys going through Provo for an extended period of time.

quency prevention as an example. The Chicago Area Project, one of the oldest programmes, was in existence for over twenty-five years, but after all that time a review could provide only interesting anecdotal and incidental information on what it had accomplished.[9] As late as 1963 a review found not a single vigorous evaluation of a delinquency programme to have been made in all of Europe.[10] Indeed in a later review Logan was able to find only four evaluative studies of delinquency prevention that met minimal standards in terms of control groups and a sharply defined programme.[11]

Using the procedures outlined above — before and after measurements in experimental and control groups created by random assignment — we can compare the before-and-after difference in the experimental group with the before-and-after difference in the control group. If the before-after differences are not the same in the two groups, it is possible that the disparity is due to the introduction of x into the experimental group. Statistical analysis can then provide the numerical probability that the differences observed between the experimental and control groups were due to chance alone or, as is hoped, due to the effects of intervention — the independent variable, x. This design is the simplest that can be employed: in effect, it tells us — within a certain margin of error — *whether the treatment made any difference at all*. At first glance this does not appear particularly useful, but, to the contrary, the fact is that there have been many highly touted programmes which, on later evaluation, were seen to have made virtually no difference at all.

The British psychologist Eysenck has written a widely known series of articles and a book carefully examining the effects of interpretive (non-directive) psychotherapy. After surveying some nineteen studies, and taking into account the natural (un-

9. See Solomon Kobrin, "The Chicago Area Project: A 25-Year Assessment," in *Prevention of Delinquency*, edited by John Stratton and Robert Terry, New York: Macmillan, 1968.
10. Eugene Doleschal and I. Anttia, *Crime and Delinquency Research in Selected European Countries*, Rockville, Maryland: National Institute of Mental Health, 1971.
11. Charles Logan, "Evaluation Research in Crime and Delinquency: A Reappraisal," *Journal of Criminal Law, Criminology, and Police Science*, 63, 1972, pp. 378-387.

treated) recovery rate, he concluded that, "with the single exception of psychotherapeutic methods based on learning theory, results of published research ... suggest that the therapeutic effects of psychotherapy are small or non-existent. ..."[12] Some of the studies he utilized had less than perfect procedures, but one study in particular had considerable significance. The Cambridge Somerville study was an effort to prevent delinquency by administering individual therapy to half of a number of boys, randomly chosen. The conclusions were extensive, but the one of interest here was that "the treatment did not ... reduce the incidence of (subsequent) adjudged delinquency in the treatment group."[13]

The findings cited above do not necessarily indicate that non-directive psychotherapy should be scrapped. Subsequent writers have noted that there is considerable variability in the effects of therapy on different individuals: some do better than the control group and some do worse. Only the *average* effects in the experimental group equate to the control group. If the operative factor behind these different individual reactions could be isolated, it might be possible to apply therapy *only* to those persons it will help and not to those it might actually hinder. If this were effected, the results might be very different.[14] Nevertheless, the findings of Eysenck and his followers have shocked the psychiatric and psychoanalytic communities.[15] Therefore, the very basic question of whether a programme has had any effects whatsoever is not a waste of time at all. It is, in fact, the first question that should be asked.

12. H.J. Eysenck, "The Effects of Psychotherapy," in *Handbook of Abnormal Psychology*, edited by H.J. Eysenck, London: Pitman Medical Pub. Co., 1960. See also Eysenck's *The Effects of Psychotherapy*, New York: Science House, 1969.
13. N. Teuber and E. Powers, "Evaluating Therapy in a Delinquency Prevention Program," *Proceedings of the Association on Nervous Mental Disorders*, 3, 1953, pp. 138-147.
14. See for the full rationale of this approach C. Truax and R. Carkhuff, *Toward Effective Counselling and Psychotherapy*, Chicago: Aldine, 1967.
15. It should be noted that not all evaluation research finds less effectiveness than anticipated. For instance, a monumental non-experimental study of the effectiveness of U.S. prisons by Daniel Glaser found the recidivist (return to prison) rate far lower than most earlier writers had assumed. See his *The Effectiveness of a Prison and Parole System*, Indianapolis: Bobbs-Merrill, 1969. The rate of recidivism was still unpleasantly high, however.

EXTENSIONS OF THE BASIC DESIGN

Even with success, researchers have to be careful in their evaluation, for it could well be the case that it is not the intended
treatment *per se* that has reduced the problem but certain side
aspects. For instance, if we wanted to improve the mental health
of children and young adults, we might adopt a programme in
which babies and young children were taken out of their homes
to a specialized daycare centre every day. If evaluation showed a
significant difference between children so treated and children
in a control group, the difference might not be due to improved
child-rearing but to other unsuspected factors. Perhaps because
the mother was unburdened and relieved of her duties several
hours daily, she was more receptive to the child upon its return
and in a better frame of mind herself. This could have a favoura-
ble effect on the child's mental health. If the family were poor,
the child might have obtained better food at the daycare centre
than at home, and this might have improved his overall health. It
might also be that the parents were intrigued (and flattered) by
the experiment and, as a consequence, involved themselves
more with the child.[16] These examples are sufficient to indicate
that, not only do researchers have to use a control group, but
also, whenever feasible, the treatment procedure has to be sub-
divided into categories or parts, each part being applied to
different persons in the experimental group. For instance, a
group of children could have been taken to the daycare centre
but, once there, given only the necessary minimal amount of
attention. This could be a partial check against the effect of
attention and novelty on the children as well as the effect of time
off for the mother. Another group could, in addition, be fed at the
centre. Then a third group could receive the "enriched" programme. Hopefully, the second group would fare better than the
first, and the third better than the second—as well as better than
the controls.

Therefore, our initial design, considered above, although in-
valuable for certain problems, is inadequate for many issues in
evaluation. Instead of ascertaining whether a given programme

---

16. Readers familiar with experimental design will recognize this to be an
instance of the Hawthorne effect, or placebo effect as it is known in medicine.

had any effect at all, we might wish to isolate the most significant components of a programme or compare the results of two or more competing programmes.[17] Perhaps — to return to the discussion of "strategies" in Chapter 1—we wish to compare the utility of two alternative approaches to the same problem. Or possibly we wish to determine the best "mix" for a single programme, or which component of a given programme produced the desired effect.[18]

To perform any of the these evaluations, a change in the design becomes necessary. Instead of an experimental group and control group we may now have numerous groups (all hopefully still formed by a process of random assignment), each of which receives a treatment somewhat different from any of the others. In the diagrams below, the first is known as the factorial design; the second is the randomized groups design where only one treatment is provided, at various intensities.

Since we are in this case confident that all treatments produce *some* effects, we need no control group *per se*. The before and after changes in the dependent variable within each of the groups can be analyzed by statistical techniques to show (again with statements of probability) which treatments and mixes were productive of *greater* changes in the desired direction.[19]

Excellent examples of such research are underway in several quarters on the feasibility of guaranteed annual income, or "negative income tax." A series of experiments known as Mincome Manitoba (for Manitoba Basic Annual Income Experiment) is in progress in Canada, and in the United States there is a series of studies on minimum income that include the New Jersey-Pennsylvania Negative Income Tax Experiment, the

17. Ironically, it was through the questions about labeling that this chapter was introduced, yet the effects of labeling are among the hardest to ascertain because the process is so inexorably intermeshed with other components.
18. As an example of empirically appraising the value of a basic intervention strategy, see B.F. Skinner's negative evaluation of "aversive reinforcement" (what we may crudely call punishment) in B.F. Skinner, *Beyond Freedom and Dignity*, New York: Bantam Books, 1972; or see Zimring and Hawkins on deterrence in Franklin Zimring and Gordon Hawkins, *Deterrence*, Chicago: University of Chicago Press, 1973.
19. It should be noted that an implicit assumption of all evaluation research is that past outcomes will continue to hold in the future. But this is an assumption necessary for *any* sort of prediction.

before			
after			

Treatment	Treatment	Treatment
A	B	C
group	group	group

before			
after			

Level 1	Level 2	Level 3
group	group	group

Treatment A

Graduated Work Incentive Experiment, the Seattle-Denver Income Maintenance Experiment, and others.[20] These efforts have been hailed as the first large-scale field experiments in the history of the social sciences. In essence, the negative income tax or guaranteed annual income is a device seen as a supplement to, or replacement of, the current welfare system. Everyone would have a minimal guaranteed income, but, to increase the incentive to work, a person who obtained a job would find his welfare cheque reduced by *less* than his gain from his new work. One of the key questions is how *much* less a reduction would motivate people to find work — hence the variations (graduated work incentives) in the experiment.

The idea is that, before implementing any one income policy, the costs and effects of various options are being experimentally

20. For the Canadian study see Tom Atkinson, *et al., Public Policy Research and the Guaranteed Annual Income,* Downsview, Ont.: Institute for Behavioural Research (York University), 1973.

determined. In Canada this is a joint federal-provincial project, with the main study underway in Manitoba and a possible project indicated for Ontario. Mincome Manitoba centres around Winnipeg and the rural community, using eight variations systematically varied. The project is slated to run for several years before evaluations are completed.

Experiments of this kind have been all too rare. Typically, solutions to social problems are approached in a pseudo-confident fashion in which, after debate, one — and only one — programme is implemented. There is enormous pressure, particularly in programmes initiated by governments, to adopt one measure immediately rather than undertaking a trial period in which several candidate measures undergo evaluation. As a case in point, there are indications that ministers may proceed with the guaranteed annual income without waiting for the Manitoba results. Undoubtedly strains engendered by the political process produce such decisions, but they are doubly unfortunate because, as we shall see, the findings of evaluation research encounter entrenched resistance when they cast doubt on the value of established, ongoing projects. As Campbell puts it, "if the political and administrative system has committed itself in advance to the correctness and efficacy of its reforms, it cannot tolerate learning of failure."[21]

Some important questions cannot be resolved through the use of a standard experiment. Although the efficacy of Provo might be ascertainable by a control group which was randomly assigned, the perennial arguments over the efficacy of the death penalty cannot be — for obvious ethical and practical reasons. Other methods of systematic comparison are still possible for such issues, but the conclusions drawn must be regarded with great caution. The issue of capital punishment is instructive in both an historical and a methodological sense.

There are numerous arguments respecting the use of the death penalty which do not rely on whether or not it helps deter future crime, but that question has nonetheless assumed a central position in the debate. From time to time social scientists have

---

21. Donald T. Campbell, "Reforms as Experiments," *American Psychologist*, 24, 1969, pp. 409-429. Quote is from p. 410.

manifested extreme skepticism respecting the efficacy of legal punishment of any sort on the pervasiveness of crime, maintaining that deterrent doctrines are outmoded and totally out of place in a modern society.[22] For generations the debate continued at a purely polemical level, with no recourse to the empirical evidence. In the 1950's two separately conceived studies, one by Thorsten Sellin and one by Karl Schuessler, broke from this tradition. Sellin took advantage of the fact that under American law each state has the right to establish its own policies with respect to capital punishment. Some states had abolished it; some retained it. By examining pairs of adjoining states, in which one state in each pair was abolitionist and the other was not, Sellin came to the conclusion that retention of the death penalty did not diminish capital crime. Schuessler examined single jurisdictions at different points in time, considering whether the existence or lack of executions at any one time made an impact on subsequent rates of capital crime. He concluded they did not. These studies have been criticized on methodological grounds, but their important contribution was simply that they quit arguing over the doctrine and started looking systematically at the data.

Since that time the empirical study of questions of deterrence has expanded enormously. After a period in which only the death penalty was investigated, researchers have started to look at whether deterrence might be effective for other types of sanctions, for example, such seemingly simple matters as increasing parking fines.[23] And the methodological sophistication of such studies has increased to the point where early efforts seem very crude indeed.[24] The case of deterrence is instructive on several counts. It is a basic strategy (as defined in Chapter 1); it serves to illustrate how researchers might evaluate measures without using a controlled experiment; and it shows an historical progression from argument to empirical analysis.

22. See, for example, Karl Menninger, *The Crime of Punishment*, New York: Viking Press, 1968.
23. See, for example, William Chambliss, "The Deterrent Influence of Punishment," *Crime and Delinquency*, 12, January, 1966, pp. 20-75.
24. An excellent overall summary is found in Zimring and Hawkins, *op. cit.*

It is worthwhile repeating that *the foregoing discussion of experimental design is extremely limited.* Many of the questions of policy analysis require much more elaborate techniques. As a single example, the researchers in the American income tax experiment wanted to determine whether the amount of income maintenance paid should be varied by age and sex of the recipient as well as by income. Once again they might have created additional groups, by randomization, to study this, but eventually this becomes impracticable if one really wants to look at a large number of variables. Hence, the researchers resorted to other techniques.[25] Serious readers are referred to the additional references mentioned earlier for a more extensive treatment of these topics.

THEORETICAL WEAKNESSES OF EVALUATION RESEARCH

Having examined some of the basic procedures behind evaluation, it is now obligatory that we look at some of the weaknesses of this tool.[26] We can roughly divide these weaknesses into two parts, disregarding occasional instances of overlap. On the one hand there are *conceptual and methodological weaknesses* in the methods themselves, and on the other hand there are the *political problems* involved in doing the research and in implementing one's findings in the real world. We shall start with the conceptual and procedural difficulties.

The foremost conceptual difficulty has already been discussed in the opening section of the chapter. To reiterate: how does one decide which aspects of the treatment are to be considered as costs, and which as gains? To what audience does one refer? If a gain for one group is a cost for another, how can one meaning-

---

25. See Robert A. Scott and Arnold Shore, *op. cit.*
26. See Howard Freeman and Clarence Sherwood, *Social Research and Social Policy*, Englewood Cliffs, N.J.: Prentice-Hall, 1970, for a good treatment of pitfalls and problems in policy research in general and evaluation research in particular. Other book-length treatments include Francis G. Caro, ed., *Readings in Evaluation Research*, New York: Russell Sage Foundation, 1971; Edward J. Mullen, *et al.*, *Evaluation of Social Intervention*, San Francisco: Jossey-Bass, 1972; Edward A. Suchman, *Evaluation Research*, New York: Russell Sage Foundation, 1967.

fully evaluate success or failure?[27] Typically, the expedient is to seek some countable, "objective" measure of success for the project (for example, reducing the suicide rate), but obviously this may be a greater gain for some segments of the population than for others.[28] It is in the very indicators of success or failure that some of the most intractable controversies develop.

Assuming for the moment that minimal agreement can be reached on the dimension to be evaluated, the next hurdle consists of what are together called *measurement problems*. The abstract dimension selected for evaluation must be translated into practical measurements. This is often far more difficult than it sounds. What is a "cure" in the case of psychotherapy? How does one measure the reduction of inter-group tensions? How is greater worker participation in industry to be examined, speaking concretely? To all such questions tentative answers can and have been offered, but the problem is often not so much that no measurement solution can be proposed but that more than one is available — and all seem reasonable yet yield different conclusions. How, for example, might one measure the success of criminal rehabilitation?[29] Does one look at inmate adjustment while in the prison, reduction in number of prison incidents and increase in volunteerism, length of time after release before new offences are committed, degree of severity of subsequent offences? Reasonable arguments can be advanced for all these approaches, yet — and this is the heart of the problem — pro-

27. There is also the issue of who gains the most, even if a programme is clearly beneficial to several parties. For instance, in terms of cooperative spending this issue has become a major point of conflict between federal and provincial governments. See discussions in J. Peter Meekison, ed., *Canadian Federalism: Myth or Reality*, 2nd ed., Toronto: Methuen, 1971.

28. Possibly this is the time to reemphasize that there may well be some forms of intervention that sizable portions of a population *hope* will fail. This is true to a limited extent with most measures, but it becomes especially acute with repressive doctrines. Unfortunately, they too can be evaluated, and "improved."

29. Since the author's criminology background shows up clearly in this chapter, perhaps it is important to emphasize that evaluation research has been carried out in many other areas — psychotherapy, encounter groups, suicide prevention, anti-poverty policies, housing reform, and education. All these and doubtless others have employed sophisticated evaluation of the type described here. Some of these efforts will be referenced shortly.

grammes successful on one of these scales are not necessarily successful on another. [30]

Assuming that agreement is reached on both the dimension of success to be evaluated and on the concrete measurement to be made, there are usually great practical difficulties in *translating* this into meaningful data. To continue the example of criminal rehabilitation, if one chooses to examine in-prison adjustment, one must be especially wary of "evaluation apprehension."[31] A prison is a hostile institution; inmates in a climate of deprivation and powerlessness may tend to tell a researcher what they believe he wants to hear instead of what they really think, regardless of guarantees of anonymity. If, on the other hand, one chooses to examine post-release adjustment, one is hampered by lack of cooperation or, again, by less than honest responses. There may be difficulty in locating former inmates if they have completed their period of parole reporting. Even if one chooses to look at rates of return to prison — a purely objective index known as recidivism — one is troubled by widespread failure to identify former convicts as such, especially if the offender is apprehended in a district far from the site of the previous offence. (Obviously, few repeat offenders will care to volunteer the information that they are ex-convicts.) Finally, the approach which examines the number of prison incidents (riots, escape attempts, sit-downs, etc.) can be attacked on the grounds that it does not really measure rehabilitation at all — technically, this is raising the question of the "validity" of the procedure.[32] It

30. In spite of this, it is usually seen as desirable to construct measures of social science concepts that use more than one single indicator. (See this point made in Amitai Etzioni and Edward W. Lehman, "Some Dangers in 'Valid' Social Measurement," *The Annals*, 373, September, 1967, pp. 1-15.) With regard to the general issue of the choice of measure, often called the "criterion" in evaluation research, some have called attention to a peculiar dilemma: one's theoretical framework can on occasion determine the measurements to be used — for example, in measuring social class or poverty. See Gideon Sjoberg and Roger Nett, *A Methodology for Social Research*, New York: Harper & Row, 1968, for a discussion.
31. See Robert Rosenthal and Ralph N. Rosnow, eds., *Artifact in Experimental Research*, New York: Academic Press, 1969.
32. For further discussion of the specific difficulties of evaluating criminal rehabilitation, see Daniel Glaser, "The Assessment of Correctional Effectiveness," in *Law Enforcement Science and Technology*, edited by S. Yefsky, New York: Academic Press, 1967, pp. 181-189; and Leslie Wilkins, *Evaluation of Penal Measures*, New York: Random House, 1969.

follows from this illustration that the researcher must be intimately familiar with the situation and its various machinations.

Another problem, inherent in many other areas of social research as well as the study of social problems, is the *reactivity* of the persons studied. The simple act of gathering information may affect, in very unexpected ways, the behaviour of the individuals or groups being investigated. There are several reasons for this, but essentially the problem is that people who are aware that they are being observed, or interviewed, sometimes alter their behaviour — even if unconsciously.[33] There are ways to surmount this problem, but the possibility of reactivity considerably increases the difficulty in obtaining meaningful results.[34]

Another conceptual problem exists which must not be ignored. There is an urge to move into *quantitative* measures of success and failure: number of cures, suicide rates, crime rates, recidivism, worker absenteeism, magnitude of income disparities, proportion of national budgets spent on war preparations, and so on. This is a natural and ordinarily laudable tendency, due for the most part to a desire to obtain the greatest possible objectivity in evaluation. What may become damaging, however, is when this urge is carried to a particular form of excess. In the rush to quantify, there is a tendency to ignore, to brush aside, that which cannot be quantified. It is as though evaluators were tacitly accepting the statement of extreme empiricism that "if it cannot be measured, it cannot be known." Since it is impossible to attach a figure to the anguish of a suicide's family, to the happiness given up because people are afraid to use the streets at night, and many other important elements, these factors are sometimes completely ignored — or relegated to a footnote in the overall examination. Some things which are impossible to quantify are none the less extremely important in evaluating the success or failure of a programme. The Croll committee investigating poverty in Canada put it this way:

33. For details, see Rosenthal and Rosnow, *op. cit.* Some commonly recognized forms of reactivity include evaluation apprehension, demand characteristics, and Hawthorne or placebo effects.
34. For possible resolutions, see Rosenthal and Rosnow, *ibid.*; and E.J. Webb, *et al., Unobtrusive Measures: Nonreactive Research in the Social Sciences*, Chicago: Rand McNally, 1972.

> We cannot afford to use . . . economic evaluations [only] of services that ease the misery of the old, the chronically ill, and disabled, or aid the mothers with small children . . . . We must consider our "profit" in terms of human and moral values as well as in dollars and cents.[35]

The urge to quantify leads to another potential problem: what is known in education circles as "teaching to the test." Thus if teachers are evaluated by how well their students do on a standard test, the tendency is to concentrate teaching on those particular subjects that will be examined. In general, there may be a tendency to concentrate on where one will be subjected to quantitative evaluation. But we may ask: is this always a disadvantage? At least in the teaching situation the students are taught some things well.

The problem of excluding nonquantifiable factors becomes especially acute in a form of evaluation known as *cost-benefits analysis* (or cost-gains analysis, or cost-effectiveness analysis). In this process — a great favourite with technocratically-minded governments in the past decade — one attempts to create a sort of balance sheet for each proposed alternative, listing the various costs of each given programme on the one hand and the gains expected on the other. The object, of course, is to maximize what might be figuratively termed "social profit" (gains over losses) by selecting the best programme out of the competition. This differs little from the ordinary evaluation except that, instead of a single dimension being considered, the candidate programmes are evaluated simultaneously in terms of multiple criteria.[36]

It has become clear that in cost-benefits analysis one must be very wary of "hidden" costs in particular programmes — eventually the analysis becomes almost an exercise in accounting as one grapples with whether certain items such as training costs should be included. What is more, nonquantifiable items have a

35. Special Senate Committee on Poverty, *Poverty in Canada*, Ottawa: Information Canada, 1971. Reproduced by permission of Information Canada.
36. This explanation oversimplifies a highly complex process, but it is adequate for the present discussion. For an extended treatment see Thomas Goldman, ed., *Cost-Effectiveness Analysis: New Approaches in Decision-Making*, New York: Praeger, 1967.

way of appearing in a footnote in the introduction and of disappearing thereafter. In principle, a cost-effectiveness analysis is supposed to first quantify that which can logically be quantified and then give a decision maker the tools for making a decision that *incorporates* the *intuitive* aspects, but in practice the latter are often simply ignored. Even without such problems, no foolproof calculus exists to take into account simultaneously gains and losses of differing kinds; ultimately it is an individual decision to determine which items should be more heavily weighted than others. (Only rarely can all items be truly reduced to a common monetary unit of analysis.) Again, in principle, cost-benefits analysis is supposed to place all judgements in plain view and show clearly the logic used throughout. In a sense this is true: analyses of this sort do indeed spell out in detail the analytical procedures they are using. But again, in practice the logic and quantitative procedures are often so difficult for administrators not used to such tools to follow that they tend to accept uncritically the choice of the expert. The latter, in turn, is loathe to emphasize the numerous intuitive judgements at the base of his immaculate, imposing edifice.

In essence, in spite of its great recent popularity, cost-benefits analysis comes down ultimately to a series of political acts — sometimes quite consciously so. That is, it often lends a veneer of objectivity and quantification to a political decision.[37] Only in rather mechanical cases does it really become worthwhile. For instance, one can use the tool to select with reasonable objectivity the best car to be purchased for a police motor pool (even here, some assumptions might be challenged), but to use cost-benefits analysis to determine whether it would be better to replace the existing motor pool at all or to spend the money on improved training is an exercise in futility — or politics. Although promising considerably less than cost-benefits analysis, the basic experimental format of evaluation research —random assignment, experimental and control groups, before and after

37. Although not so critical of the process, the political acceptability and economic rationale of cost-benefits analysis is taken up in J. Wolfe, *Cost Benefit and Cost Effectiveness*, London: Allen and Unwin, 1973. For a skeptical, sophisticated treatment, see Peter Rossi and Walter Williams, eds., *Evaluating Social Programs: Theory, Practice, and Politics*, New York: Seminar Press, 1972.

measurements — poses far fewer questions of validity. Without minimizing the difficulties discussed earlier, it holds out a reasonable promise of meaningful answers to a limited list of questions.

POLITICAL AND ETHICAL CONSIDERATIONS

Before exploring the political weaknesses of evaluation, it should be noted that certain types of experimental programmes are simply impossible for a government to establish within a given cultural milieu because of a legislative or administrative fear of popular outcry. A governmental proposal has to take into account the probable reaction of media gate-keepers and others with influence. It is for this reason that, as Boguslaw has pointed out, it is ordinarily not possible to conduct "live" studies which involve fundamental changes in the social environment. Such changes might provide offense to community sentiment. For, again as he pointed out, although it is feasible to do research and experimentation on social problems in contexts that are socially acceptable at a given time and place, it is usually not possible to obtain support for research which would seriously investigate alternatives to existing institutional arrangements. What the evaluative results of such programmes would be can never be known for they are usually strangled in their infancy; neither the programme nor its evaluation can be initiated. On the other hand, private or cooperative programmes outside of the government can sometimes surmount the limitations imposed by "consensus politics." We shall have more to say about this in the final section.

Political considerations surround every step in the initiation of social intervention. A lack of fit between the perceived cause of a problem and the means used to combat it may, of course, be due to ideological factors, but it may also be due to administrative inefficiency on the part of the bureaucrats charged with programme implementation. Alternatively, lack of fit between cause and attempted solution may be due to ambiguous transmission of instructions through the administrative hierarchy, with lower echelons employing their own interpretations or selectively paying attention to only certain parts of their instructions. There may be insufficient resources (money or personnel) to carry out the programme actually needed. In such cases there is often a political need to appear to be "doing something," even when it is clear to those directly involved that little benefit will come from the option chosen. Likewise, in governmental bureaucracy unspent funds are supposedly indicative of "slack"; the agency which does not allocate all of its resources finds its future budgets reduced. Hence activity itself comes to be a prime concern, and the worth of the activity tends to become secondary.

Failure to offer the best programme to counter the perceived cause of a problem may be a result of insufficient popular consensus, support, and cooperation, especially if the public would be inconvenienced by truly effective measures. There may be powerful interests that would have to be challenged were the proper means implemented or, conversely, vested interests that are served by the option chosen (such as the training of new personnel, or the satisfaction of a powerful movement). Finally the administrators themselves may be uncertain of which programme to employ, leading them to adopt a mid-point policy which is useless.

Practical difficulties are compounded by the failure of most agencies to collect evaluation data on their own. This task has not usually been seen as a part of the obligation of organizations which deal with social problems. To be sure, most organizations gather statistical information about some aspects of their work, but data specifically related to whether the activity is meeting its ultimate purpose is rarely collected. Paradoxical as it may seem, organizations are far more likely to seek and systematically collect information which helps in their day-to-day functioning, irrespective of whether this routine functioning ever does any good.

When official statistics do become available, they are at times tainted with such pronounced political overtones that they are virtually worthless as means of evaluation. To take a single example, consider the compilation of statistics on volume of crime.[38] Clearly, it would be highly desirable to compare crime

---

38. We ignore here certain aspects which render such data even more suspect, such as the large volume of crime never reported to the police. For weaknesses of

rates in order to determine, for instance, the effects of various policing policies. We could either look at the same place at different times or, preferably, at the results of allocating new policies in a random selection of precincts or districts. Indeed the former approach has been successfully utilized on occasion. But the difficulties introduced by politics are enormous. Total volume of crime, it appears, is a highly sensitive issue. A city or a region could look very bad if it were to appear at the top of an index of crime. Tourism, industry, and economic growth could decline. Pressure is often brought to bear by city fathers to "dampen" these statistics. Then too, police departments themselves look bad if there is a high proportion of unsolved crime. Some cities have been notorious for "wiping the blotter clean" at the end of the year.

Criminal statistics can thus become a political football that even reform administrations are loathe to touch: whoever is the first political leader to improve a poor statistical system can later be condemned by the opposition for the "fantastic growth in crime" during his period in office. (Despite this, brave or foolhardy administrators do on occasion reform the accounting system, sometimes generating "increases" in crime over one hundred per cent in a single year.) More recently it has occurred to official compilers that certain advantages, in terms of increased financial support to combat the crime wave, may accrue from *over*-estimating volume of crime. Hence today inaccuracies can be introduced in *both directions*. Because of these inaccuracies the research situation has seemed so desperate that independent surveys have been conducted in recent years to approach more exactly the actual rate of crime.[39] Such surveys have been so helpful that in some places they have graduated

---

a supposedly sophisticated crime reporting system, see Marvin Wolfgang, "Uniform Crime Reports: A Critical Appraisal," *University of Pennsylvania Law Review*, 3, 1963, pp. 708-738. For further information on the weakness of available statistics on crime, see Nicholas Zay, "Gaps in Available Statistics on Crime and Delinquency in Canada," *Canadian Journal of Economics and Political Science*, 29, February, 1963, pp. 75-90.

39. For an early model see James F. Short, Jr. and F. Ivan Nye, "Reported Behavior as a Criterion of Deviant Behavior," *Social Problems*, 5, 1957, pp. 207-213. Again we note that inadequate police reporting is by no means the only reason for inaccuracies in estimating volume of crime.

from one-time affairs into systematic, recurring measurements.

The example of crime statistics illustrates, without exaggerating, the difficulties of using officially compiled statistics that purport to show how an agency is accomplishing its job.

To round out this long list of difficulties there are times when a control group is simply inappropriate or, indeed, unethical. If one strongly suspects that a reform measure will be beneficial, to withhold it from a control group merely to have a tidy experiment might be construable as an unnecessary perpetuation of misery. The issue is a difficult one, centring around the degree of people's need of some helpful development, and the degree of certainty about the proposed programme. Neither component can be ignored: even with the most serious of diseases, doctors do not administer a new drug to every patient until it has been exhaustively evaluated with experimental and control groups.[40] However, if one is reasonably sure of at least some beneficial effects, it would not do to withhold treatment even for less serious matters.

One of the most serious ethical cases concerning a control group was only recently discovered. In 1932 officials of the U.S. Public Health Service decided to see what the difference in prognosis was for treated and untreated cases of syphilis. A large group of poor black men with syphilis were located in Alabama and were randomly assigned to treatment and control groups. The men in the control group were paid a small sum periodically for their continuing participation in the experiment, but over a period of some forty years they received no medication whatsoever, meanwhile suffering progressive deterioration from the disease.[41] When at last the scandal was uncovered, it was noted that in the earliest days of the study there was no effective cure for syphilis, and the treatment then was considered by many to be as bad as the disease. But penicillin had been discovered less than ten years into the experiment and yet the control group was maintained for another thirty years without treatment. A court

40. The typical progression in medical research is from animal experimentation to terminal cases (as a last resort), then to controlled experimentation, and finally to general use.

41. See Bernard Barber, et al., *Research on Human Subjects: Problems of Social Control in Medical Experimentation*, New York: Russell Sage Foundation, 1973.

award of $37,500 to each survivor appeared to many observers to be far too little, too late. This senseless cruelty contrasts with the occasional use of a false "ethics" issue as a facade to hide behind for those anxious to avoid evaluation.

For years the ethical issue formed a part of the rationale behind the refusal of the psychoanalytic profession to submit to controlled experimentation: ethically it could not refuse to treat a part of the population that badly needed its help merely in order for others to ascertain the natural untreated recovery rate. Of course this argument assumes that one knows that psychoanalysis is indeed beneficial — the very question which needed to be studied. George Fairweather relates one such incident.

> The experimenter came under severe criticism from prac-
> titioners [service personnel] who were advocates of either
> group or individual psychotherapy. From their point of view,
> people in the fourth group were being denied one of the best
> treatments. It must be noted here that the adoption of this
> position rests upon the assumption that the merits of the three
> psychotherapy conditions had already been established. As
> far as experimental verification was concerned, however, it
> was equally tenable that the no-psychotherapy fourth condi-
> tion might bring about the same or even more desirable results
> than any of the three psychotherapy programs. The research
> eventually did proceed, but only with great misgivings on the
> part of these service personnel.[42]

In the end, the experimental results showed that the no-psychotherapy fourth group fared just as well after eighteen months' community living as those receiving one or the other form of psychotherapy.

When an evaluation is made, it runs considerable risk of being ignored — not because of its technical defects but because of a number of practical and/or political reasons. To begin with, a considerable time-lag between programme implementation and

42. George Fairweather, Methods for Experimental Social Innovation, New York: Wiley, 1967, p. 31.

evaluation may be politically indefensible. New programmes usually emerge as the direct result of social crises. The lead time required before results may be known through systematic evaluation research is always considered excessive by administrators and political figures, and in some cases it may in truth be too slow to cope with a rapidly evolving situation.[43]

Popular demand may override findings which run contrary to common-sense appraisals. The politicians and bureaucratic élite may themselves be only vaguely familiar with evaluation research; like the general public, they may not accept conclusions which conflict with their own intuition. This seems to have occurred, for example, with research showing no deterrent effects from capital punishment. Then too, appraisal results may be demanded with such persistence, and accepted with such alacrity, that programmes are prematurely evaluated. Potentially worthwhile efforts may thus be rejected as unproductive before the project staff has had time to make necessary adjustments. Finally, politically or ideologically distasteful findings can simply be *suppressed*, with the study never released to the public or surrounded with copyright restrictions and printed obscurely. For this reason the sponsorship of research is very important with regard to honesty—the social organization of the research effort is a critical issue.

It has been suggested that evaluation research can at times result in the loss of the more progressive administrative staffs since they are more likely to sponsor an evaluation of their own programmes. Goffman speaks of "latent secrets," meaning facts incompatible with the impression fostered by an agency, which have not yet been collected and organized into a usable form.[44] In the bureaucratic morass, volunteering to have one's latent secrets analyzed amounts to exposing oneself to a form of criticism which the traditionalist avoids. Among traditional programmes, Hackler points out, evaluative research will encounter not only antipathy but downright hostility. "To say that the

---

43. There is a short but excellent overview of the political dilemmas of social policy research on pp. 172-176 of Walter Buckley, *Sociology and Modern Systems Theory*, Englewood Cliffs, N.J.: Prentice-Hall, 1967.
44. Erving Goffman, *The Presentation of Self in Everyday Life*, Garden City, N.Y.: Doubleday, 1959, p. 144.

status of the evaluator is 'ambiguous' is to put it nicely. Evaluators are damned unpopular people in the eyes of those who are being evaluated."[45]

The preceding discussion should suffice to show the grave difficulties involved in conducting evaluation research. It is by no means a simple, straightforward process. Indeed, the types of problems enumerated above are of such magnitude that some observers have concluded that the results of evaluation research are meaningless and that such research should therefore be abandoned.[46] Yet it should be realized that projects rarely encounter more than a small fraction of the *potential* political difficulties described above, and means to overcome the technical problems have been found and continue to be suggested.[47] We have of necessity been able to review only the most basic techniques in this chapter. Unless we are to return to an era in which sheer argumentative power carried the day, in which "common-sense logic" dictated the programmes to be employed, and anecdotal examples (or "testimonials") constituted the only feedback on the success of a programme, evaluation research—difficult as it is to carry out in practice—is a necessity.

EVALUATION RESEARCH AND NONGOVERNMENTAL INTERVENTION

To this point we have concentrated on a sort of "establishment" research—that is, on the evaluation of programmes of the kind that a *government* might generate. Actually, of course, programmes to counter social problems can arise not only from governmental intervention but also from private sources external to government, and these sources can be either cooperative with or hostile to the established political and social structure. Some critics have regarded techniques of assessment and decision-making as simply parts of the strategies of rulers to control the populace. What, if anything, does evaluation re-

45. James Hackler, *Why Delinquency Prevention Programs Should NOT be Evaluated*, Edmonton: University of Alberta, 1973, p. 56.
46. See Hackler, *ibid.* For a strong defence of evaluation see Chapter 1 of Leslie T. Wilkins, *Social Deviance*, Englewood Cliffs, N.J.: Prentice-Hall, 1965.
47. See, as examples, the techniques proposed in Campbell, 1969, *op. cit.*; and Fairweather, *op. cit.*

search have to say in terms of the latter two responses to social problems?

Evaluation research is clearly compatible with some forms of intervention not associated with governments. Traditional psychotherapy has been evaluated, against fierce resistance, and lately results—largely negative—have been forthcoming on the encounter group (sensitivity training, T-group) movement.[48]

What is the usefulness of evaluation research for movements that are hostile to a prevailing government? Can the procedures outlined in this chapter be of any assistance for the strategy of social reorganization as outlined in Chapter 1? Let us take up the stage of actual reorganization, assuming that a movement has *attained* sufficient power to implement fundamental changes. Use of evaluation research here seems less likely than it would be for the private agency, not because there is any obstacle to using evaluation research on radical programmes *per se*, but because there is, rather, an inherent difficulty involved in evaluating *any* programme in which the unit of analysis is the whole society. For programmes that require the restructuring of a complete society, there can ordinarily be no control groups in the usual sense of the word; hence it becomes impossible to isolate the effects of the intended structural change from influences of ongoing historical events (for instance, counter-revolutionary uprisings) which take place simultaneously. This is also a problem in properly evaluating certain programmes ordinarily considered non-revolutionary. For instance, historians continually argue over whether the Great Depression was really being defeated by economic counter-measures before the Second World War broke out. Did economies heal only because of war production or were they already being mended by the recommendations of Keynesian economics?[49] A revolutionary programme which proposes, for example, to abolish the market economy, *cannot* be tested in one small quadrant of a

48. Morton Lieberman, *et al.*, *Encounter Groups: First Facts*, New York: Basic Books, 1973. See also sections of N. Solomon and Betty Berson, eds., *New Perspectives on Encounter Groups*, San Francisco: Jossey-Bass, 1972.
49. In addition to the lack of control groups, such programmes are also difficult to evaluate because they often change many features at once. A sophisticated experimental design, however, can cope with this particular problem.

society since the beneficial effects that are purported for such a programme would ensue, gradually, only if society as a whole were affected, rather than particular sectors or individuals.

How have programmes such as these been evaluated traditionally? Although no one has the power to assign randomly whole cultures and societies into experimental and control groups, nevertheless some societies will embark on a particular programme at a certain time while others will not, thereby constituting a form of "natural experiment." Of course the missing randomization procedure makes all comparisons on such "experiments" terribly risky. We see, for instance, a programme apparently producing benefits. The society in which it is introduced appears better off than societies without it. But the programme may have been introduced where it was only because that society was *already* more "advanced," or more conducive to beneficial outcomes, than any other. The true effects of the programme itself, vis-à-vis other concurrent historical events, is thus extraordinarily difficult to isolate. Nevertheless, people do not give up on analysis in such cases.

The tendency is to revert back to simpler before-and-after arguments or comparisons across societies at a single point in time, simply because that is the best that can be done.[50] One can look, for instance, at the experience of workers' control of industry in Yugoslavia, compare it with the Saab approach in Sweden, contrast it with "soviets" of workers in the Soviet Union.[51] It is quite reasonable to say, on the one hand, that such comparisons are better than nothing, but, on the other hand, it is foolhardy— and possibly a source of human misery—to place great confidence in such inherently inadequate evaluations by themselves. Still, can one give up this challenge?

Is it true, then, that evaluation research as described in this chapter is of no use for a radical movement? This may be the case in the early formative stage of the movement. But all movements

50. In cases where a sizable number of societies changed, it may be possible to control statistically for some of the sources of error without randomization. Even where this is possible, conclusions about the effects of a programme must be approached with great caution.
51. See the work of Jerry Hunnius in *The Case for Participatory Democracy*, edited by George Benello and Dimitrios Roussopoulos, New York: Viking Press, 1972.

hope to succeed, and they cherish visions of a period in which the desired structural changes can be made. Unless one is prepared to defend the notion that revolution will usher in the millenium, one must concede that even a post-revolution society will be beset with problems of a social nature. Insofar as some of these may be resolvable at the microlevel, they are amenable to evaluation research. In fact, can one conceive of a society that could *not* find a use for this tool?

Somehow, the notion of a radical movement in the role of programme evaluator does seem incongruous. But this is because of a growing distrust of expertise, technocracy, and technologism — a distrust which is coming to be more and more closely associated with radical thinking. It is time to pursue systematically a line of thought that recurs throughout this book: the tension between expertise and humanity — between bureaucracy and efficiency, on the one hand, and compassion and concern on the other. It is time to examine that tension in the arena of social problems.

5   In The End: Expertise And Persisting Social Problems

A BRIEF REVIEW

As we begin the final chapter, a brief review of the uses of this book seems apropos. As we remarked in the opening chapter, the book is intended neither to provide remedies for specific social problems nor to discuss the causes of these problems. Our focus, rather, has been on the efforts of humanity to cope with its problems, with the strategies and issues attendant thereto. We have tried to grapple with some of the broader issues: the basic strategies of intervention; how the "mix" has changed over time; why people of earlier eras did not intervene in certain problems; some of the hidden pitfalls, the unanticipated consequences of intervention; how we can be sure we are producing any results; and how we can, perhaps, choose between competing remedies. As we noted in the preface, these are terribly important questions, yet treatments of social problems usually ignore them. Of course this book omits the treatment of specific problems found in other works; the two efforts complement each other.

Our study commenced with an analysis of the strategies and doctrines which have been employed against social problems in various times and places. We noted the preponderance of punitive measures in earlier periods and the conspicuous absence until historically recent times of the strategy of social reorganization. Some of the reasons for the latter's absence were the subject of Chapter 2, which emphasized those aspects of the history of ideas which have provided obstacles or objections to certain forms of intervention. The intellectual élite of earlier centuries, instead of providing a base of dissent, was the staunch supporter of the establishment; Chapter 2 reviewed and examined critically the intellectual justifications for this stance. We reserved for a separate chapter the discussion of one particular conceptual obstacle to intervention: the problem of unanticipated consequences. But, as Chapter 3 made clear, the significance of unanticipated consequences is far broader than providing another objection to intervention. One form of unintended consequence received special attention: the consequences of official labeling were examined in detail, demonstrating that the concept of unanticipated consequences can provide support for both conservative and radical positions. Finally, Chapter 4 presented the multiple advantages of evaluation research, sketched some of the basic approaches, and described the attendant difficulties.

We have saved for the last what may be the most important issue: where are we going in terms of coping with social problems? Are current trends hopeful or discouraging? Are we becoming more or less effective today in coping with problem conditions, and why?

A full treatment of this question would require an historical survey of the gradual development of new tools for combating social ills. We might consider the emergence of formal codes of law, of self-conscious law-making, taxation, and state service, the first gathering of social statistics. If we chose more recent developments, we might examine centralized planning, or the creation of economic and social indicators. It is important to recognize that modern modes of coping with social problems are the result of numerous social inventions. Many of these innovations seem so commonplace today that it is difficult to conceive of their having a definitive period of origin, in the same manner as a physical invention, yet their advent is a matter of historical record. We shall concentrate on one development with marked implications for the future of social intervention: the triumph of the expert and the specialized group. The chapter will consider the growth of *technique* and *specialization*, the advantages this provides for combating social problems in terms of competence, and its drawbacks in terms of ethical blindness and impersonality.

In the first section below we lay the groundwork by examining the meaning of technicism. The third section traces the historical emergence of experts and specialized social problem agencies up to the present day. The tendencies within technicism that are conducive to ethical blindness are explored in detail. Finally, we look at some of the advantages of specialization, and see clearly the dilemma before us: how can we obtain the blessings of efficient expertise and yet escape its terrible costs?

TECHNICISM IN MODERN SOCIETY

A favourite theme of critics of modern society is the extent to which technology has come to dominate the life of man. One perceptive observer, Jacques Ellul, has penetrated beyond this commonplace insight to attack what he sees as a far broader problem, the problem of technicism. We shall want to discuss the rise of technicism in the treatment of social problems, but, first, it is essential to understand precisely what technicism is.

By now we have numerous books and countless articles on the problems attendant on the ascendancy of technology in modern society.[1] It is true, as the writers of such works say, that modern technology has rendered the contemporary world more remote from the life of eighteenth-century Europe than that life was from the life of ancient Rome.[2] Within the period since the industrial revolution, the vision of man being warped by the machines he supposedly controls is a recurring theme. One thinks of Charlie Chaplin pathetically ruled by machines in the movie "Modern Times," of the nineteenth-century Luddites smashing the machinery which had taken away their jobs, or of the modern phobias about computers and IBM cards, and the transfer of the plea "do not fold, spindle or mutilate" to the

1. For example, Jean Meynaud, *Technocracy*, New York: Free Press, 1969; or Hans Morgenthau, *Scientific Man Versus Power Politics*, Chicago: Phoenix Books, 1965. Lewis Mumford, *Technics and Civilization*, New York: Harcourt, Brace, 1934, was an early precursor, as was, in its way, Norbert Weiner's *The Human Use of Human Beings: Cybernetics and Society*, New York: Avon Books, 1967 (original, 1950). Harold Innis takes up the theme in his *The Bias of Communication*, Toronto: University of Toronto Press, 1951.
2. Herbert J. Muller, *The Children of Frankenstein: A Primer on Modern Technology and Scientific Values*, Bloomington: Indiana University Press, 1971. This chapter has been profoundly influenced by Muller's insights, sometimes in ways not suitable for citation. The intellectual debt is considerable.

persons whom the cards affect. Assaults on technology started with the revulsion of the Romantic writers at the excesses of the early industrial revolution. Their protests were directed more against the historical by-products—human suffering in factory towns, loss of contact with nature, uprooting of families—than against the triumph of machine civilization itself.[3] "Technologism" is the word in common usage that refers either to the glorification of technology or to the social condition in which technology is ascendant.

Ellul's analysis is considerably broader and more profound than the standard critique of technologism. As noted in Robert Merton's introduction to the English translation, the title of Ellul's book has been mistranslated.[4] The book is really a critique of *the encroachment of "technique" or expertise into all aspects of life*—certainly not just in technology! To be sure we find technicism, if we may use the word, in technology, but we also find it today in such widely diverse areas as politics (the selling of the political candidate), the "art" of sex (the legion of "how to do it better" books), personal manipulation (from Dale Carnegie's old *How to Win Friends and Influence People* to the recent *Games People Play*), or negotiation ("psychological strategies for gaining negotiating advantages" as a series of recent management seminars were called).

Technicism, *the transformation of all aspects of life into the realm of technique*, is an amorphous, difficult concept.[5] Yet one feels it is a profoundly important insight. Ellul calls technicism "the real religion of our times." The foundations of advancing expertise across all fields of endeavour and the spread of technicism can be detected in the decline of the realm of the sacred and the sacrosanct. As Max Weber pointed out, we live in a world that has become, in a special sense of the word, "dis-enchant-

3. A good modern equivalent is Everett C. Hughes' description of a factory town in French Canada. See his *French Canada in Transition*, Chicago: University of Chicago Press, 1963.
4. Jacques Ellul, *The Technological Society*, Introduction by Robert K. Merton, New York: Vintage Books, 1967 (original, 1954).
5. Ellul's usage is important but risks being carried too far. Is an opera singer's technique "technicism" in a meaningful sense? For an attempt to sort out the definition, see Victor Ferkiss, *Technological Man: The Myth and the Reality*, New York: Mentor, 1969, pp. 37-38.

ed." Every social convention and arrangement can be subjected to today to examination and challenge: patriotism, religion, paternalism, the family, etc. In place of the sanctity of the traditional comes increasing *rationalization* of all sectors of society, a long-term trend to which many writers, especially Max Weber, have called attention. And linked with the extension of rationalization and technicism to all quarters is the growth of what Weber called the rational bureaucracy.[6] Bureaucracy is a modern social invention having few parallels in earlier cultures, yet today an increasingly standardized organizational structure can be found in contexts as diverse as organized religion, the military, big business, big unions, and the university.[7] And, according to Weber, bureaucracy is ubiquitous in all modern societies, capitalist and socialist.[8]

Bureaucracy seems to be both a prominent outcome of inreased rationalization as well as one of its sources. The existence of representative democracy cannot be taken as any assurance against incursion of bureaucratic control. For that matter, the decisions of a legislative body are today *carried out* by bureaucracies, a point long ago noted by Weber. Even at the turn of the century it was becoming clear that "the day-to-day exercise of authority was in the hands of the bureaucracy, and even success in the struggle for votes and in parliamentary debate and decision-making would come to naught unless it was translated into effective control over administrative implementation."[9]

6. For Weber's ideas on bureaucracy see Reinhard Bendix, *Max Weber: An Intellectual Portrait*, Garden City, N.Y.: Doubleday, 1962. Many of the topics to be discussed here, including the professionalization of society, bureaucratization, and secularization, are excellently treated in Guy Rocher, *A General Introduction to Sociology: A Theoretical Perspective*, Toronto: Macmillan Co. of Canada, 1972. See the section on "Technological Society." For an old but outstanding treatment of bureaucratic structure and personality, see Chapter 6 in Robert K. Merton, *Social Theory and Social Structure*, rev. ed., Glencoe, Ill.: Free Press, 1957.
7. See William H. Whyte, Jr., *The Organization Man*, Garden City, N.Y.: Doubleday, 1956. For a discussion of proto-bureaucracies in earlier societies, see William Delaney, "The Development and Decline of Patrimonial and Bureaucratic Administrations," *Administrative Science Quarterly*, 7, March, 1963, pp. 458-501.
8. See S. M. Lipset, *Political Man*, New York: Doubleday, 1963, p. 10.
9. Bendix, *op. cit.*, p. 433. See also the reference to Michel's iron law of oligarchy at the end of Chapter 2.

Nor could socialism be counted upon to answer the bureaucratic challenge; according to Weber, socialism merely extends and multiplies the existing bureaucracy to such an extent that it penetrates into every nook and cranny of the society, resulting in a "dictatorship of the bureaucrats," not of the proletariat. A variant of modern socialist thought strongly agrees. Distinguishing "élite socialism" from "socialism-from-below," Oppenheimer notes that "a simplistic either-or view of the future (either capitalism or socialism) blinded socialists to the dangers of bureaucracy as an independent force which could (become) a third alternative." The growth of bureaucracy was for Weber one of the most ubiquitous, and unpleasant, developments in modern society; indeed it was "the most crucial phenomenon of the modern Western state."[10]

Ellul, of course, is adamantly opposed to technicism, and there is an affinity between Ellul's work and Kafka's fictional masterpiece, *The Trial*, with its emphasis on the nightmarish qualities of an uncaring, unfeeling bureaucracy. It is simplistic to treat the bureaucratic phenomenon as an unmitigated evil, but important to recognize the trend toward technicism in its various manifestations.[11]

Not only the physical machinery used in work but also the very *organization of work* itself has become a matter of technicism — symbolized in the twentieth century by the efficiency expert with time-and-motion studies and the rationalization of industrial work. The early decades of the century were especially congenial to "Taylorism," the introduction of the so-called "scientific management" approach. Although later decades have softened its rough corners with "human relations" in the factory, this softening merely blurs the outlines of the triumph of technicism in the organization of work: production schedules, assembly lines, time clocks. All, difficult as it may be

10. Martin Oppenheimer, "The Limitations of Socialism," in *The Case for Participatory Democracy*, edited by C.G. Benello and D. Roussopoulos, New York: Viking Press, 1971; Max Weber, "The Essentials of Bureaucratic Organization," in *Reader in Bureaucracy*, edited by Robert K. Merton, *et al.*, Glencoe, Ill.: Free Press, 1952, p. 24.

11. For surveys of the many modern studies of bureaucracy, see Richard H. Hall, *Organizations: Structure and Process*, Englewood Cliffs, N.J.: Prentice-Hall, 1972; Charles Perrow, *Complex Organizations*, Glenview, Ill.: Scott, Foresman, 1972.

to believe, are social inventions of the present century. The factory itself is a social invention only a few centuries old.

So great is the triumph of technicism that the search for new technologies, and the rapid introduction of these innovations into the mainstream of economic and social life, has itself become a matter of expertise. Whereas inventions were formerly created haphazardly, there has been, first, a gradual (sometimes reluctant) mating of science and technology[12] and, more recently, the emergence of research and development as an industry in its own right. We are, as has been remarked, the first civilization to *systematize* the processes of innovation and discovery. Alfred North Whitehead once noted that the greatest invention of the nineteenth century was the comprehension of the method of invention. In the United States research and development has become a multi-billion dollar activity, with support coming from government as well as from business interests, while throughout the Western world the "knowledge industry" is today one of the largest economic units. Numerous scholars — notably Daniel Bell and John Kenneth Galbraith — have forecast that the production of knowledge will be the most important institution in the "post-industrial" or "technocratic" society. Technicism, thus, is introduced at the very creation of new technology; *we are now expert at creating new areas of expertise.*

As a result of these trends, and the concomitant occupational shifts, the professional and technical class emerges as the dominant occupational group in the "post-industrial society." According to many writers (prominently, Daniel Bell, S.M. Lipset, J.K. Galbraith), the creation and utilization of theoretical knowledge will become the central, axial principle of society, with decision-making itself the subject of an "intellectual technology," run by technocrats.[13] In the society of the future a predom-

12. The exact degree of interdependence of science and technology in various historical periods has been a continuing source of debate. For contrasting views on the strength of interrelationship, see Robert K. Merton, "Science and Economy of 17th Century England," in his *Social Theory and Social Structure, op. cit.*, and A. Rupert Hall, "Engineering and the Scientific Revolution," *Technology and Culture*, 2, Fall, 1961, pp. 333-341.
13. See, for example, Daniel Bell, *The Coming of Post-Industrial Society*, New York: Basic Books, 1973.

inant role will be played by scientists, professionals, technicians, and technocrats. Our purpose in the remainder of this chapter is to examine the triumph of technicism in the treatment of social problems and to consider the ethical and practical consequences of this ascendancy.

HISTORICAL INTERLUDE: THE GROWTH OF TECHNICISM IN INTERVENTION

In the early 1800's a new development appeared in the treatment of social problems. Facilities that we take for granted today — mental hospitals (formerly insane asylums), penitentiaries, orphanages, etc.—were developed in this period. These *asylums* were regarded at the time as a great innovation.[14] Given the difficulties subsequently experienced with large centralized facilities, it is painful to recall the enthusiasm with which they were once greeted. Today, of course, we know by experience the severe disadvantages of placing all criminals into a single facility, where they can reinforce each other's attitudes and learn new techniques of crime.[15] We know also the disadvantages of the centralized mental institution: the patient's isolation, cut off as he is from family and friends, in itself retards improvement.[16] The isolation of a large central facility from public view also increased the ease of mistreatment of its inmates.

But such reflections were far in the future of the heady reform atmosphere surrounding the emergence of the asylum. In centralized facilities treatment would be possible, humane intentions made workable at last. To be sure the period's idea of

14. See David Rothman, *The Discovery of the Asylum*, Boston: Little, Brown, 1971.
15. The earliest prisons tried to avoid this problem through segregation of prisoners or by rules of silence, but these attempts disintegrated in practice. It is tragic that large penal institutions are still being considered in Canada, despite opposition. See Department of the Solicitor General, *Report of the Working Group on Federal Maximum Security Institutions Design*, Ottawa: Queen's Printer, 1971.
16. The trend today in mental health care is toward community-centred facilities. Interestingly, the early asylums in the United States followed similar patterns. See Norman Dain, *Concepts of Insanity in the United States 1759-1865*, New Brunswick, N.J.: Rutgers University Press, 1964, p. xiii. See also comments on the cyclical nature of reforms later in this chapter.

"humane" differed radically from our own, incorporating ideas of orderliness that we would find abhorrent. But the central point was that instead of detaining-centres for the infliction of physical pain, prisons would be places where habits of industry and religious belief could be incubated. In retrospect, although the degree of enthusiasm was naive, asylums did make treatment *possible*—however much it was subsequently neglected in practice. And although the earliest asylums were undifferentiated, with old and young, sane and insane, criminals and paupers mixed together, the development of specialized *institutions* paved the way for the creation of specialized *treatment personnel*. Taken in sum, then, the asylum was a major development in the transformation of intervention.

The *social problems concept*, as currently conceived, is also a relatively recent development in the history of Western culture. The existence of such conditions as mental illness, crime, and poverty is well documented in historical records, and a deleterious quality about such conditions has long been recognized. But these undesirable conditions were generally viewed within a fatalistic perspective with religious and/or military overtones. They were not generally seen as problems that could be treated socially. Most social problems in the past were defined as problems against order, against nature, against God, or, perhaps, as manifestations of God's will. And it is only toward the end of the eighteenth century that many of the problems we now consider as social emerged as such in the public consciousness. This change toward a perception of problems was related to other developments in modern Western thought and social structure which have been discussed in previous chapters.

Social problems — as a new conceptualization, not a new phenomenon — emerged around the turn of the eighteenth and nineteenth centuries as a result of several mutually reinforcing developments.[17] On the structural level were the severe stresses created by industrialization and urbanization. Accompanying these structural developments were marked changes on the cul-

17. The passages on the social problems concept and the development of the social sciences are taken from Chapter 2 of Richard L. Henshel and Anne-Marie Henshel, *Perspectives on Social Problems*, Don Mills, Ont.: Longman Canada, 1973.

tural level in social thought: a growing humanitarianism, democratic trends, and a new scientific ideology and secular rationality.[18]

The factors which finally led to the perception of deleterious conditions as social problems and to the questioning of the prevailing order are finely and intricately interwoven. Along with the new drive toward humanitarian reform, a scientific value system and a new conception of progress emerged from the successes of the physical sciences. Secular rationalism, or the secularization of formerly sacred thought, was a development that paralleled the development of the scientific orientation. One effect of this development meant that men no longer viewed the social order as dictated by divine will and therefore irremediable. This new perception of the situation permitted the rise of reformers and of social movements in ways previously incompatible with the vision of an unalterable status quo.[19] These factors were prerequisite to the concept of a social problem and, especially, its rational study. The successes of the natural sciences and the secularization of thought led intellectuals to consider applying the principles of science to the human realm as well. In the seventeenth and eighteenth centuries scientific developments led to a more optimistic and active view of mankind, and to consideration of the possibility of applying scientific rules for the betterment of humanity.

We thus have the timely beginning of the *social sciences.* Social science associations were created in England (1857), in France (1862), and in the United States (1865). One purpose of these early associations was to find ways through scientific means to alleviate the social injustices that were recognized at the time. Conversely, any situation that was felt to be in need of remedy by middle-class reformers became a social problem. In spite of its early ameliorative emphasis under Saint-Simon and Comte, European sociology developed with considerably less

18. Jessie Bernard, *Social Problems at Midcentury*, New York: Dryden Press, 1957, pp. 90-91.
19. Rudolph Heberle, "Social Movements," in *International Encyclopedia of the Social Sciences*, Vol. 14, New York: Crowell, Collier and Macmillan, 1968, p. 440.

emphasis on social problems than its American counterpart.[20] In 1897 the French sociologist, Emile Durkheim, attacked the problem of suicide from this new scientific perspective.[21] His work is now a classic in sociology, and it encouraged the first, slow beginnings of the scientific study of social problems. In the meantime, social problems had already become a matter of academic interest in the United States, although several years had to elapse before a work of great empirical importance was produced.[22] Nevertheless, under the impetus of the now defunct American Association of Social Sciences, courses on social problems were offered in universities and colleges beginning in 1865 and reaching an early peak between 1885 and 1895.[23] Courses on social problems did not attain such popularity in Canada until much later because the establishment of the social sciences took place after the initial ferment was already over in the United States. The first sociology course in Canada was offered in 1908.[24]

We should not convey the erroneous impression that the social sciences in their formative years were unequivocally in favour of active amelioration of social problems. The concept of laissez faire itself had developed at the hands of the classical economists, Adam Smith and Ricardo. Even the founder of sociology, Auguste Comte, was by no means an unequivocal

20. J. Graham Morgan, "Contextual Factors in the Rise of Academic Sociology in the United States," *Canadian Review of Sociology and Anthropology*, 7, 1970, pp. 159-171.

21. Emile Durkheim, *Suicide*, Glencoe, Ill.: Free Press, 1951 (original, 1897).

22. W.E.B. DuBois' study of the Negro in Philadelphia, published in 1899, and Thomas and Znaniecki's study of the Polish peasant in Europe and America, in 1918, are considered the best early American studies on social problems. See for the latter the treatment in John Madge, *The Origins of Scientific Sociology*, Glencoe, Ill.: Free Press, 1962.

23. Edwin M. Lemert, "Social Problems," in *International Encyclopedia of the Social Sciences*, Vol. 14, *op. cit.*, p. 452.

24. For historical accounts of the development of sociology, see Howard Becker and H.E. Barnes, *Social Thought from Lore to Science*, 3rd ed., New York: Dover Publications, 1961, especially Chapters 14 and 16; Desmond M. Connor and James E. Curtis, *Sociology and Anthropology in Canada*, Montreal: Canadian Sociology and Anthropology Association, September, 1970; Roscoe C. Hinkle and Gisela Hinkle, *The Development of Modern Sociology*, New York: Random House, 1962; and Frank Manuel, *The Prophets of Paris*, Cambridge, Mass.: Harvard University Press, 1962.

advocate of reform, and two of the most prominent early sociologists, Summer and Spencer, were ideologically reactionary. In spite of this, however, the thrust of early social science was clearly reformative and ameliorationist in character, with most early American sociologists, for example, having backgrounds in the clergy.[25]

In the realm of personnel the gradual growth of a *body of experts* in particular types of social problems followed the emergence in the nineteenth century of the social problem concept and the creation of the asylum. In the early stages of the asylum there was very little specialization and virtually no training of personnel.[26] The keeper at the insane asylum was largely interchangeable with the prison guard or, for that matter, the caretaker of an orphanage. Many of the public specialties that are taken for granted today, such as policemen or firemen, were nonexistent.[27] When the police first came into existence around 1830, the composition and organization was highly similar to that of the military, a relationship hardly surprising since it was through the inadequacies of the traditional intervention by the military in civil disturbances that the police originally came into being. As Bordua puts it, "the establishment of the modern uniformed police constituted a recognition that coercive social control could not remain in the hands of nonspecialists."[28] Gradually, a special body of technique evolved for civilian police that decisively distinguished them from their military forebears.[29] (Indeed the police detective was

25. Hinkle and Hinkle, *op. cit.* Consider in this context the rise of the social gospel in the same period, as discussed in Chapter 2.

26. One historian, noting that the insane were, as a rule, locked up with criminals in prisons, has maintained that there were no real hospitals for the treatment of the mentally ill up to the end of the eighteenth century — only places where they were kept. See George Rosen, *Madness in Society*, New York: Harper & Row, 1968, p. 151.

27. An early effort to provide such services in eighteenth-century Prussia was largely abortive. See Reinhold Dorwart, *The Prussian Welfare State Before 1740*, Cambridge, Mass.: Harvard University Press, 1971.

28. David J. Bordua, ed., *The Police*, New York: Wiley, 1967, p. vii.

29. For the history of the early police see Charles Reith, *The Police Idea*, London: Oxford University Press, 1938 and *A New Study of Police History*, London: Oliver and Boyd, 1956; and T.A. Critchley, *A History of Police in England and Wales, 900-1966*, London: Constable, 1967. For an excellent analysis of the novelty of the idea of police (something we take for granted

among the earliest true specialists in social problems.) Other specialized roles gradually emerged in a process of differentiation that continues unabated to the present day. Meanwhile, the now-familiar body of specialized agencies of the state — police, fire, prison, orphanage, insane asylum, homes for the blind, war veterans — was replacing church-based organizations or largely undifferentiated, primitive state arrangements.[30]

The social worker made an appearance on the scene in the 1880's.[31] Around this time the idea developed that charity by itself was not enough if it was not translated into the actual good of the deprived and unfortunate, and that such benefits did not automatically follow from mere benevolent intent. To ensure the translation of good intentions into beneficial results required expertise and special capabilities — hence the need for special training in social work.[32] Consider this statement by Rabbi Abba Silver in 1928:

The last few decades have introduced a purposefulness and an intelligence which have made [charity] more helpful than heretofore. The sporadic giving of doles became, in the hands of trained and capable administrators, an organized system of service, of study, of investigation and supervision, so that the recipient of aid was not pauperized, and the public not victimized. Charity has become more scientific. This does not mean that it has lost spontaneity, or that it has become cold, tardy and impersonal. Rather, it has become more expert.[33]

---

today), see Allan Silver, "The Demand for Order in Civil Society: A Review of Some Theories in the History of Urban Crime, Police, and Riot," pp. 1-24 in Bordua, *op. cit.*

30. Hospitals, courts, and jails were considerably earlier developments.

31. See Roy Lubove, *The Professional Altruist: The Emergence of Social Work as a Career 1880-1930*, Cambridge, Mass.: Harvard University Press, 1971; Kathleen Woodroofe, *From Charity to Social Work in England and the United States*, Toronto: University of Toronto Press, 1962.

32. For a general treatment of the rise of bureaucracies within the welfare apparatus, and the increasing emphasis on efficiency, see Guy Rocher, "Bureaucracy and Welfare," *Canadian Welfare*, 39, March-April, 1963, pp. 55-61.

33. Abba Hillel Silver, "The Widening Horizon of Social Service," *Proceedings of the First Annual Meetings*, Canadian Council on Social Work, 1928, pp. 21-24. Quote is from p. 21.

Observe the confidence! We shall look at the drawbacks of "expertise" momentarily.

The slow conversion, among the educated, of beliefs about insanity — from divine retribution (or divine will) to organic brain damage — led to the establishment in the United States of some carefully planned, medically oriented regimes, with medical superintendents as directors.[34] Canadian asylums at first resembled British country asylums, but their administration more closely resembled the American type with medical superintendents.[35] Technical training specifically for the care of the insane began in the late nineteenth century.

The early decades of the twentieth century witnessed the emergence of what historians today call the child-saving movement.[36] This movement generated increased specialization in a number of institutions. Juvenile delinquents who had formerly been housed with adult offenders were now provided separate facilities that, in a naive way, were focused specifically on delinquency. In addition to these reformatories, the movement also produced the institution known as juvenile court, an innovation about which we will have more to say later in the chapter. The emergence of the social problems expert was unmistakable by the early twentieth century.

THE TRIUMPH OF TECHNICISM IN INTERVENTION

The developments described above have been augmented in recent decades with some important additional trends. To begin with, there has been a growing acceptance by both the public and governmental authorities of the need for specialists in fields of social problems. There is increasing recognition of the exper-

34. However many so-called medical men of the 1800's were charlatans; most did not possess medical degrees, nor was the possession of a medical degree a guarantee of sophistication, especially in psychiatric affairs. See Dain, *op. cit.*, p. 25.
35. See D.G. McKerracher, *Trends in Psychiatric Care*, Royal Commission on Health Services, Ottawa: Queen's Printer, 1966, pp. 5-6. Asylums in Quebec were of a different nature; patients were under the care of religious orders and treatment was influenced by the French tradition.
36. Anthony Platt, *The Child Savers: The Invention of Delinquency*, Chicago: University of Chicago Press, 1969.

tise of professionals and semi-professionals in several fields: criminologists, prison psychologists, social workers, sex counselors, marriage counselors, psychiatrists, psychoanalysts, labour/management mediators, suicidologists — the list grows lengthy. In addition, one can detect increasing acceptance of training programmes. Formal training grows in importance, at the expense of skills learned on the job. In recent years there has been a burgeoning demand for college-level courses and programmes in skills relating to social problems. And in each of the emerging specialties there exists a steady drive for the trappings of "professionalism," as this is variously defined by the practitioners in each specialty. Associations are formed; gradations of rank appear and proliferate. Following increasingly vocal demands for certification by the state (ostensibly to weed out incompetents, in practice to eliminate practitioners without formal training), there has been a slow but steady growth in credentialism. And demands arise for accreditation of institutions which teach the requisite skills. In these respects, as in others, specialization in social problems parallels the development of "professions" in other areas.[37] Although most of the specialties existed prior to their "professionalization," newer fields are composed almost exclusively of professionals, in the traditional sense (for example, suicidology, conflict resolution), with exceptions appearing only where the new field offers unusually lucrative financial inducements (for example, in marriage counseling or encounter groups).

Two of the most frequent recommendations today for combating social problems involve the training of additional personnel and the expansion of existing research. Both of these proposals furnish their most direct support in furtherance of the *careers* of the professional and the technician, although they also may aid the target population that has the problem. It is true that virtually every sector of social services needs more personnel; the creation of new skills and the development of new professionals

---

37. See Harold Wilensky, "The Professionalization of Everyone," *American Journal of Sociology*, 70, September, 1964, pp. 137-158. Some of John Porter's observations on bureaucracy are very apropos. See *The Vertical Mosaic*, Toronto: University of Toronto Press, 1965.

should in most cases be considered a positive accomplishment. And who could argue that additional research on a social problem is not needed? But it is a question of *priorities*. In some cases problems have been "studied to death" and training programmes can barely replace resignations due to lack of support. The two recommendations have been cited separately, but it should be recognized that there is a considerable overlap: one of the principal ways to train aspiring professionals is to involve them in funded research. After the training and research handouts are completed, there is all too often very little left to "trickle down" to the target population — the poor, the handicapped, the unemployed.

All too often grants designed to help people with problems finish by feeding more graduate students than by taking care of the persons the students study. This should scarcely evoke surprise when it is remembered that the technicians and the experts are members of the middle and upper-middle classes, while most of the target populations are working class — even, in many cases, the "unreachables" at the bottom of the working class. Most pressure groups, it will be recalled, are middle class or higher in composition. Ironically, when the student completes his training, he is often priced out of the market.

The longer the time spent in the training of a specialist, the higher the price of his service. It follows that the higher the price, the farther removed it is from the reach of the poor.[38]

In the triumph of the expert there is great demand for educational "upgrading," but there seems to be little reflection and less real research on whether formal training really improves one's capacity to deal with social problems. This strange situation poses serious questions about how helpful some of the training actually is. Research on empathy, for instance, seems to show that social scientists are somewhat less competent in judging persons than lay individuals without professional

38. William C. Richan and Allan R. Mendelsohn, *Social Work: The Unloved Profession*, New York: New Viewpoints, 1973, p. 8.

training.[39] After an exhaustive review Hakeen concluded that "It is astounding that judges and correctional officials continue to view psychiatrists as experts on human behavior when there is considerable experimental evidence and other research which shows laymen superior to psychiatrists . . . in the judgement of people's motives, abilities, personality traits, and action tendencies."[40] In recent years it has been repeatedly noted that many job requirements are "overqualified" in terms of excessive demand for formal educational attainments. Meanwhile, however, the trends towards specialization, formal training, and certification continue; the process appears inexorable.[41]

In addition to the fact that training is sometimes of questionable value, and unquestionably diverts funds, there is growing evidence that for many types of problems it is better to use someone with background and experience similar to those being helped, even at the cost of supposedly essential expertise. Workers who come from the "problem" neighbourhood itself, or who have been through similar experiences, understand the "street-scene" much better than an outsider. Although this is a venerable concept in such organizations as Alcoholics Anonymous or Synanon (its drug-use companion), it is resisted in many parts of the social work and penal bureaucracies — for instance, in the use of ex-convicts in prisons. In part, such non-expert workers may experience hostility from the professional because they do not come from the same social background, but in part they are resisted because they do not possess

39. See, for example, R. Taft, "The Ability to Judge People," *Psychological Bulletin*, 52, 1955, pp. 1-28; M. Hakeen, "A Critique of the Psychiatric Approach to Crime and Corrections," *Law and Contemporary Problems*, 23, 1958, pp. 650-682.
40. *Ibid.*, p. 682.
41. Without exception, experts on future trends expect these developments to continue. For one forecast see Herman Kahn and Anthony Wiener, "A Framework for Speculation," in the initial reports of the Commission on the Year 2000. Those interested in the reasons for these developments might look at the literature on the sociology of occupations. It covers such issues as the growth of credentialism and professionalization. See Wilbert E. Moore, *The Professions: Roles and Rules*, New York: Russell Sage Foundation, 1970. For the case of medicine see Eliot Freidson, *The Profession of Medicine*, New York: Dodd, Mead, 1970.

the proper credentials. Regardless of demonstrated effectiveness they are regarded as a threatening step backwards because they work, and even succeed, without the usual training.[42]

To this point we have concentrated on technicism among the practitioners themselves. But there is another major way in which technicism is relevant for intervention. Expertise has triumphed in the *"people-handling"* groups that relate to social problems (a) by convincing people that a particular problem does or does not exist, (b) by convincing them to follow a particular course of action to counter it. The social definition of social problems is treated in several chapters of Henshel and Henshel,[43] which demonstrates by repeated example that there is a major process involved in transforming an objective problem *condition* into one which is in the forefront of the public's consciousness. The means by which this is accomplished are familiar — advertising, special pleading lobbies, propaganda, demonstrations. Behind the concrete techniques—even behind supposedly spontaneous manifestations of sentiment — are an extensive armory of manipulative techniques. *Technicism has come to the marshalling of public support.* An extensive literature on mass persuasion exists[44] and in this area the findings of social science research have diffused to the practitioners—to the propagandists, the public relations men, the advertisers, and to leaders of social movements. As Martinson has put it, "We live in an age in which 'people-changing' has become a skill, a profession . . . . This is what is new. It should not be confused with the pledge, the moral campaign, or frenzied efforts to promote virtue historically engaged in by concerned amateurs."[45]

42. See Lubove, *op. cit.* In social work in particular there is a threat perceived in the very idea that a person without expertise can be an effective altruist.
43. *Op. cit.*
44. See, as illustrative examples, Arthur Cohen, *Attitude Change and Social Influence*, New York: Basic Books, 1964; Joseph Klapper, *The Effects of Mass Communication*, New York: Free Press, 1960; and Philip Zimbardo and Ebbe Ebbeson, *Influencing Attitudes and Changing Behavior*, Reading, Mass.: Addison-Wesley, 1969.
45. Robert Martinson, "The Age of Treatment," in *Crisis in American Institutions*, edited by Jerome Skolnick and Elliott Currie, Boston: Little, Brown, 1970. For a famous exposé see Vance Packard, *The Hidden Persuaders*, New York: McKay, 1957.

Demand for a product or service is created by plan — through advertising campaigns and promotional "blitzes." Advertising is an entire industry consisting of experts in the manipulation of public buying habits.[46] (Muller has called them specialists in psychological technology.) In the United States, with the world's largest advertising business, it is a thirty-one billion dollar a year activity today. As Galbraith has pointed out in *The New Industrial State*, demand is manufactured along with the products themselves, and in many cases advertising creates new wants and "needs" at the service of the highest bidder.[47] But more than new products and services are advertised. As government penetrates ever farther into the marketplace to regulate (or subsidize) businesses, the use of advertising to put across a particular industry's *policy* to the public has come increasingly into use.[48] The vast expenditures of the oil industry in "public service" advertisements that promote their positions on the oil crisis are merely the latest illustrations. Social science findings on the dynamics of social influence are also being applied to public relations drives and to political campaigns.[49] We can now speak without exaggeration of "the engineering of consent," meaning technicism in the realm of public policy in a democracy.[50]

Technicization extends also to the anti-establishment. In con-

46. See Herbert Schiller, *The Mind Managers*, Boston: Beacon Press, 1973.

47. John Kenneth Galbraith, *The New Industrial State*, New York: Houghton-Mifflin, 1967. For a critical review of the concept of the "managed" consumer, see Irving Kristol, "Professor Galbraith's 'New Industrial State'," *Fortune*, July, 1967, pp. 90-91 and 194-195.

48. Hydro is an interesting example — a monopoly yet an advertiser. The reason, of course, is to influence governmental policy via public opinion. While extolling free enterprise, the large corporation is far more likely to be accepting governmental subsidies or, as David Lewis has put it, playing the role of the "corporate welfare bum."

49. See Walter Stewart, *Shrug: Trudeau in Power*, Toronto: New Press, 1971, Chapter 13; Joe McGinnis, *The Selling of the President, 1968*, New York: Trident Press, 1969. See also Harold Mendelsohn and Irving Crespi, *Polls, Television and the New Politics*, Scranton, Pa.: Chandler, 1970.

50. Marcuse makes a point about the repressive nature of tolerance in a manipulative society, calling for a denial by the left of tolerance of "oppressive" points of view. See Herbert Marcuse, "Repressive Tolerance," in Robert Paul Wolff, *et al., A Critique of Pure Tolerance*, Boston: Beacon Press, 1965. For an agonizing rejection of this argument, see Barrington Moore, Jr., *Reflections on the Causes of Human Misery*, Boston: Beacon Press, 1972, pp. 81-82.

trast to the formless, inchoate protests and social movements of the past,[51] the *techniques of dissent* have become increasingly systematized. Books are written on how to organize, how to sustain "spontaneous" mass mobilization. Saul Alinsky has prepared handbooks on the proper procedures for organizing protest.[52] The organizers of mass demonstrations often undergo role-playing sessions before assuming their leadership functions. In the United States the new "counter-advertising" (for example, anti-smoking spots on television) has been based on the same motivational analysis as the commercial advertising it contends with. Literature such as *The Organizer's Handbook* is readily available.[53] Piven and Cloward, after detailing the debilitating tyranny of conventional institutions designed to help the poor, suggest tactics such as intentionally overburdening the welfare system in order to obtain reforms.[54] Jay Schulman and his associates have perfected a computerized method of jury selection for defence attorneys, provided only for radical defendants, in which the background characteristics of the most favorable jurors of previous trials are isolated to aid in the selection of new jurors. So far their success rate in terms of acquittals is virtually perfect.[55] Sink has written a technical book on how the defence at political trials should operate in order to win.[56] And of course the expertise of the cadre of underground left and right wing movements has long been

51. See Eric Hobsbawm, *Primitive Rebels: Studies in Archaic Forms of Social Movements*, New York: Norton, 1965; George Rudé, *The Crowd in History, 1730-1848*, New York: Wiley, 1964.

52. See his *Reveille for Radicals*, New York: Random House, 1969, and *Rules for Radicals: A Pragmatic Primer for Realistic Radicals*, New York: Vintage Books, 1972. Some typical rules include: "A good tactic is one that your people enjoy," "The threat is usually more terrifying than the thing itself," "Pick the target, freeze it, personalize it . . ." (pp. 128, 129, 130).

53. Martin Oppenheimer and George Lakey, *A Manual for Direct Action: Strategy and Tactics for Civil Rights and All Other Nonviolent Protest Movements*, Chicago: Quadrangle, 1964; The O.M. Collective, *The Organizer's Manual*, New York: Bantam Books, 1971.

54. Frances Fox Piven and Richard A. Cloward, *Regulating the Poor: the Functions of Public Welfare*, New York: Pantheon Books, 1971.

55. See Jay Schulman, *et al.*, "Recipe for a Jury," *Psychology Today*, May, 1973, pp. 37-44 and 77-84.

56. John M. Sink, *Political Criminal Trials: How to Defend Them*, New York: Clark Boardman Co., 1974.

recognized. In this realm, the laudatory notion is that of a "vanguard party;" the negative that of an "organizational weapon."[57] In summary, technicism is *dominant* today in both establishment and anti-establishment handling of social problems.[58]

THE ETHICAL BLINDNESS OF TECHNICISM

Ellul takes note of a general emphasis in technicism on goal attainment rather than ethics, of a narrowing of the focus of the specialist to the point that broader standards of principle are ignored in the quest for achievement of narrow objectives. Capability tends to define what is "good" — "can" implies "should" not only in technology[59] but in all spheres touched by technicism. A symptom is the oft- noted emphasis on *pragmatism* in bureaucracies: if something works to further organizational objectives, the feeling grows that it should be used, regardless of its other consequences. Weber made its pragmatic character one of the central characteristics of bureaucracy.

In many cases an organization's pragmatism is manifested principally in ensuring *self-perpetuation* and self-aggrandizement.[60] What this may do to an agency's capacity to deal with social problems was noted in the political section of the last chapter. Self-perpetuation occurred, for example, when a fund-raising organization called the National Foundation (the "March of Dimes") was about to go out of business because a cure had been found for poliomyelitis. Rather than proclaim

57. See Philip Selznick, *The Organizational Weapon*, New York: McGraw-Hill, 1952.
58. Wherever labour unions fall along this continuum—and some would argue they have become a part of the establishment — the complexity of labour-management negotiations and tactics makes it clear that expertise has triumphed in the realm of work problems, as elsewhere.
59. See H. Ozbekhan, "The Triumph of Technology: 'Can' Implies 'Ought'," in *An Introduction to Technological Forecasting*, edited by Joseph P. Martino, London: Gordon and Beach, 1972.
60. These objectives seem to hold true even in organizations ostensibly motivated by the pursuit of profits. Large corporations do seek profits, but even more they choose perpetuation and self-aggrandizement. Galbraith, *op. cit.*, talks of organizational continuity and predictability of operations as the main objectives of the modern corporation. For an interpretation of social work agencies in these terms, see Richan and Mendelsohn, *op. cit.*

success and fade away, its directors suddenly found new diseases with which the foundation could be identified. So too
when American aerospace companies found their budgets
dwindling, they shifted to earthbound projects, with varying
success, and defence "think tanks" shifted to thinking about
domestic problems. Organizations, it is said, have "negative
entropy" — they do not die easily.

What comes to pass, then, is a condition in which the dominant tendency is to

> ... treat man as an object to be calculated and controlled,
> exemplified in the almost overwhelming tendencies in the
> Western world to make human beings into anonymous units
> to fit like robots into the vast industrial and political collec-
> tivisms of our day.[61]

The problem with pragmatism is that it leads to a condition in
which the goals of the organization are pursued by any means,
irrespective of the larger goals of society as a whole or of the
needs of individuals. A kindred problem is that of "ritualism," a
condition in which persons lose sight altogether of the ultimate
ends and purposes of their actions — even the goals of the
organization — yet continue ritually to observe the "proper"
means without understanding why they exist.[62]

We have all encountered ritualists — the nurse who wakes the
patient so he can take his sleeping pill, the fictional sergeant in
From Here to Eternity who refuses to unlock the armory during
the attack on Pearl Harbor because he has not received proper
authorization. The means tend to become ends in themselves,
perhaps the only ends that the actor respects, a process known
variously as the displacement of goals or the autonomy of
means.

Although pragmatism may be an important attribute of the
bureaucracy, in actual operation the erection of rules and stan-

---

61. Rollo May, *Love and Will*, New York: W.W. Norton & Co., 1969. See also the
discussion of Roszak's "objective consciousness" later in this chapter.
62. Merton, *Social Theory and Social Structure*, *op. cit.*

dard operating procedures is highly conducive to the creation of ritualism. The apparent paradox of a bureaucratic system, which is oriented around the pragmatic approach, becoming entrapped in ritualistic adherence to formula can be explained in terms of the central fact that one pragmatic way a bureaucracy can increase efficiency in most cases is to set up standardized rules and require adherence by the functionaries. But the rules ultimately come to be treated as absolutes instead of useful tools, and when new phenomena emerge for which the rules do not work, they tend to be followed anyway. Thus, as Merton puts it, "the very elements which conduce toward efficiency in general produce inefficiency in specific instances."[63] The process has also been analyzed, in psychological terms, as the "functional autonomy of motives."

The modern bureaucracy erects a shield of secrecy around its activities that gives it a measure of power over its clientele and an unanticipated degree of autonomy from supposedly overwatching agencies. The importance of secrecy for the bureaucracy was recognized long ago by Weber.[64] (See also the discussion of latent secrets in the previous chapter.) Speaking of the specialist and the consumer of his services (for example, doctor-patient, lawyer-client), Moore and Tumin stress the importance of secrecy, and of ignorance on the client's part, in maintaining the authority and legitimacy of the specialist.[65] As George Bernard Shaw once put it, all professions are conspiracies against the laity. But the experts often suffer from their own unique shortsightedness so that the normal patterns of secrecy become ethically questionable.

However well the expert can perceive some aspects of a situation which escape a layman, some very important mechanisms still operate in rather systematic fashion to maintain a degree of ignorance and blindness — although the expert's ignorance is

63. *Ibid*, chapter on "Bureaucratic Structure and Personality." Philip Selznik has dubbed this the "organizational paradox."
64. Hans H. Gerth and C. Wright Mills, eds., *From Max Weber: Essays in Sociology*, New York: Oxford University Press, 1958, p. 233.
65. Wilbert E. Moore and Melvin Tumin, "Some Social Functions of Ignorance," *American Sociological Review*, 14, 1949, pp. 787-795.

much more selective.[66] In order to appreciate the expert's ignorance, a few lines should be devoted to current thinking on distortions of reality; some of the social dynamics of reality distortion in modern society have by now become well documented. First, *occupational selection*, whereby persons with specific personalities or values are attracted or repelled by particular occupations, plays a major role in producing different orientations toward identical facts by those in various areas of expertise. Then too, occupational selection is also based on various *educational attainments* which further differentiate the members of different areas. And the educational requisites themselves constitute a mode of *shared experience* which again differentiates occupational groups from one another, while at the same time heightening the similarity of views within each group. Evidence from a wide variety of sources confirms that once similar persons are attracted to certain niches, "consensual affirmation" of norms and *consensual validation* of the attitudes they share intensifies their eccentricity of thought, as do the *common experiences* which those with highly similar jobs tend to acquire. The occupational viewpoints which emerge are then stabilized by *group censure* for participation in disapproved experiences or in reading disapproved literature, and further stabilized by *psychological* mechanisms: selective exposure to new ideas, selective perception, and selective retention.[67] These and other obstacles to the spread and acceptance of innovations in thought or method are well covered in Rogers and Shoemaker.[68] Experts, in short, come to share and maintain a particular set of blinders which shut off certain aspects of reality, a problem reinforced in a way by their very competence and arrogance about their expertise. Ultimately, they may develop

66. The following passage is taken from Richard L. Henshel and Robert A. Silverman, eds., *Perception in Criminology*, New York: Columbia University Press, 1975.
67. See the literature on these strong tendencies reviewed in Klapper, *op. cit.*, pp. 19-25 and 64-65; Bernard Berelson and Gary F. Steiner, *Human Behavior: An Inventory of Scientific Findings*, New York: Harcourt, Brace, & World, 1964, pp. 529-533.
68. Everett Rogers and F. Shoemaker, *Communication of Innovations*, New York: Free Press, 1971.

what Veblen called a "trained incapacity" to observe or deal with situations except in the traditional ways to which they are accustomed.[69]

Accompanying the general advance of bureaucratization and rationalization has been what some observers see as a basic change in the modal personality in modern society. Admittedly, such alterations are difficult to isolate (and still more difficult to prove), but analysts in the 1950's seemed to agree that there had been a fundamental long-term shift. David Riesman and his co-workers wrote of the "lonely crowd," of a long-term change in personal character from what they called "inner-directed" to "other-directed." The other-directed man takes his own positions not on the basis of values received early in life (Riesman used the gyroscope as his analogue for this) but on the basis of his immediate surrounding associates (a sensitive radar was Riesman's analogue here).[70] Similarly, Whyte wrote in the same period of the replacement of the Protestant ethic pattern of conscientious individualism with the conformist pattern (what he called the social ethic). In the place of the independent entrepreneur he saw the rise of the "organization man," a man whose chief loyalties are to the organization of which he is a part, and who is found, in virtually interchangeable settings, in big business, big labour, organized religion, the university, and the military.[71] There will be more to say about *recent changes* in personal character in the final section.

Accompanying the rationalization of society, Theodore Roszak speaks of an "objective consciousness," a mode of thought which allows one to avoid thinking about the likely consequences of one's actions by reverting to cold, impartial, scientific language. For one example he quotes from a British medical journal the description of an experiment in which a rabbit is

69. We must note parenthetically that the same dynamics are at work among the academic sociologist, even if we wish it were otherwise. See Chapter 6 of Henshel and Henshel, *op. cit.*, "Defining Social Problems: the Intellectual, the Professional."

70. David Riesman, *et al.*, *The Lonely Crowd*, New Haven: Yale University Press, 1950.

71. W.H. Whyte, *op. cit.* See especially pages 4-22. Galbraith, *op. cit.*, agrees with Whyte on the fundamentally bureaucratic nature of the modern business corporation.

given Lewisite gas in its eye, which proceeds to rot away over a period of several weeks. The language is virtually one of engineering, describing a mechanical process as if there was no beast there at all. "Note how the terminology and the reportorial style distance us from the reality of the matter," Roszak says, and he is entirely accurate.[72] Only a short quote can be included here.

> Very severe lesions ending in loss of the eye: . . . in two eyes of the 12 in the series of very severe lesions the destructive action of the Lewisite produced necrosis (decay) of the cornea before the blood vessels had extended into it. Both lesions were produced by a large droplet. In one case the rabbit was anaesthetized, in the other it was not anaesthetized and was allowed to close the eye at once, thus spreading the Lewisite all over the conjunctival sac (eyeball). The sequence of events in this eye begins with instantaneous spasm of the lids followed by lacrimation in 20 seconds (at first clear tears and in one minute 20 seconds milky Harderian secretion). In six minutes the third lid is becoming oedematous (swollen) and in 10 minutes the lids themselves start to swell. The eye is kept closed with occasional blinks. In 20 minutes the oedema (swelling) is so great that the eye can hardly be kept closed as the lids are lifted off the globe. In three hours it is not possible to see the cornea and there are conjunctival petechiae (minute hemorrhages). Lacrimation continues.
>
> In 24 hours the oedema is beginning to subside and the eye is discharging muco-pus. There is a violent iritis (inflammation) and the cornea is oedematous all over in the superficial third . . . On the third day there is much discharge and the lids are still swollen. On the fourth day the lids are stuck together with discharge. There is severe iritis. The corneae are not very swollen. . . . On the eighth day there is hypopyon (pus), the lids are brawny and contracting down on the globe so that the eye cannot be fully opened. . . . In 10

---

72. Theodore Roszak, The Making of a Counterculture, Garden City, N. Y.: Anchor Books, 1969, p. 276. The Appendix of this book, "Objectivity Unlimited," pp. 269-289, is the most valuable part of the work.

days the cornea is still avascular, very opaque and covered with pus. On the 14th day the center of the cornea appears to liquefy and melt away, leaving a descemetocoele (a membrane over the cornea), which remains intact till the 28th day, when it ruptures leaving only the remains of an eye in a mass of pus.[73]

Roszak provides similarily striking "objective" analyses of an experiment on a feeble-minded woman, an investigation of the effects of nuclear bombardment, and of the emotions of prisoners awaiting execution.[74]

Similarly, Abraham Maslow recites his own experiences in medical school:

The first operation I ever saw was almost a representative example of the effort to desacralize, i.e. to remove the sense of awe, privacy, fear, and shyness before the sacred and of humility before the tremendous. A woman's breast was to be amputated with an electrical scalpel that cut by burning through. As a delicious aroma of grilling steak filled the air, the surgeon made carelessly "cool" and casual remarks about the pattern of his cutting, paying no attention to the freshmen rushing out in distress, and finally tossing this object through the air onto the counter where it landed with a plop. It had changed from a sacred object to a discarded lump of fat.... This was all handled in a purely technological fashion — emotionless, calm, even with a slight tinge of swagger.

The atmosphere was about the same when I was introduced — or rather not introduced — to the dead man I was to dissect. I had to find out for myself what his name was and that he had

---

73. Ida Mann, et al., "An Experimental and Clinical Study of the Reaction of the Anterior Segment of the Eye to Chemical Injury, with Special Reference to Chemical Warfare Agents," British Journal of Ophthalmology, Supplement XIII, 1948, pp. 146-147, as quoted in Roszak, ibid., pp. 276-277.
74. Merton calls this "sociological euphemism" when conducted by sociologists. See his "Insiders and Outsiders: A Chapter in the Sociology of Knowledge," American Journal of Sociology, 78, July, 1972, pp. 9-47, especially pp. 38-39.

been a lumberman and was killed in a fight. And I had to learn to treat him as everyone else did, not as a dead person but without ceremony, as a "cadaver." . . .

The new medics themselves tried to make their deep feelings manageable and controllable by suppressing their fears, their compassion, their tender feelings, their awe before stark life and death, their tears as they all identified with the frightened patients. Since they were young men, they did it in adolescent ways, e.g. getting photographed while seated on a cadaver and eating a sandwich. . . .

This counterphobic toughness, casualness, unemotionality and profaning (covering over their opposites) was apparently thought to be necessary, since tender emotions might interfere with the objectivity and fearlessness of the physician. I myself have often wondered if this desacralizing and desanctifying was really necessary. It is at least possible that a more priestly and less engineerlike attitude might improve medical training.[75]

Maslow concludes that such "insensitivity training" may be necessary for surgeons, but it is very questionable for the average doctor and totally counter productive for the psychotherapist.

Of course it is possible to reveal even more horrible examples if one is willing to accept the *actor's view* that he is helping alleviate a social problem. The Nazis officially regarded the continued existence of Jews as a pressing social problem and their extermination as its "final solution." Europe, especially Germany, had to become *Judenrein* — literally "clean of Jews." Raul Hilberg has described not only the technological/ organizational feat of the destruction of six million people, but he has also given us a sense of how, by translating genocide into terms of transportation problems, organizational structure problems, and similar routine activities, the German bureaucrat was able to

75. Abraham Maslow, The Psychology of Science, New York: Harper & Row, 1966, pp. 139-140. Of course one can go too far in attacking the real defects of scientism. For a reasoned defence of objective consciousness, see the postscript to Frank Cunningham, Objectivity in Social Science, Toronto: University of Toronto Press, 1973.

cope psychologically with his task.[76] Especially through a translation process in which death became "cleansing" (and similar euphemisms existed for every stage) the "objective consciousness" of the bureaucracy in charge of the programme obscured its horrible reality.[77] Again Max Weber:

> *The more the bureaucracy is "dehumanized," the more completely it succeeds in eliminating from official business love, hatred, and all purely personal, irrational, and emotional elements which escape calculation. This is the specific nature of bureaucracy and it is appraised as its special virtue.*[78]

But of course in the handling of a social problem it may be these human qualities which are of the greatest value. Again and again we see this all-encompassing emphasis on the organization's goals, and a blindness, heightened by a style of thought and language, toward any ethical standards outside of it.

If we study the historical development of intervention, we begin to sense what some have seen as the *cyclical nature of reform*. Cycles can easily be found in periodic movements of political reform — "throw the rascals out" campaigns, which last until public apathy resumes.[79] But we find cycles also in reform situations where the practical idealism of reformers leads them to set up an *institutional structure*; then the new system gradually loses sight of its origins and reason for being. Positions come to be filled by careerist time-servers and, if lucrative, by opportunists. (The concept of "generations," i.e., individuals who join a movement at different times, before and after it

76. Raul Hilberg, "The Destruction of the European Jews," in *Mass Society in Crisis*, edited by Bernard Rosenberg, et al., New York: Macmillan, 1964.

77. But ironically, the very force and impact of Hilberg's account is intensified by the objectivity and dispassionate style in which he describes the phenomenon. The impact comes from reading page after page of horrors, described dispassionately and — thereby — believably.

78. Gerth and Mills, *op. cit.*, p. 236.

79. Piven and Cloward, *op. cit.*, have called attention to the cyclical nature of relief for the poor in modern societies. Their evidence shows that relief approaches adequacy only in times of widespread unemployment — when large numbers of vocal, articulate people are out of work. This goes against the common thesis that welfare has steadily improved in the present century.

attains power or popularity, is very significant in understanding the routinization of once-dynamic movements.) Eventually, pragmatism and, finally, ritualism sets in among the functionaries of the now- routinized, smug institution. And in the end a new reform wave is needed to sweep clean what was once a reform itself. *One generation's reforms have become the scandals of the next generation.* Let us consider two cases:

1. The creation of juvenile courts and reformatories were part of the "child-saving movement" of the first decades of the century.[80] There can be little doubt that the creation of these institutions was brought about by a social movement, or that the movement was reformative in temper. The juvenile court was an effort to remove the child from the harsh world of the adult criminal justice system. A new set of informal procedures was adopted. The adversary concept was abandoned, with the judge now sitting down with the delinquent and the parents and "trying to do what was best." There were "determinations" instead of verdicts, and "dispositions" instead of sentences. But, like the adult prison — itself a distinct reform in an earlier era — the juvenile reform began to take on the aspects of a major scandal. Fifty years after the movement, conditions had deteriorated to such an extent that, in the United States, a Supreme Court decision (the Gault case) initiated essential reforms in the juvenile courts themselves.[81] As Justice Abraham Fortas wrote at that time, "There may be grounds for concern that the child gets the worst of both worlds: that he gets neither the [legal] protection accorded to adults nor the solicitous care and regenerative treatment postulated for children." Although decisions have not been so clear, much the same difficulties are apparent in the Canadian juvenile system.

2. The mental health movement in the early twentieth century was a vigorous effort to provide mental hospitalization for the insane and socially to substitute the concept of mental sickness for weakness of will. It, again, was obviously humane in intent.

80. Anthony M. Platt, *op. cit.* Platt provides beautiful examples of the cyclical aspect of social reform.
81. W. Vaughn Stapleton and Lee E. Teitelbaum, *In Defense of Youth: A Study of the Role of Counsel in American Juvenile Courts*, New York: Russell Sage Foundation, 1972.

In order to economize and provide for ease of handling patients, however, large centralized hospitals were created. Isolated from the community they became final dumping grounds for a large proportion of cases. Inspections were lax, funding inadequate, facilities overcrowded. Sadism became a major problem, as did sexual assaults on female inmates. Later, electro-shock and tranquilizing drugs were abused, in non-therapeutic contexts, as punishment or control measures. Safeguards against improper involuntary commitment were unconscionably poor; periodic review of involuntary cases was in many instances nonexistent or insufficient. The right of involuntary patients to receive treatment or be released has become a major issue, as has the question of whether a patient can refuse treatment.[82] Whereas at one time only eccentrics and members of the far right. attacked mental health, today it is increasingly the intellectuals, including liberals and radicals, who are in the forefront of attacks on what is now termed the mental health establishment.[83] As Kopkind and Ridgeway put it,

> Mental Health as a social campaign began early in the century in conjunction with the generalized psychiatric movement.... For their time, the movements were in many ways revolutionary — that is, they organized people to deal with themselves, their fellows, and their world in radically new ways....
>
> As revolutions will, the psychiatric one began to deteriorate as it achieved power in its institutionalized forms, and as its organizers found status in their managerial roles.... (Today) you don't have to be crazy to be against Mental Health.[84]

82. See discussion of these and related issues in B.B. Swadron and D.R. Sullivan, eds., The Law and Mental Disorder, Toronto: Canadian Mental Health Association, 1973.
83. See especially the works of Thomas Szasz: The Myth of Mental Illness, rev. ed., New York: Harper & Row, 1974; Psychiatric Justice, New York: Macmillan, 1971; and The Manufacture of Madness, New York: Harper & Row, 1970; the labeling school (discussed in Chapter 3); and The Radical Therapist, New York: Ballantine Books, 1971 and Rough Times, New York: Ballantine Books, 1973.
84. Andrew Kopkind and James Ridgeway, "The Mental Health Industry: This Way Lies Madness," Ramparts, February, 1971, pp. 38-44.

With discouragement it can be noted that this is not the first "cycle" in the history of psychiatric treatment. The enthusiasm and progressivism of the late 1700's (reviewed in Chapter 2 under conceptions of progress) led to numerous innovations in thought and reforms in method: the unchaining and humane treatment of inmates, the direct involvement of medicine, a belief in the curability of insanity, an emphasis on "environmental" factors — considered somewhat differently than they are today, to be sure — as causes and, hence, as possible means of "cure," even the ideas of open-hospital, non-restraint, and individual care in small institutions — all were present, in theory at least, in the early 1800's.[85] It will not do to present too rosy a picture of the "moral treatment," but it is its contrast to the substantial degeneration of treatment that subsequently occurred (so that by the 1800's there was again public concern about brutality)[86] and the regression of ideas (to an hereditary, incurable conception of insanity, which meant more custodial care), that is so striking.

Other examples of the cyclical nature of reform can be seen in the civil service and in urban renewal.[87] It is true that later attacks on measures previously regarded as reformative stem not only from their eventual regression but also from the growth of new concepts of human rights and dignity, or from the expansion of old concepts of fair treatment into newer areas. But, this reservation notwithstanding, the examples of repeating cycles of reform and malaise are too numerous and too obvious to be ignored.

85. Dain, *op. cit.*, pp. xiii and 12; Ruth B. Caplan, *Psychiatry and the Community in Nineteenth Century America*, New York: Basic Books, 1969.
86. Caplan, *ibid.*
87. See E.S. Savas and Sigmund Ginsburg, "The Civil Service: A Meritless System?" *The Public Interest*, 32, Summer, 1973, pp. 70-85. For readers interested in urban problems, the example of the downfall of American urban renewal programmes may hold special interest. Originally presented as a liberal proposal, and attacked by conservatives as "socialistic," urban renewal was seized upon by promoters, developers, and contractors, and ultimately became a programme of "Negro removal" instead of urban renewal. See the decline and fall of the programme treated with appropriate indignation in William Ryan, *Blaming the Victim*, New York: Vintage Books, 1971, pp. 175-182; Jane Jacobs, *The Death and Life of Great American Cities*, New York: Vintage Books, 1961. See Donald Clairmont and Dennis Magill, *Nova Scotian Blacks*, Halifax: Inst. of Public Affairs, 1970, for urban renewal in Halifax.

It would be comforting to be able to exclude the practitioners of social science from this survey of ethical myopia, but in truth they too, the experts in the social sciences themselves, have been attacked more than once as the "servants of power."[88] Already mentioned are the uses of social influence findings in public relations, advertising, and propaganda. We have a superfluity of studies of the poor (the better to manipulate them, say the critics)[89] yet few studies of the rich and powerful. Of course it is easier to study the poor: they cannot erect the barriers that the upper class can afford. A few "élite studies" are only now emerging, and it becomes clear that there are reasons behind the hiatus which go beyond the sheer technical difficulties of such studies and into subtle matters of ideology. It seems that we have a social problem of poverty but not one of wealth; the very choice of which end of the spectrum is to be designated the "problem" seems instructive.

Other evidence of a tendency of social science to sell to the highest bidder are unhappily not difficult to find. Military psychology and sociology for long concentrated on how best to bring the wayward soldier into line, or how to increase troop morale, with little, if any, attention to the involuntary servitude aspects of conscription, or military inequities. Project Camelot was an ill-fated effort by the United States Army to look at the "preconditions of internal conflict," especially in Latin America. After it was publicized, an intense outcry arose, and the project was ulitimately cancelled.[90] The Mayo school of industrial sociology felt that the principle source of labour difficulties involved a breakdown of contact between management and the worker — a failure to communicate. It therefore sponsored the training of management personnel in human relations approaches to employees. The possibility of an *inherent* conflict of interest between labour and management was scarcely consi-

88. Loren Baritz, *The Servants of Power*, New York: Wiley, 1965. The book deals exclusively with the social sciences.
89. Alvin Gouldner presents strong criticism of sociological work for the "welfare state," with respect to providing legitimacy for controlling the poor. See his *The Coming Crisis of Western Sociology*, New York: Basic Books, 1970.
90. Gideon Sjoberg, ed., *Ethics, Politics and Social Research*, Morristown, N.J.: General Learning Corp., 1967.

dered, and the human relations approach has been bitterly criticized as a manipulative tool for management to use. At one time
or another, industrial sociology, personality measurement, and
motivational psychology have been singled out as the servants
of power.[91] As Muller says, "If the new élite is not actually
corrupted by its eminence, at least it is not inclined to be highly
critical of the powers that employ it. And its professional devo-
tion to method or technique raises the usual questions about its
ruling values, or the measure of its wisdom."[92]

Nor may the far left be declared free of the ethical blindness of
technicism. The left has developed its own theories of how to
deal with social problems. Typically these call for a basic restructuring of the social arrangements of society. But although
the old emphasis on radical criticism of contemporary society
remains intact, another focus of the "old left" has disappeared.
No longer do we find "blueprints" of what the new order will
look like; instead the emphasis has shifted increasingly to the
technique of revolution itself. Techniques and tactics of disrup-
tion become more and more polished and sophisticated, but
there are no longer any coherent programmes at the end.[93] In
addition, a new factor has come into play: the romantic *mystique*
of revolution, of revolution as a cleansing end in itself, of revolution itself as the blueprint.[94] Such orientations are implicit in
some of the writings of Guevara and Lin Piao (especially Lin's
"Long Live the Glory of People's War!"); they are made quite
explicit in Régis Debray's internationally popular *Revolution
within the Revolution?* Frantz Fanon in particular places great

91. See especially Loren Baritz, *op. cit.*; Martin L. Gross, *The Brain Watchers*,
New York: Random House, 1962.
92. Muller, *op. cit.*, p. 354.
93. To be sure, in a way, the new route is ideologically *safer*, since one of the
principal ways to attack the old left was to criticize its proposed programmes. It
is sometimes argued with false humility that not enough is known to provide a
blueprint at this point in time. But to encourage revolution without a programme
invites the worst excesses of a pragmatic, *ad hoc* tyranny once a conflict is
underway, a point well drawn by Karl Popper in *The Poverty of Historicism*,
London: Routledge and Kegan Paul, 1957.
94. Some have termed this position "revolutionism." See Kenneth Boulding, *A
Primer on Social Dynamics: History as Dialectics and Development*, New York:
Free Press, 1970; Abdul Said and Daniel Collier, *Revolutionism*, Boston: Allyn
and Bacon, 1971.

emphasis on the necessity and virtue of violence. Following Georges Sorel's early eulogizing of the virtues of violence in principle, Fanon develops an idea of the cathartic effect of violence in a revolution.[95] But as McRae maintains, "To favor revolution and oppose power is a temporary stance at best, for one is driven to ask: Revolution for what?"[96] Thus we witness a retreat from the explicit post-revolutionary programmes of old-line socialism toward a vague romanticizing of the revolution itself, at the extreme of which we find Debray and Abbie Hoffman's *Revolution for the Hell of It.*[97] Again, there is an almost obscene triumph of technique (and left-ritualism) and, in spite of the excellent critiques of the status quo, an uncomfortable measure of ethical blindness.[98]

IN THE END: THE ADVANTAGES OF COMPETENCE

We have of course been unfair. We have been unfair, first, in concentrating exclusively on the ethical blindness of technicism. Not all agencies are full of ritualists and time-servers.[99] Nor does all reform apparently end in futility.[100] Not all of social

95. Régis Debray, *Révolution dans la Révolution?*, Paris: Maspero, 1967. Translated as *Revolution in the Revolution?*, New York: Grove Press, 1967. Frantz Fanon, *The Wretched of the Earth*, New York: Grove Press, 1963.
96. Duncan McRae, Jr., "A Dilemma of Sociology: Science versus Policy," *The American Sociologist*, 6, June, 1971, pp. 2-7. Even those highly sympathetic to the general call for revolution can take revolutionism to task. Thus, A. Norman Klein notes that it is one thing to direct and mobilize a people for the trials of guerilla warfare; it is a different matter to rhapsodize on the virtues of violence. See his "On Revolutionary Violence," *Studies on tihe Left*, 6, 1966, pp. 83-89.
97. Abbie Hoffman, *Revolution for the Hell of It*, New York: Pocket Books, Inc., 1970.
98. Always the realist, Saul Alinsky faces squarely such issues as the use of harsh means to justify good ends. See his chapter on "Of Means and Ends," (1972, *op. cit.*) He presents a rationale for justifying virtually any means in terms of the ends to be gained, and notes that "the tenth rule . . . is that you do what you can with what you have and clothe it with moral garments." p. 36.
99. Analysis shows that many of the apparently ritualist qualities of such agencies as social welfare are actually due to the legally mandated welfare structure in which social workers have to operate. See Nina Toren, *Social Work: The Case of a Semi-Profession*, Beverley Hills, Calif.: Sage Publications, 1972.
100. As pointed out earlier, some of the apparently cyclical quality of reform measures really comes from the growth of new standards of what constitutes decent treatment.

science has been a servant of the powerful. Not all of its "human relations" courses for industry were without effect except for a manipulative fraud.[101] For that matter, not all corporate public relations has resulted in deception of the public.[102] Certainly many radical groups have not become mesmerized by the revolutionary process. There are serious thoughts devoted to developing alternative social structures.[103] The defects we have examined are *tendencies*; they are ethical traps for the persons and groups involved with defining or handling social problems, but they are traps which can be surmounted. The analysis was not intended to evoke a sense of defeatism. It is distinctly unfair, too, to attribute all ills to technicism, as though separate causes could not be found for some of the disorders mentioned. As Muller notes, it is too easy to blame everything on technology.[104] Indeed there is a danger of substituting an unreasoning hatred for science and technology (the "new devils," as they have been called) for our earlier uncritical worship of scientism and "progress." But there was a reason for emphasizing the defects of technicism: its advantages are so open and obvious, and so often glibly stated, that it is especially worthwhile to point out that the drift to expertise, the fascination with technique, is no panacea. It carries with its advantages severe tendencies toward distortion and ethical blindness.

What are some of the advantages of technicism? Certainly the availability of expert knowledge does make a difference in many cases, and technical agencies possess the facilities and resources to effect positive intervention. With respect to bureaucracy, it is accepted because it seems so efficient,[105] and it probably is in

101. Muller points out that the human relations approach assured at least a measure of dignity to the worker, however superficial, and constituted a vast improvement over the "brutal impersonality" of the last century.

102. Robert Heilbroner notes that "if public relations has cheapened the face value of good conduct, at the same time it has enormously increased the prevalence of good conduct." ("Public Relations: The Invisible Sell," in *Voice of the People*, edited by R.M. Christenson and R.O. McWilliams, New York: McGraw-Hill, 1962, pp. 473-486. Quote is from p. 486.) This may indeed be true, but only by way of contrast with the robber-baron mentality of the late 1800's.

103. See, for example, C. George Benello and Dimitrios Roussopoulos, eds., *The Case for Participatory Democracy*, New York: Viking Press, 1971.

104. Muller, *op. cit.*, p. 412.

105. See, on the conditions for compliance with bureaucracy, Gerth and Mills, *op. cit.*, pp. 214-216. Merton (*Social Theory and Social Structure, op. cit.*) lists

fact more efficient than alternatives. When their efforts are not misdirected, the legitimacy that intervention agencies maintain in the public eye increases their effectiveness. And, in terms of inaugurating needed reform, expertise in the care and feeding of social movements is clearly required when so many of the vested interests can command their own experts in public relations and infinitely greater resources of wealth and power. If protest has become professionalized, so has the management or containment of protest. Revolution is sometimes justified, always difficult, and impossible without technique. This is part of what Barrington Moore has called the "iron law of revolutionary politics." Even the emphasis on pragmatism and goal attainment is beneficial under the right circumstances, where the goals sought are ethical, humane, and meaningful. It is even more difficult to imagine evaluation research being conducted by dilettantes than by bureaucracies.

If we are to accept the impressions of a later generation of writers on changes in modal character, we might be somewhat more optimistic than Riesman or Whyte. Charles Reich's "consciousness IV" individual (epitomized by the socially conscious, skeptical member of the emerging generation) surmounts the other-directedness of the middle-class organization man, and is apparently growing in numbers and influence.[106] Pitirim Sorokin's classic work on social and cultural dynamics also provides a challenge to the Weberian vision of everincreasing rationalization in society. According to Sorokin, cultural phenomena such as rationalization move in great cycles hundreds of years in duration, oscillating between what he termed sensate, ideational, and idealistic forms.[107] Before his death Sorokin predicted that the sensate mentality had nearly reached its peak and would shortly begin the long change-over to ideational. The entirely unanticipated re-birth of anti-science,

---

the presumed virtues of bureaucracy as precision, speed, expert control, continuity, discretion, and optimal returns on input.

106. Charles Reich, *The Greening of America*, New York: Bantam Books, 1970. See also Theodore Roszak, *Where the Wasteland Ends*, New York: Doubleday, 1973.

107. Pitirim Sorokin, *Social and Cultural Dynamics*, Totowa, N.J.: Bedminster Press, 1962 (original, 1941).

anti-technology, astrology, occult explanations of man's past, satan worship, Jesus cults, and Eastern gurus in the last ten years might be taken for initial confirmation. There is certainly a counterculture today which had no counterpart in the 1950's, and it is true that conventional values are being challenged as never before. Sorokin's vision must command careful attention.

Nevertheless, the agencies that deal with social problems remain bureaucritized, and the type of life they foster seems to "turn off" critical persons to such an extent that they rarely volunteer to work in these agencies. The agencies' traditional mode of existence thus seems little threatened by "consciousness IV" people, and many of the viewpoints popularized by Whyte and Riesman still seem valid today in terms of the workings of the social problem agency itself. Where Reich and others may have a point is in the emergence of entirely *new* organizations, which do attract the socially conscious person — consumer groups, legal aid groups, women's liberation.

There is also increasing dissent on whether other-directed men are so undesirable as was thought. Muller notes that "the goals of other-directed men who seek security and happiness are not necessarily more . . . inhuman than the goals of wealth, power, or fame sought by inner-directed men, who could easily be ruthless or . . . aggressive."[108] Riesman has reconsidered his position on other-directedness, and in a sequel to *The Lonely Crowd* he noted that "groupism" possesses many virtues, especially the capacity to adjust to a rapidly changing society.[109] Muller echoes this theme, noting the powers of resilience of people that enable them to cope with widely varying environments and still to be happy and even noble on occasion. Even the bureaucrat turns out to be somewhat different from what critics have maintained. In a very enlightened study Melvin Kohn found empirical evidence that supported the conclusion that

There is a small bu t consistent tendency for men who work in bureaucratic organizations to be more intellectually flexible, more open to new experience, and more self-directed in their

108. Muller, *op. cit.*, p. 346.
109. David Riesman, *Individualism Reconsidered*, Glencoe, Ill.: Free Press, 1954.

values than are men who work in non-bureaucratic organizations.[110]

Kohn also analyzed the reasons for this finding:

This may in part result from bureaucracies' drawing on a more educated work force. In larger part, though, it appears to be a consequence of occupational conditions attendant on bureaucratization — notably, far greater job protection, somewhat higher income, and substantively more complex work.[111]

This finding is amazing in view of the standard stereotype of the bureaucrat, but perhaps it is the most odious, officious bureaucrats whom people remember best. In any event the effects of bureaucratization are considerably more complex than they appear to be at first; certainly there are positive consequences.

The shift toward technically proficient but impersonal agencies to deal with social problems seems inevitable in a modern, complex, highly differentiated society. Older forms of helping — the church, the family, mutual aid among neighbours — cannot work as well as in previous eras. Increased geographical mobility and what Toffler terms the transcience of interpersonal relationships slowly break down the feasibility of mutual aid, as the old theories of social disorganization long maintained. The extended family is weakening; the established church no longer gathers enough money or patrons to fill the need for help with social problems. To be sure, the help from these institutions remains useful, but the trend is toward the assumption by the state of more and more control over the traditional forms of intervention and complete ascendancy of the state with respect to many newly conceived forms of intervention.

110. Melvin L. Kohn, "Bureaucratic Man: A Portrait and an Interpretation," *American Sociological Review*, 36, June, 1971, pp. 461-474.
111. *Ibid*. There are also indications, examined by Bennis, Janowitz, Likert, Parsons, and others, that we are moving toward a post-bureaucratic model with greater sharing of decisions. See these writings reviewed in Delany, *op. cit.*

This chapter has concentrated on the less obvious, on the drawbacks of expertise, but the common-sense idea that expertise is valuable is not without merit. Although compassion and altruism are always desirable, an impersonal expert is (usually) of greater benefit than an impersonal novice or dilettante. What would be best, of course, would be the *compassionate expert*, but training and cynical attitudes among the professional groups themselves seem to drive out the novice's compassionate impulses with discouraging regularity. There are some unique structural advantages which are conducive to improvement in the long run. For instance, the emphasis on originality in academia and in scientific research has led to a continual challenge of established ideas about social problems. Ignoring the inevitable fads and false starts, this is almost certainly a unique advantage accruing to the ascendancy of the expert.

The experiences of the Company of Young Canadians seem to exemplify many of the dilemmas just discussed. Formed by the government in 1966 as a volunteer group to work for social change within Canada, it survived a series of mounting crises only to be ultimately eviscerated in 1970, largely as a result of its own internal mismanagement.[112] On the one hand, the volunteers in the field were virtually without training or expertise of any sort, and yet their enthusiasm and dedication carried the day in many instances, leading to some remarkable achievements in a relatively brief span of existence. But their amateurism also caused unnecessary antagonism and resulted in the collapse of many projects. On the other hand, the CYC in Quebec (which became *de facto* independent of the rest of the organization very early) developed the virtues and vices of the *expert*. Recruiting and organization was entirely different here, and resulted in efforts that were at once far more professional and efficient and yet far more élitist in terms of presuming to know what was best for the people.[113] In microcosm, the CYC

112. Like virtually all statements about the CYC, the one just given is doubtless subject to challenge. For an excellent and sympathetic insider's book, see Ian Hamilton, *The Children's Crusade*, Toronto: Peter Martin, 1970.
113. Again, no fact about the CYC is beyond dispute; these are the best personal interpretations.

represented the strengths and weaknesses of amateurish enthusiasm and élitist expertise.

Jack Douglas frames the dilemma of the future:

> *Ironically, ordinary people will see the solution of their objective problems coincide with their greater estrangement from the decision-making process . . . . (T)echnocracy will overtake democracy. Truth will achieve power, but will it be content?*[114]

Can we have the best of both worlds? Can we have true expertise, a willingness to examine all alternatives, evaluation research, and organizational efficiency without impersonal coldness, cynicism, élitism, and perhaps sale to the highest bidder, and ritualism? Can we have both compassion and competence? These are the great challenging questions to those who would reconstruct society or society's assault on social problems. Not to do away with expertise but to humanize it, to make it harmonious with human dignity.

114. Jack D. Douglas, ed., *The Relevance of Sociology*, New York: Appleton Century-Crofts, 1970, p. 183.

References

Aberle, D.F. et al., "The Functional Prerequisites of a Society," Ethics, 60, 1950, pp. 100-113.

Abrahamson, Mark, "Functionalism and the Functional Theory of Stratification: An Empirical Assessment," American Journal of Sociology, 78, March, 1973, pp. 1236-1246.

Adams, Ian et al., The Real Poverty Report, Edmonton, Alta.: Hurtig, 1971.

(Report of the) Advisory Committee to the Surgeon General, "Beneficial Effects of Tobacco," in Smoking and Health, Washington, D.C.: U.S. Government Printing Office, 1964.

Alexander, Tom, "The Social Engineers Retreat Under Fire," Fortune, October, 1972.

Alinsky, Saul, Reveille for Radicals, New York: Random House, 1969.

Alinsky, Saul, Rules for Radicals: A Pragmatic Primer for Realistic Radicals, New York: Vintage Books, 1972.

Allen, A.R., The Social Passion: Religion and Social Reform in Canada, 1914-1928, Toronto: University of Toronto Press, 1971.

Armor, David J., "The Evidence on Busing," The Public Interest, 28, Summer, 1972, pp. 90-126.

Anderson, Dorothy and Lenora McClean, eds., Identifying Suicide Potential, New York: Behavioral Publications, 1969.

Aronson, Sidney H., "The Sociology of the Telephone," International Journal of Comparative Sociology, 12, 1971, pp. 153-167.

Asimov, Isaac, ed., Soviet Science Fiction, New York: Collier, 1962.

Atkinson, Tom et al., Public Policy Research and the Guaranteed Annual Income, Downsview, Ont.: Institute for Behavioral Research (York University), 1973.

Baran, Paul A. and Paul H. Sweezy, Monopoly Capital, New York: Monthly Review Press, 1966.

Barber, Bernard, "Structural-Functional Analysis: Some Problems and Misunderstandings," *American Sociological Review*, 21, April, 1956, pp. 129-135.

Barber, Bernard et al., *Research on Human Subjects: Problems of Social Control in Medical Experimentation*, New York: Russell Sage Foundation, 1973.

Baritz, Loren, *The Servants of Power*, New York: Wiley, 1965.

Barnes, Harry Elmer, *The Story of Punishment: A Record of Man's Inhumanity to Man*, Montclair, N.J.: Patterson Smith, 1972 (original, 1930).

Beach, Frank, "The Descent of Instinct," *Psychological Review*, 62, 1955, pp. 401-410.

Becker, Howard S., *Outsiders: Studies in the Sociology of Deviance*, New York: Free Press, 1963 and 1973.

Becker, Howard and Harry Barnes, *Social Thought from Lore to Science*, 3rd edition, Volume II, New York: Dover Publications, 1961 (original, 1938).

Bell, Daniel, *The Coming of Post-Industrial Society*, New York: Basic Books, 1973.

Bell, Wendell and James A. Mau, "Images of the Future: Theory and Research Strategy," in *Theoretical Sociology*, edited by J. McKinney and E. Tiryakian, New York: Appleton-Century-Crofts, 1970.

Bendix, Reinhard, *Max Weber: An Intellectual Portrait*, Garden City, N.Y.: Doubleday, 1962.

Benedict, Ruth, *Patterns of Culture*, New York: Mentor, 1934.

Benello, C. George and Dimitrios Roussopoulos, eds., *The Case for Participatory Democracy*, New York: Viking Press, 1971.

Berelson, Bernard and Gary F. Steiner, *Human Behavior: An Inventory of Scientific Findings*, New York: Harcourt Brace and World, 1964.

Bernard, Jessie, *Social Problems at Midcentury*, New York: Dryden Press, 1957.

Berton, Pierre, *The Last Spike*, Toronto: McClelland & Stewart, 1971.

Bettelheim, Bruno, *The Informed Heart*, Glencoe, Ill.: Free Press, 1960.

Blalock, Hubert M., Jr., *Social Statistics*, New York: McGraw-Hill, 1960.

Blalock, Hubert M., Jr., *Causal Inferences in Nonexperimental Research*, Chapel Hill, N.C.: University of North Carolina Press, 1964.

Blum, Zahava D. and Peter H. Rossi, "Images of the Poor," in *On Understanding Poverty*, edited by Daniel P. Moynihan, New York: Basic Books, 1969.

Blumer, Herbert, "Social Problems as Collective Behavior," *Social Problems*, 18, 1971, pp. 298-306.

Bordua, David J., ed., *The Police*, New York: Wiley, 1967.

Boulding, Kenneth, *A Primer on Social Dynamics: History as Dialectics and Development*, New York: Free Press, 1970.

Bremner, Robert, "Shifting Attitudes," in *Social Welfare Institutions: A Sociological Reader*, edited by Mayer Zald, New York: Wiley, 1965.

Brenner, M. Harvey, *Mental Illness and the Economy*, Cambridge, Mass.: Harvard University Press, 1973.

Bruner, Jerome S., "On Perceptual Readiness," in *Current Perspectives in Social Psychology*, edited by E.P. Hollander and Raymond G. Hunt, New York: Oxford University Press, 1963.

Buckley, Walter, *Sociology and Modern Systems Theory*, Englewood Cliffs, N.J.: Prentice-Hall, 1967.

Bullock, Henry A., "Significance of the Racial Factor in the Length of Prison Sentence," *Journal of Criminal Law, Criminology, and Police Science*, 52, 1961, pp. 411-417.

Cameron, Mary Owen, *The Booster and the Snitch*, Glencoe, Ill.: Free Press, 1964.

Campbell, Donald T., "Factors Relevant to the Validity of Experiments in Social Settings," *Psychological Bulletin*, July, 1957, pp. 297-312.

Campbell, Donald T., "Reforms as Experiments," *American Psychologist*, 24, 1969, pp. 409-429.

(Canada) Department of Justice, *Juvenile Delinquency in Canada*, Ottawa: Queen's Printer, 1965.

(Canada) Department of the Solicitor General, *Report of the Working Group on Federal Maximum Security Institutions Design*, Ottawa: Queen's Printer, 1971.

Canadian Civil Liberties Education Trust, *Due-Process Safeguards and Canadian Criminal Justice: A One-Month Inquiry*, Toronto: 1972.

Canadian Committee on Corrections, *Toward Unity: Criminal Justice and Corrections*, Ottawa: Queen's Printer, 1969.

Caplan, Ruth B., *Psychiatry and the Community in Nineteenth Century America*, New York: Basic Books, 1969.

Cardinal, Harold, *The Unjust Society*, Edmonton, Alta.: Hurtig, 1969.

Caro, Francis G., ed., *Readings in Evaluation Research*, New York: Russell Sage Foundation, 1971.

Catton, William R., Jr., *From Animistic to Naturalistic Sociology*, New York: McGraw-Hill, 1966.

Chambliss, William, "The Deterrent Influence of Punishment," *Crime and Delinquency*, 12, January, 1966, pp. 20-75.

Chiricos, Theodore G. *et al.*, "Inequality in the Imposition of a Criminal Label," *Social Problems*, 19, 1972, pp. 553-572.

Clairmont, Donald and Dennis Magill, *Nova Scotian Blacks*, Halifax, N.S.: Inst. of Public Affairs, 1970.

Clark, John P., "Isolation of the Police: A Comparison of British and American Situations," *Journal of Criminal Law, Criminology, and Police Science*, 56, 1965, pp. 307-319.

Cohen, Arthur, *Attitude Change and Social Influence*, New York: Basic Books, 1964.

Cohen, Stanley, ed., *Images of Deviance*, Harmondsworth, Eng.: Penguin, 1971.

Cohn, Norman, *The Pursuit of the Millennium*, revised edition, Cambridge: Oxford University Press, 1970.

Connor, Desmond M. and James E. Curtis, *Sociology and Anthropology in Canada*, Montreal: Canadian Sociology and Anthropology Association, September, 1970.

Coser, Lewis A., *The Functions of Social Conflict*, New York: Free Press, 1966.

Coser, Lewis A., "Some Social Functions of Violence," *The Annals*, 304, March, 1966, pp. 8-18.

Coser, Lewis A., "Unanticipated Conservative Consequences of Liberal Theorizing," *Social Problems*, 16, Winter, 1969, pp. 263-272.

Cousineau, Douglas F. and Jean Veevers, "Incarceration as a Response to Crime: The Utilization of Canadian Prisons," *Canadian Journal of Criminology and Corrections*, 14, 1972, pp. 10-36.

Critchley, T.A., *A History of Police in England and Wales, 900-1966*, London: Constable, 1967.

Crow, Duncan, *The Victorian Woman*, London: Allen and Unwin, 1971.

Cunningham, Frank, *Objectivity in Social Science*, Toronto: University of Toronto Press, 1973.

Dain, Norman, *Concepts of Insanity in the United States 1759-1865*, New Brunswick, N.J.: Rutgers University Press, 1964.

Davis, Arthur K., "Social Theory and Social Problems," *Philosophy and Phenomenological Research*, 18, December, 1957, pp. 190-208.

Davis, Kingsley, "Population Policy: Will Current Programs Succeed?", *Science*, 158, Nov. 10, 1967, pp. 730-739.

Davis, Murray S., "That's Interesting! . . . ," *Philosophy of the Social Sciences*, 1, 1971, pp. 309-344.

Davis, Kingsley and Wilbert E. Moore, "Some Principles of Stratification," *American Sociological Review*, 10, 1945, pp. 242-249.

Debray, Régis, *Révolution dans la Révolution?*, Paris: Maspero, 1967. Translated as *Revolution in the Revolution?*, New York: Grove Press, 1967.

De Vos, George A., *Socialization for Achievement: Essays on the Cultural Psychology of the Japanese*, Berkeley University of California Press, 1973.

Delany, William, "The Development and Decline of Patrimonial and Bureaucratic Administrations," *Administrative Science Quarterly*, 7, March, 1963, pp. 458-501.

Diamond, Arthur S., *The Evolution of Law and Order*, London: Watts, 1951.

Doleschal, Eugene and I. Anttia, *Crime and Delinquency Research in Selected European Countries*, Rockville, Maryland: National Institute of Mental Health, 1971.

Dore, Ronald P., "Function and Cause," *American Sociological Review*, 26, December, 1961, pp. 843-853.

Dorwart, Reinhold, *The Prussian Welfare State Before 1740*, Cambridge, Mass.: Harvard University Press, 1971.

Douglas, Jack D., ed., *The Relevance of Sociology*, New York: Appleton-Century-Crofts, 1970.

Dugdale, Robert, *The Jukes: A Study in Crime, Pauperism, Disease, and Heredity*, New York: 1877.

Duncan, Kenneth, "Irish Famine Immigration and the Social Structure of the Canadian West," *Canadian Review of Sociology and Anthropology*, Special Edition on Aspects of Canadian Society, 1974, pp. 140-162.

Durkheim, Emile, *Suicide*, Glencoe, Ill.: The Free Press, 1951 (original, 1897).

Edwards, R.D. and W.T. Desmond, eds., *The Great Famine*, 2nd edition, New York: Russell and Russell, 1975.

Ellul, Jaques, *The Technological Society*, New York: Vintage Books, 1967 (original, 1954).

Empey, Lamar T. and Jerome Rabow, "The Provo Experiment in Delinquency Rehabilitation," *American Sociological Review*, 26, 1961, pp. 679-695.

Erikson, Kai T., "Notes on the Sociology of Deviance," *Social Problems*, 9, Spring, 1962, pp. 307-314.

Erikson, Kai T., *Wayward Puritans*, New York: Wiley, 1966.

Etzioni, Amitai, "Human Beings are not Very Easy to Change After All," *Saturday Review*, June 3, 1972, pp. 45-47.

Etzioni, Amitai and Edward W. Lehman "Some Dangers in 'Valid' Social Measurement," *The Annals*, 373, September, 1967, pp. 1-15.

Eysenck, H.J., "The Effects of Psychotherapy," in *Handbook of Abnormal Psychology*, edited by H.J. Eysenck, London: Pitman Medical Pub. Co., 1960.

Eysenck, H.J., *The Effects of Psychotherapy*, New York: Science House, 1969.

Fairweather, George, *Methods for Experimental Social Innovation*, New York: Wiley, 1967.

Fanon, Frantz, *The Wretched of the Earth*, New York: Grove Press, 1963.

Farson, Richard, *Birthrights: A Bill of Rights for Children*, New York: Macmillan, 1974.

Fattah, E.A., *A Study of the Deterrent Effect of Capital Punishment with Special Reference to the Canadian Situation*, Ottawa: Office of the Solicitor General, 1972.

Feingold, Adolf, "Technology Assessment: A Systematic Study of Side-Effects of Technology," *The Canadian Forum*, February, 1974, pp. 10-11.

Ferkiss, Victor, *Technological Man: The Myth and the Reality*, New York: Mentor, 1969.

Foucault, M., *Madness and Civilization*, New York: Pantheon Books, 1965.

Frazer, James G., *Folklore in the Old Testament*, New York: Tudor, 1923.

Freeman, Howard and Clarence Sherwood, *Social Research and Social Policy*, Englewood Cliffs, N.J.: Prentice-Hall, 1970.

Freeman, Linton and Robert F. Winch, "Societal Complexity: An Empirical Test of a Typology of Societies," *American Journal of Sociology*, 62, March, 1957, pp. 461-466.

Freidson, Eliot, *The Profession of Medicine*, New York: Dodd, Mead, 1970.

Fromm, Erich, *Escape from Freedom*, New York: Holt, 1941.

Galbraith, John Kenneth, *The New Industrial State*, New York: Houghton-Mifflin, 1967.

Gans, Herbert J., "The Positive Functions of Poverty," *American Journal of Sociology*, 78, September, 1972, pp. 275-289.

Garfinkel, Harold, "Conditions of Successful Degradation Ceremonies," *American Journal of Sociology*, 61, March, 1956, pp. 420-424.

Gerth, Hans H. and C. Wright Mills, eds., *From Max Weber: Essays in Sociology*, New York: Oxford University Press, 1958.

Gibbs, Jack P., "Conceptions of Deviant Behavior: The Old and the New," *Pacific Sociological Review*, 9, 1966, pp. 9-14.

Gibbs, Jack P., *Sociological Theory Construction*, Hinsdale, Ill.: Dryden Press, 1972.

Giffen, P.J., "The Revolving Door: A Functional Interpretation," *Canadian Review of Sociology and Anthropology*, 3, 1966, pp. 154-166.

Glaser, Daniel, "The Assessment of Correctional Effectiveness," in *Law Enforcement Science and Technology,* edited by S. Yefsky, New York: Academic Press, 1967.

Glaser, Daniel, *The Effectiveness of a Prison and Parole System,* Indianapolis, Ind.: Bobbs-Merrill, 1969.

Glaser, Daniel, *Social Deviance,* Chicago: Markham, 1971.

Goffman, Erving, *The Presentation of Self in Everyday Life,* Garden City, N.Y.: Doubleday, 1959.

Goldman, Thomas, ed., *Cost-Effectiveness Analysis: New Approaches in Decision-Making,* New York: Praeger, 1967.

Gottlieb, David, ed., *Children's Liberation,* Englewood Cliffs, N.J.: Prentice-Hall, 1973.

Gould, Leroy, "Who Defines Delinquency?", *Social Problems,* 16, Winter, 1969, pp. 325-336.

Gouldner. Alvin W., *The Coming Crisis of Western Sociology,* New York: Basic Books, 1970.

Gouldner, Alvin W., "The Sociologist as Partisan: Sociology and the Welfare State," reprinted in *The Sociology of Sociology,* edited by Larry T. Reynolds and Janice M. Reynolds, New York: McKay, 1970.

Gove, Walter R., "Societal Reaction as an Explanation of Mental Illness: An Evaluation," *American Sociological Review,* 35, 1971, pp. 873-884.

Green, Edward, *Judicial Attitudes in Sentencing,* London: Macmillan, 1961.

Gross, Martin L., *The Brain Watchers,* New York: Random House, 1962.

Grupe, Stanley, ed., *Theories of Punishment,* Bloomington: Indiana University Press, 1971.

Hackler, James, "An 'Underdog' Approach to Correctional Research," *Canadian Journal of Criminology and Corrections,* 9, 1967, pp. 27-36.

Hackler, James, "Predictors of Deviant Behaviour: Norms Versus the Perceived Anticipations of Others," *Canadian Review of Sociology and Anthropology,* 5, 1968, pp. 92-106.

Hackler, James, *Why Delinquency Prevention Programs Should NOT Be Evaluated,* Edmonton, Alta.: University of Alberta, 1973.

Hagan, John, "The Labelling Perspective: The Delinquent and the Police," *Canadian Journal of Criminology and Corrections,* 14, 1972, pp. 150-162.

Hakeen, M., "A Critique of the Psychiatric Approach to Crime and Corrections," *Law and Contemporary Problems,* 23, 1958, pp. 650-682.

Hall, Richard H., *Organizations: Structure and Process*, Englewood Cliffs, N.J.: Prentice-Hall, 1972.

Hall, Rupert A., "Engineering and the Scientific Revolution," *Technology and Culture*, 2, Fall, 1961, pp. 333-341.

Hamilton, Edith, *Mythology*, New York: Mentor, 1940.

Hamilton, Ian, *The Children's Crusade*, Toronto: Peter Martin, 1970.

Hardin, Garrett, "The Tragedy of the Commons," *Science*, 162, December, 1968, pp. 1243-1248.

Harrington, Michael, *The Other America: Poverty in the United States*, New York: Macmillan, 1962.

Harris, Marvin, *The Rise of Anthropological Theory*, New York: Thomas Y. Crowell Co., 1968.

Heberle, Rudolph, "Social Movements," in *International Encyclopedia of the Social Sciences*, Volume 14, New York: Crowell, Collier, and Macmillan, 1968.

Hecksher, E.F., *Mercantilism*, (Trans. Meyer Shapiro), London: Allen and Unwin, 1935.

Heilbroner, Robert, "Public Relations: The Invisible Sell," in *Voice of the People*, edited by R.M. Christenson and R.O. McWilliams, New York: McGraw-Hill, 1962.

Henshel, Richard L., "Ability to Alter Skin Color: Some Implications for American Society," *American Journal of Sociology*, 76, January, 1971, pp. 734-742.

Henshel, Richard L., *On the Future of Social Prediction*, Indianapolis, Ind.: Bobbs-Merrill, 1976.

Henshel, Richard L. and Anne-Marie Henshel, *Perspectives on Social Problems*, Don Mills: Longman Canada, 1973.

Henshel, Richard L. and Leslie W. Kennedy, "Self-Altering Prophecies: Consequences for the Feasibility of Social Prediction," *General Systems*, 18 (annual), 1973, pp. 119-126.

Henshel, Richard L. and Robert A. Silverman, eds., *Perception in Criminology*, New York: Columbia University Press, 1975.

Herskovits, M.J., *Cultural Relativism: Perspectives in Cultural Pluralism*, edited by Frances Herskovits, New York: Random House, 1972.

Hilberg, Raul, "The Destruction of the European Jews," in *Mass Society in Crisis*, edited by Bernard Rosenberg et al., New York: Macmillan, 1964.

Hinkle, Roscoe C. and Gisela Hinkle, *The Development of Modern Sociology*, New York: Random House, 1962.

Hobsbaum, Eric, *Primitive Rebels: Studies in Archaic Forms of Social Movements*, New York: Norton, 1965.

Hoebel, E. Adamson, *The Law of Primitive Man*, Cambridge, Mass.: Harvard University Press, 1954.

Hoffer, Eric, *The True Believer*, New York: Mentor, 1951.

Hoffman, Abbie, *Revolution for the Hell of It*, New York: Pocket Books, 1970.

Hogarth, John, *Sentencing as a Human Process*, Toronto: University of Toronto Press, 1971.

Hollander, Paul, "Sociology, Selective Determinism, and the Rise of Expectations," *The American Sociologist*, 8, November, 1973, pp. 147-153.

Hopkins, C.H., *The Rise of the Social Gospel in American Protestantism, 1865-1915*, New Haven, Conn.: Yale University Press, 1967.

Hughes, David R. and Evelyn Kallen, *The Anatomy of Racism: Canadian Dimensions*, Montreal: Harvest House, 1974.

Hughes, Everett C., *French Canada in Transition*, Chicago: University of Chicago Press, 1963.

Hunnius, Jerry, ed., *Participatory Democracy for Canada*, Montreal: Black Rose Books, 1971.

Hurry, Jamieson B., *Poverty and Its Vicious Circles*, London: J. & A. Churchill, 1917.

Ichheiser, Gustav, *Appearances and Realities*, San Francisco: Jossey-Bass, 1970.

Innis, Harold, *The Bias of Communication*, Toronto: University of Toronto Press, 1951.

Innis, Harold, "Government Ownership and the Canadian Scene," in his *Essays in Canadian Economic History*, Toronto: University of Toronto Press, 1956.

Irving, J., *The Social Credit Movement in Alberta*, Toronto: University of Toronto Press, 1959.

Jacobs, Jane, *The Death and Life of Great American Cities*, New York: Vintage Books, 1961.

James, Bernard, *The Death of Progress*, New York: Knopf, 1973.

James, Sidney V., *A People among Peoples: Quaker Benevolence in Eighteenth Century America*, Cambridge, Mass.: Harvard University Press, 1963.

Jeffery, C. Ray, *Crime Prevention Through Environmental Design*, Beverly Hills, Calif.: Sage Publications, 1971.

Johnson, Elmer H., *Crime, Correction, and Society*, revised edition, Homewood, Ill.: Dorsey Press, 1968.

Johnson, Roger N., *Aggression in Man and Animals*, Philadelphia: Saunders, 1972.

Joravsky, D., "The Lysenko Affair," *Scientific American*, 207, November, 1962, pp. 41-49.

Kadish, Sanford, "The Crisis of Over-Criminalization," *The Annals*, 374, 1967, pp. 157-170.

Kavolis, V., *Comparative Perspectives on Social Problems*, Boston: Little, Brown, 1969.

Kay, A. William, *Moral Development*, revised edition, London: Allen and Unwin, 1970.

Killian, Lewis M., "Optimism and Pessimism in Sociological Analysis," *The American Sociologist*, 6, 1971, pp. 281-286.

Kirkconnell, W., "Religion and Philosophy: An English Canadian Point of View," in *Canadian Dualism: Studies in French-English Relations*, edited by Mason Wade, Toronto: University of Toronto Press, 1960.

Kitsuse, John I., "Societal Reaction to Deviant Behavior: Problems of Theory and Method," *Social Problems*, 9, Winter, 1962, pp. 247-256.

Klapper, Joseph, *The Effects of Mass Communication*, New York: Free Press, 1960.

Klein, A. Norman, "On Revolutionary Violence," *Studies on the Left*, 6, 1966, pp. 62-82.

Kluckhohn, C., "Cultural Relativity," in *A Dictionary of the Social Sciences*, edited by J. Gould and W. Kolb, New York: Free Press, 1964.

Kobrin, Solomon, "The Chicago Area Project: A 25-Year Assessment," in *Prevention of Delinquency*, edited by John Stratton and Robert Terry, New York: Macmillan, 1968.

Kohn, Melvin L., "Bureaucratic Man: A Portrait and an Interpretation," *American Sociological Review*, 36, June, 1971, pp. 461-474.

Kopkind, Andrew and James Ridgeway, "The Mental Health Industry: This Way Lies Madness," *Ramparts*, February, 1971, pp. 38-44.

Kriesberg, Louis, *Mothers in Poverty*, Chicago: Aldine, 1970.

Kristol, Irving, "Professor Galbraith's 'New Industrial State'," *Fortune*, July, 1967, pp. 90-91, 194-195.

Kropotkin, P., *Mutual Aid*, London: 1902.

Kuhn, Thomas, *The Copernican Revolution: Planetary Astronomy in the Development of Western Thought*, Cambridge, Mass.: Harvard University Press, 1957.

Kunkel, John and Michael Garrick, "Models of Man in Sociological Analysis," *Social Science Quarterly*, 50, June, 1969, pp. 136-152.

LaBarre, Weston, *The Ghost Dance: The Origins of Religion*, New York: Delta Books, 1972.

LaFave, Wayne R., *Arrest: The Decision to Take a Suspect into Custody*, Boston: Little, Brown, 1964.

Lange, J., *Crime as Destiny*, New York: Boni, 1930.

Laskin, Richard, ed., *Social Problems: A Canadian Profile*, Toronto: McGraw-Hill Co. of Canada, 1964.

Laxer, R.M., ed., *Canada, Ltd.*, Toronto: McClelland & Stewart, 1973.

Leacock, E.B., ed., *The Culture of Poverty: A Critique*, New York: Simon and Schuster, 1971.

LeDain, G. et al., *Interim Report of the Commission of Inquiry into the Non-Medical Use of Drugs*, Ottawa: Queen's Printer, 1970.

Lemert, Edwin M., *Social Pathology*, New York: McGraw-Hill, 1951.

Lemert, Edwin M., *Human Deviance, Social Problems, and Social Control*, Englewood Cliffs, N.J.: Prentice-Hall, 1967.

Lemert, Edwin M., "Social Problems," in *International Encyclopedia of the Social Sciences*, Volume 14, New York: Crowell, Collier, and Macmillan, 1968.

Lévi-Bruhl, Lucien, *Primitive Mentality*, London: Allen and Unwin, 1923.

Levy, Marion J., Jr., *The Structure of Society*, Princeton, N.J.: Princeton University Press, 1952.

Lewis, Oscar, *La Vida*, New York: Random House, 1966.

Lieberman, Morton et al., *Encounter Groups: First Facts*, New York: Basic Books, 1973.

Lippmann, Walter, *The Public Philosophy*, Boston: Little, Brown, 1955.

Lipset, S.M., et al., *Union Democracy*, Glencoe, Ill.: Free Press, 1956.

Lipset, S.M., *Political Man*, New York: Doubleday, 1963.

Lipset, S.M., *The First New Nation*, New York: Basic Books, 1963.

Lipset, S.M. and R.B. Dobson, "The Intellectual as Critic and Rebel: With Special Reference to the United States and the Soviet Union," *Daedalus*, 101, 1972, pp. 137-198.

Logan, Charles, "Evaluation Research in Crime and Delinquency: A Reappraisal," *Journal of Criminal Law, Criminology, and Police Science*, 63, 1972, pp. 378-387.

Lombroso, Cesare, *L'uomo Deliquente*, (expanded version), Torino: Bocca, 1896.

Lowie, Robert H., *The History of Ethnological Theory*, New York: Rinehart, 1937.

Lowry, Ritchie P., *Social Problems*, Lexington, Mass.: D.C. Heath & Co., 1974.

Lubove, Roy, *The Professional Altruist: The Emergence of Social Work as a Career 1880-1930*, Cambridge, Mass.: Harvard University Press, 1971.

Ludwig, Arnold M., *The Importance of Lying*, Springfield, Ill.: Charles C. Thomas, 1965.

Madge, John, *The Origins of Scientific Sociology*, Glencoe, Ill.: Free Press, 1962.

Malinowski, Bronislaw, *Magic, Science, and Religion*, Glencoe, Ill.: Free Press, 1948.

Mankoff, Milton, "Societal Reaction and Career Deviance: A Critical Analysis," *Sociological Quarterly*, 12, Spring, 1971, pp. 204-218.

Mann, Ida et al., "An Experimental and Clinical Study of the Reaction of the Anterior Segment of the Eye to Chemical Injury, with Special Reference to Chemical Warfare Agents," *British Journal of Ophthalmology*, Supplement XIII, 1948, pp. 146-147.

Mann, W.E., ed., *Deviant Behaviour in Canada*, Willowdale, Ontario: Social Science Publishers, 1968.

Manuel, Frank, *The Prophets of Paris*, Cambridge, Mass.: Harvard University Press, 1962.

Marcuse, Herbert, *Eros and Civilization*, Boston: Beacon Press, 1955.

Marcuse, Herbert, "Repressive Tolerance," in *Political Elites in a Democracy*, edited by P. Bachrach, New York: Atherton, 1971.

Martingdale, Don, ed., "Functionalism in the Social Sciences," *The Annals*, special edition on functionalism , February, 1965.

Martinson, Robert, "The Age of Treatment," in *Crisis in American Institutions*, edited by Jerome Skolnick and Elliott Currie, Boston: Little, Brown, 1970.

Marx, Gary T., *Protest and Prejudice*, New York: Harper & Row, 1967.

Marx, Karl, *Capital*, Volume I, New York: E.P. Dutton & Co., 1930.

Maslow, Abraham, *The Psychology of Science*, New York: Harper & Row, 1966.

Matza, David, *Becoming Deviant*, Englewood Cliffs, N.J.: Prentice-Hall, 1969.

May, Rollo, *Love and Will*, New York: W.W. Norton & Co., 1969.

Mayhew, Henry, *Those That Will Not Work*, London: 1861.

McGinniss, Joe, *The Selling of the President, 1968*, New York: Trident Press, 1969.

McGrath, W.T., *Crime and Its Treatment in Canada*, Toronto: Macmillan Co. of Canada, 1965.

McKerracher, D.G., *Trends in Psychiatric Care*, Royal Commission on Health Services, Ottawa: Queen's Printer, 1966.

McLuhan, T.C., ed., *Touch the Earth*, Toronto: New Press, 1971.

McRae, Duncan, Jr., "A Dilemma of Sociology: Science Versus Policy," *The American Sociologist*, 6, June, 1971, pp. 2-7.

Medvedev, Zhores, *The Rise and Fall of T.D. Lysenko*, New York: Columbia University Press, 1969.

Meekison, J. Peter, ed., *Canadian Federalism: Myth or Reality*, 2nd edition, Toronto: Methuen, 1971.

Melville, Herman, *Moby Dick*, New York: Rinehart, 1959 (original, 1851).

Mendelsohn, Harold and Irving Crespi, *Polls, Television and the New Politics*, Scranton, Pa.: Chandler, 1970.

Menninger, Karl, *The Crime of Punishment*, New York: Viking Press, 1968.

Merton, Robert K., "Insiders and Outsiders: A Chapter in the Sociology of Knowledge," *American Journal of Sociology*, 78, July, 1972, pp. 9-47.

Merton, Robert K., *Science, Technology and Society in Seventeenth Century England*, New York: Howard Fertig, 1970.

Merton, Robert K., "The Self-Fulfilling Prophecy," *Antioch Review*, 8, Summer, 1948, pp. 193-210.

Merton, Robert K., *Social Theory and Social Structure*, revised edition, Glencoe, Ill.: Free Press, 1957.

Merton, Robert K., "The Unanticipated Consequences of Purposive Social Action," *American Sociological Review*, 1, December, 1936, pp.894-904.

Merton, Robert K. and Robert Nisbet, eds., *Contemporary Social Problems*, 3rd edition, New York: Harcourt, Brace & World, 1971.

Meynaud, Jean, *Technocracy*, New York: Free Press, 1969.

Michels, Robert, *Political Parties*, Glencoe, Ill.: Free Press, 1949 (original in German, 1911).

Milosz, Czeslaw, *The Captive Mind*, New York: Vintage Books, 1955.

Miner, Horace, "A New Epoch in Rural Quebec," *American Journal of Sociology*, 62, July, 1956, pp. 1-10.

Montagu, Ashley, *Man's Most Dangerous Myth*, New York: Columbia University Press, 1942.

Montagu, Ashley, *The Idea of Race*, Lincoln: University of Nebraska Press, 1965.

Moore, Barrington, Jr., *Reflections on the Causes of Human Misery*, Boston: Beacon Press, 1970.

Moore, Wilbert E., *Social Change*, Englewood Cliffs, N.J.: Prentice-Hall, 1963.

Moore, Wilbert E., *The Professions: Roles and Rules*, New York: Russell Sage Foundation, 1970.

Moore, Wilbert E. and Melvin Tumin, "Some Social Functions of Ignorance," *American Sociological Review*, 14, 1949, pp. 787-795.

Morgan, J. Graham, "Contextual Factors in the Rise of Academic Sociology in the United States," *Canadian Review of Sociology and Anthropology*, 7, 1970, pp. 159-171.

Morgenthau, Hans, *Scientific Man Versus Power Politics*, Chicago: Phoenix Books, 1965.

Mowat, Farley, *The People of the Deer*, Toronto: Little, Brown, 1952.

Mullen, Edward J., et al., *Evaluation of Social Intervention*, San Francisco: Jossey-Bass, 1972.

Muller, Herbert J., *The Children of Frankenstein: A Primer on Modern Technology and Scientific Values*, Bloomington: Indiana University Press, 1971.

Mumford, Lewis, *Technics and Civilization*, New York: Harcourt, Brace, 1934.

Myrdal, Gunnar, *An American Dilemma*, New York: Harper, 1944.

Neale, R.S., *Class and Ideology in the Nineteenth Century*, London: Routledge and Kegan Paul, 1972.

Nettler, Gwynn, *Explaining Crime*, New York: McGraw-Hill, 1974.

Nettler, Gwynn, *Social Concerns*, Toronto: McGraw-Hill Ryerson, 1976.

Newman, Oscar, *Defensible Space: Crime Prevention Through Urban Design*, New York: Macmillan, 1973.

Nicholson, H.G., *The Age of Reason, the 18th Century*, New York: Doubleday, 1961.

Nisbet, Robert A., *Social Change and History: Aspects of the Western Theory of Development*, Cambridge: Oxford University Press, 1969.

Ogburn, William F., *The Social Effects of Aviation*, Boston: Houghton Mifflin, 1946.

O.M. Collective, (The), *The Organizer's Manual*, New York: Bantam Books, 1971.

Oppenheimer, Martin, "The Limitations of Socialism," in *The Case for Participatory Democracy*, edited by C.G. Benello and D. Roussopoulos, New York: Viking Press, 1971.

Oppenheimer, Martin and George Lakey, *A Manual for Direct Action: Strategy and Tactics for Civil Rights and All Other Nonviolent Protest Movements*, Chicago: Quadrangle Books, 1964.

Ozbekhan, Hasan, "The Triumph of Technology: 'Can' Implies 'Ought'," in *An Introduction to Technological Forecasting*, edited by Joseph P. Martino, London: Gordon and Beach, 1972.

Packard, Vance, *The Hidden Persuaders*, New York: D. McKay Co., 1957.

Packer, Herbert L., *The Limits of the Criminal Sanction*, Stanford: Stanford University Press, 1968.

Pareto, V., *The Mind and Society*, New York: Harcourt, Brace, 1935 (original, Florence, 1916).

Pearson, Lester, *Peace in the Family of Man*, London: Oxford University Press, 1969.

Perrow, Charles, *Complex Organizations*, Glenview, Ill.: Scott, Foresman, 1972.

Petras, John W., "George Herbert Mead's Theory of Self: A Study in the Origin and Convergence of Ideas," *Canadian Review of Sociology and Anthropology*, 10, 1973, pp. 145-159.

Phillips, Bernard, *Social Research: Strategy and Tactics*, 2d ed., New York: Macmillan, 1971.

Piliavin, Irving and Scott Briar, "Police Encounters with Juveniles," *American Journal of Sociology*, 70, September, 1964, pp. 206-214.

Piven, Frances and Richard Cloward, *Regulating the Poor: The Functions of Public Welfare*, New York: Pantheon Books, 1971.

Platt, Anthony, *The Child Savers: The Invention of Delinquency*, Chicago: University of Chicago Press, 1969.

Polak, Fred, *The Image of the Future*, Amsterdam: Elsevier, 1973 (orginal: 1952).

Popper, Karl, *The Poverty of Historicism*, London: Routledge and Kegan Paul, 1957.

Popper, Karl, *Conjectures and Refutations*, New York: Basic Books, 1963.

Porter, John, *The Vertical Mosaic*, Toronto: University of Toronto Press, 1965.

Price, A. Grenfell, *White Settlers and Native Peoples*, Westport, Conn.: Greenwood Press, 1972 (original, 1950).

Quinn, H.F., *The Union Nationale: A Study in Quebec Nationalism*, Toronto: University of Toronto Press, 1963.

Radical Therapist Collective, *The Radical Therapist*, New York: Ballantine, 1971.

Radical Therapist Collective, *Rough Times*, New York: Ballantine, 1973.

Reich, Charles, *The Greening of America*, New York: Bantam Books, 1970.

Reith, Charles, *The Police Idea*, London: Oxford University Press, 1938.

Reith, Charles, *A New Study of Police History*, London: Oliver and Boyd, 1956.

Remmling, Gunter, *Road to Suspicion: A Study of Modern Mentality and the Sociology of Knowledge*, New York: Appleton Century-Crofts, 1967.

Rex, J., *Key Problems of Sociological Theory*, London: Routledge and Kegan Paul, 1961.

Richan, William C. and Allan R. Mendelsohn, *Social Work: The Unloved Profession*, New York: New Viewpoints, 1973.

Riesman, David, *et al.*, *The Lonely Crowd*, New Haven, Conn.: Yale University Press, 1950.

Riesman, David, *Individualism Reconsidered*, Glencoe, Ill.: Free Press, 1954.

Rioux, M. and Y. Martin, *French Canadian Society*, Volume I, Toronto: McClelland & Stewart, 1965.

Roberts, Ron E., *The New Communes*, Englewood Cliffs, N.J.: Prentice-Hall, 1971.

Robins, Lee, *Deviant Children Grown Up*, Baltimore: Williams and Wilkins, 1966.

Rocher, Guy, "Bureaucracy and Welfare," *Canadian Welfare*, 39, March-April, 1963, pp. 55-61.

Rocher, Guy, *A General Introduction to Sociology: A Theoretical Perspective*, Toronto: Macmillan Co. of Canada, 1972.

Rogers, Everett and F. Shoemaker, *Communication of Innovations*, New York: Free Press, 1971.

Rosen, George, *Madness in Society: Chapters in the Historical Sociology of Mental Illness*, New York: Harper & Row, 1968.

Rosenberg, Bernard, *et al.*, eds., *Mass Society in Crisis*, New York: Macmillan, 1964.

Rosenthal, David, *Genetic Theory and Abnormal Behavior*, New York: McGraw-Hill, 1970.

Rosenthal, Robert and Ralph N. Rosnow, eds., *Artifact in Experimental Research*, New York: Academic Press, 1969.

Rossi, Peter and Walter Williams, eds., *Evaluating Social Programs: Theory, Practice, and Politics*, New York: Seminar Press, 1972.

Roszak, Theodore, *The Making of a Counterculture*, Garden City, N.Y.: Anchor Books, 1969.

Roszak, Theodore, *Where the Wasteland Ends*, New York: Doubleday, 1973.

Rothman, David, *The Discovery of the Asylum*, Boston: Little, Brown, 1971.

Rudé, George, *The Crowd in History, 1730-1848*, New York: Wiley, 1964.

Rusche, George, and Otto Kirchheimer, *Punishment and Social Structure*, New York: Russell and Russell, 1968 (original, 1939).

Ryan, William, *Blaming the Victim*, New York: Vintage Books, 1971.

Rytina, Joan Huber and Charles P. Loomis, "Marxist Dialectic and Pragmatism: Power as Knowledge," *American Sociological Review*, 35, April, 1970, pp. 308-318.

Safarian, A.E., *Foreign Ownership of Canadian Industry*, Toronto: University of Toronto Press, 1973.

Sagarin, Edward, *Deviants and Deviance*, New York: Praeger, 1975.

Said, Abduland Daniel Collier, *Revolutionism*, Boston: Allyn and Bacon, 1971.

Sallach, David, "What is Sociological Theory?", *The American Sociologist*, 8, August, 1973, pp. 134-139.

Savas, E.S. and Sigmund Ginsburg, "The Civil Service: A Meritless System?", *The Public Interest*, 32, Summer, 1973, pp. 70-85.

Scheff, Thomas, *Being Mentally Ill*, Chicago: Aldine, 1966.

Schervish, Paul, "The Labeling Perspective: Its Bias and Potential in the Study of Political Deviance," *The American Sociologist*, 8, May, 1973, pp. 47-57.

Schiller, Herbert, *The Mind Managers*, Boston: Beacon Press, 1973.

Schneider, Louis, *Sociological Approach to Religion*, New York: Wiley, 1970.

Schulman, Jay et al., "Recipe for a Jury," *Psychology Today*, May, 1973, pp. 37-44, 77-84.

Schur, Edwin M., *Crimes Without Victims*, Englewood Cliffs, N.J.: Prentice-Hall, 1965.

Schur, Edwin M., "Reactions to Deviance: A Critical Assessment," *American Journal of Sociology*, 75, 1969, pp. 309-322.

Schur, Edwin M., *Labeling Deviant Behavior: Its Sociological Implications*, New York: Harper & Row, 1971.

Schur, Edwin M., *Radical Non-Intervention: Rethinking the Delinquency Problem*, Englewood Cliffs, N.J.: Prentice-Hall, 1973.

Schwartz, Richard, "Functional Alternatives to Inequality," *American Sociological Review*, 20, August, 1955, pp. 424-430.

Schwartz, Richard and Jerome Skolnick, "Two Studies of Legal Stigma," *Social Problems*, 10, 1962, pp. 133-142.

Scott, Robert A. and Arnold Shore, "Sociology and Policy Analysis," *American Sociologist*, 9, 1974, pp. 51-59.

Selltiz, Claire et al., *Research Methods in Social Relations*, revised edition, New York: Holt, 1959.

Selznick, Philip, *The Organizational Weapon*, New York: McGraw-Hill, 1952.

Shafer, Stephen, "Restitution to Victims of Crime — An Old Correctional Aim Modernized," in *Criminological Controversies*, edited by Richard Knudten, New York: Appleton-Century-Crofts, 1968.

Shils, E.A., "Introduction" to Georges Sorel, *Reflections on Violence*, New York: Collier Books, 1961.

Shils, Edward, *The Intellectuals and the Powers and Other Essays*, Chicago: University of Chicago Press, 1972.

Short, James F., Jr. and F. Ivan Nye, "Reported Behavior as a Criterion of Deviant Behavior," *Social Problems*, 5, 1957, pp. 207-213.

Siegal, Morris, *Constructive Eugenics and Rational Marriage*, Toronto: Macmillan, 1934.

Silver, Abba Hillel, "The Widening Horizon of Social Service," *Proceedings of the First Annual Meetings*, Canadian Council on Social Work, 1928, pp. 21-24.

Silver, Allan, "The Demand for Order in Civil Society: A Review of Some Theories in the History of Urban Crime, Police, and Riot," in *The Police*, edited by David J. Bordua, New York: Wiley, 1967.

Simmons, J.L., "Public Stereotypes of Deviants," *Social Problems*, 13, 1965, pp. 223-232.

Sink, John M., *Political Criminal Trials: How to Defend Them*, New York: Clark Boardman, 1974.

Sjoberg, Gideon, *The Preindustrial City*, Glencoe, Ill.: Free Press, 1957.

Sjoberg, Gideon, ed., *Ethics, Politics and Social Research*, Morristown, N.J.: General Learning Corp., 1967.

Sjoberg, Gideon and Roger Nett, *A Methodology for Social Research*, New York: Harper & Row, 1968.

Skinner, B.F., *Beyond Freedom and Dignity*, New York: Knopf, 1971.

Sklair, Leslie, *The Sociology of Progress*, London: Routledge and Kegan Paul, 1971.

Small, Albion W., *General Sociology*, Chicago: University of Chicago Press, 1905.

Smith, Adam, *An Inquiry into the Nature and Causes of the Wealth of Nations*, New York: P.F. Collier, 1909 (original, 1776).

Solomon, L.N. and Berson, Betty, eds., *New Perspectives on Encounter Groups*, San Francisco: Jossey-Bass, 1972.

Sorel, Georges, *The Illusions of Progress*, Berkeley: University of California Press, 1972 (original, 1908).

Sorokin, Pitirim, *Contemporary Sociological Theories*, New York: Harper Torchbooks, 1928.

Sorokin, Pitirim, *Social and Cultural Dynamics*, Totowa, N.J.: Bedminster Press, 1962 (original, 1941).

Special Senate Committee on Poverty, *Poverty in Canada*, Ottawa: Information Canada, 1971.

Spencer, Herbert, *The Man Versus the State*, London: 1884.

Spengler, Oswald, *Decline of the West*, New York: Knopf, 1932 (original in German, 1922).

Splane, Richard, *Social Welfare in Ontario*, Toronto: University of Toronto Press, 1965.

Sraffa, Pierro, ed., *Works and Correspondence of David Ricardo*, Cambridge: Cambridge University Press, 1951.

Stapleton, Vaughn W. and Lee E. Teitelbaum, *In Defense of Youth: A Study of the Role of Counsel in American Juvenile Courts*, New York: Russell Sage Foundation, 1972.

Stark, Werner, "Max Weber and the Heterogony of Purposes," *Social Research*, 34, Summer, 1967, pp. 249-264.

Starowicz, Mark and Rae Murphy, eds., *Corporate Canada*, Toronto: James Lewis and Samuel, 1973.

Stewart, Walter, *Shrug: Trudeau in Power*, Toronto: New Press, 1971.

Stinchcombe, Arthur, *Constructing Social Theories*, New York: Harcourt, Brace & World, 1968.

Strong, Margaret K., *Public Welfare Administration in Canada*, Chicago: University of Chicago Press, 1930.

Suchman, Edward A., *Evaluation Research*, New York: Russell Sage Foundation, 1967.

Swadron, B.B. and D.R. Sullivan, eds., *The Law and Mental Disorder*, Toronto: Canadian Mental Health Association, 1973.

Sykes, Gresham, *Society of Captives*, Princeton, N.J.: Princeton University Press, 1965.

Szasz, Thomas, *Psychiatric Justice*, New York: Basic Books, 1966.

Szasz, Thomas, *The Manufacture of Madness*, New York: Harper & Row, 1970.

Szasz, Thomas, *The Myth of Mental Illness*, revised edition, New York: Harper & Row, 1974.

Taft, Donald R., *Criminology*, 3rd edition, New York: Macmillan, 1956.

Taft, R., "The Ability to Judge People," *Psychological Bulletin*, 52, 1955, pp. 1-28.

Teuber, N. and E. Powers, "Evaluating Therapy in a Delinquency Prevention Program," *Proceedings of the Association on Nervous Mental Disorders*, 3, 1953, pp. 138-147.

Thernstrom, Stephen and Richard Sennett, eds., *Nineteenth Century Cities: Essays in the New Urban History*, New Haven, Conn.: Yale University Press, 1969.

Thorsell, Bernard and Lloyd Klemke, "The Labelling Process: Reinforcement and Deterrent?", *Law and Society Review*, 6, February, 1972, pp. 393-403.

Timberlake, James H., *Prohibition and the Progressive Movement: 1900-1920*, Cambridge, Mass.: Harvard University Press, 1966.

Toffler, Alvin, *Future Shock*, New York: Bantam Books, 1970.

Toren, Nina, *Social Work: The Case of a Semi-Profession*, Beverly Hills, Calif.: Sage Publications, 1972.

Trevor-Roper, H.R., "Religion, the Reformation and Social Change," *Historical Studies*, 4, 1963, pp. 18-44.

Trilling, Lionel, *Beyond Culture*, New York: Viking Press, 1965.

Truax, C. and R. Carkhuff, *Toward Effective Counselling and Psychotherapy*, Chicago: Aldine, 1967.

Tuchman, Barbara, *The Guns of August*, New York: Macmillan, 1972.

Tumin, Melvin M., "Some Principles of Stratification: A Critical Analysis," *American Sociological Review*, 18, 1953, pp. 387-394.

Tumin, Melvin M., "The Functionalist Approach to Social Problems," *Social Problems*, 12, Spring, 1965, pp. 379-388.

Vallée, F.G., "The Emerging Northern Mosaic," in *Canadian Society: Pluralism, Change, and Conflict*, edited by R.J. Ossenberg, Scarborough, Ont.: Prentice-Hall, 1971.

Van den Berghe, Pierre, "Bringing Beasts Back In: Toward a Biosocial Theory of Aggression," *American Sociological Review*, 39, December, 1974.

Wade, Mason, *The French Canadians, 1760-1967*, Toronto: Macmillan Co. of Canada, 1967.

Wallis, Wilson D., *Messiahs: Their Role In Civilization*, Washington, D.C.: American Council on Public Affairs, 1943.

Walsh, Chad, *From Utopia to Nightmare*, New York: Harper & Row, 1962.

Walsh, G., *Indians in Transition*, Toronto: MçClelland & Stewart, 1971.

Warren, W., *Good Times: The Belief in Progress from Darwin to Marcuse*, Bloomington: Indiana University Press, 1972.

Webb, E.J. *et al.*, *Unobtrusive Measures: Nonreactive Research in the Social Sciences*, Chicago: Rand McNally, 1972.

Weber, Max, *The Protestant Ethic and the Spirit of Capitalism*, New York: Scribner's, 1930 (orginally part of a larger work, 1921).

Weber, Max, "The Essentials of Bureaucratic Organization," in Robert K. Merton *et al.*, eds., *Reader in Bureaucracy*, Glencoe, Ill.: Free Press, 1952.

Weiner, Norbert, *The Human Use of Human Beings: Cybernetics and Society*, New York: Avon Books, 1967 (original, 1950).

Westhues, Kenneth, *Society's Shadow*, Toronto: McGraw-Hill Ryerson, 1972.

Whyte, William H., Jr., *The Organization Man*, Garden City, N.Y.: Doubleday, 1956.

Wilensky, Harold, "The Professionalization of Everyone," *American Journal of Sociology*, 70, September, 1964, pp. 137-158.

Wilkins, Leslie T., *Social Deviance*, Englewood Cliffs, N.J.: Prentice-Hall, 1965.

Wilkins, Leslie, *Evaluation of Penal Measures*, New York: Random House, 1969.

Wise, S.F., "Sermon Literature and Canadian Intellectual History," in *Canadian History Before Confederation*, edited by J.M. Bumstead, Georgetown, Ont.: Irwin-Dorsey, 1972.

Wittfogel, Karl, *Oriental Despotism: A Comparative Study of Total Power*, New Haven, Conn.: Yale University Press, 1957.

Wolfe, J., *Cost Benefit and Cost Effectiveness*, London: Allen and Unwin, 1973.

Wolff, Robert Paul *et al.*, eds., *A Critique of Pure Tolerance*, Boston: Beacon Press, 1965.

Wolfgang, Marvin, "Uniform Crime Reports: A Critical Appraisal," *University of Pennsylvania Law Review*, Volume III, 1963, pp. 708-738.

Woodham-Smith, Cecil, *The Great Hunger*, New York: Harper & Row, 1963.

Woodroofe, Kathleen, *From Charity to Social Work in England and the United States*, Toronto: University of Toronto Press, 1962.

Worsley, Peter, *The Trumpet Shall Sound*, London: Macgibbon and Kee, 1957.

Wrong, Dennis H., "The Oversocialized Conception of Man in Modern Sociology," *American Sociological Review*, 26, 1961, pp. 183-193.

Yablonsky, Lewis, *Robopaths*, Indianapolis, Ind.: Bobbs-Merrill, 1972.

Young, Jock, "The Police as Amplifiers of Deviancy," in *Images of Deviance*, edited by Stanley Cohen, Harmondsworth: Penguin, 1971.

Young, Michael, *The Rise of the Meritocracy, 1870-2033*, New York: Random House, 1959.

Zay, Nicholas, "Gaps in Available Statistics on Crime and Delinquency in Canada," *Canadian Journal of Economics and Political Science*, 29, February, 1963, pp. 75-90.

Zeitlin, Irving, ed., *American Society, Incorporated*, Chicago: Markham, 1971.

Zimbardo, Philip and Ebbe Ebbeson, *Influencing Attitudes and Changing Behavior*, Reading, Mass.: Addison-Wesley, 1969.

Zimring, Franklin, and Gordon Hawkins, *Deterrence*, Chicago: University of Chicago Press, 1973.

Index